LOVE is a Start

An Adoptive Family's Journey

D1738612

DONNA

To Toni with fond regards, Donna Shu

Printed in the United States of America

First Edition

Library of Congress Cataloging-in-Publication Data

Shilts, Donna

Love is a Start...An Adoptive Family's Journey / Donna Shilts

p.   cm.

ISBN #0-9666313-0-7

1. Family. 2. Child Care. 3. Relationships.
4. Child Development. 5. Child Psychology. 6. Neuroscience.
7. Adoption. 8. Child Welfare. I. Title.

Library of Congress 98-96487

Photo on page 323 reprinted with permission of Olan Mills

Cover Design and Layout: Kathleen Krushas at
tothepoint@imagina.com

Published by: **LookAgain Publishing**

Post Office Box 17332

Portland, Oregon 97217-0332

In memory of Rosemary

This book is a tribute to the work of
the late Dr. A. Jean Ayres
and dedicated to children

LOVE
is a Start

continued

Chapter 1
A Broken Family

S am and I had not been dating long when he mentioned that his younger sister Julie had recently lost the custody of her children to child welfare. Jacob, the oldest boy, was three at the time, and Jared, the youngest boy, was almost two. "She drinks and couldn't take care of them, I guess," Sam said with a blank expression on his face and a crack in his voice. I didn't ask about the particulars because I was making a conscious effort to not get involved in other people's problems.

I was a caretaker by nature and a "sap" for a sad story my friends were always telling me. A sales pitch followed by the person saying the job was his second and a necessity in order to help pay for an elderly parent's operation, and I would consider the product whether I needed it or not. A handicapping condition never failed to get my attention. Once I bought enough light bulbs from the blind to last five years. When friends or family needed money, I'd offer to help before I was even asked. I never proclaimed such gestures as loans because I always thought that if a person is kind enough to extend, then the other would be decent enough to repay. It seldom worked out that way. "Never cast your pearls before a swine," my dad would advise, but I wasn't very good at distinguishing the deserving from the undeserving. Heartache and desolation always looked the same to me among the weak and the strong, the rich and the poor; I'd "hung" with each group at one time or another. People liked to tell me their troubles, too. I didn't mind. I wasn't a very good listener though. I was a problem solver, quick to offer advice; always surprised and a bit disgruntled when it wasn't taken.

Nearly a year passed after Sam had told me about his sister. He and I were sharing an apartment together when Julie stopped by one day unexpectedly to see her brother. She was actually four years younger than me but she seemed older dressed in a chocolate brown polyester pant suit, the likes of which I had not seen in years. Her hair was naturally wavy, like Sam's, and she had big dark brown eyes, as dark as the color of her pant suit. She didn't wear face make-up. She didn't need to; she was pretty naturally. Her good looks were undercut by a tiredness that didn't seem necessarily due to a lack of sleep. I poured her a cup of coffee, myself and Sam one, and we all sat down at the table to chat. Julie liked talking about herself and what she had been doing: working as a dishwasher, moving, seeing old friends, making new ones, and writing poetry. She especially liked talking about the things she was "gonna do."

I had a hard time tracking Julie's conversation at first because she would say something then stop midway through and start talking about something altogether different. Sam had an uncanny ability for bringing her back to the original discussion. With precise timing, he'd interject a single word and without missing a beat, Julie would refocus and continue on.

Sam eventually brought the conversation around to the subject of Jacob and Jared.* As soon as he mentioned their names I braced myself. I was about to hear a sad story. It would be a story of human suffering. Tears would flow as Julie disclosed

*all names have been changed

the details of the misfortune that had befallen her and her children. I would lend a sympathetic ear. Sam's sister would need some support, even some advice perhaps. But I didn't hear a story and there were no tears. Instead, Julie slammed her hand down on the table and lashed out defensively at the child welfare system.

"That damned Children's Services Division. They're saying I didn't take care of em' right! I have to go to parenting classes and alcohol and drug treatment before I see the judge on September 6th. I've been so lonely. I can't wait till they're back with me." When she said September 6th, I realized there was something amiss in her thinking. It was already the third week of August. I asked if she had signed up for the classes yet. "Not yet, but I'm gonna," she said.

Well, September came and went and in November a child welfare worker called Sam and his other sisters to tell them Jacob and Jared would be free for adoption soon. Evidently, there was finally enough evidence to satisfy the courts and Julie's parental rights were to be terminated. "If you folks are interested in adopting them, you need to come forward. Otherwise their names will go on our 'children in waiting' list," the worker said to Sam. Sam and his older sister Jenny wanted to see the boys right away so a visit with them at the child welfare office was arranged for the following week.

In the interim Sam started talking to me about adoption. "I wonder if the Children's Services Division would let you and me adopt them?" he asked one day in a serious tone.

I couldn't have children but I didn't want to be a parent, especially to someone else's children. I had already done that once when in my late twenties I married a man who had two teenage sons. It was disastrous; the boys wanted their own mother to parent them. We all suffered. When I looked back on it years later I realized I probably worked too hard; I should have tried to be just a friend to the kids.

Following the divorce I went to college and obtained a degree in Occupational Therapy. After college I moved to the inner city of Portland, Oregon, where I met Sam. He was thirty-three and I was thirty-five. The year was 1988 and I was deep in debt paying off student loans.

I knew Sam would want to do something to help his nephews. He was a caring person, even a little sentimental at times. But I couldn't picture him as a father. He was an artist. Up half the night painting or drawing; he lived according to his own timetable. I didn't want to discourage his interest in his nephews; however, a man needs encouragement sometimes when it comes to matters of the heart. So when he asked if I would go with him to see the boys, I said yes.

It was a wet and dark November morning when we all gathered at the child welfare office. There was Sam and I and Jenny with her husband Tom. The child welfare worker was at the helm and guided us into a room marked "reserved." It was a gloomy room, scantily furnished and lit only by a lamp standing in the corner. A one-way mirror on the south wall peered out at us silently, watching and waiting like a huge camera lens. There wasn't anyone on the other side of the mirror, we were informed, but everyone kept glancing over at it as if to make sure, even the child welfare worker.

Jacob and Jared arrived with their foster mother shortly after we did. They were cute children. Jacob was little and slim, with light brown hair, beautiful blue eyes and fair skin. Jared was even littler but plump, with olive color skin, strawberry blond hair, and enormous chocolate brown eyes like his mother's. In fact, Jared looked exactly like his mother. Jacob had his uncle's jaw line, the only hint of resemblance to Julie, and neither he nor Jared resembled each other. They were guarded and un-willing to make eye contact during introductions. Jacob had just turned four so his Aunt Jenny brought him a bucket of 'Legos' for his birthday. So he wouldn't feel left out, for Jared she brought a pull string learning toy called a 'See and Say'. Even with gifts to cast their spell and befriend, both children remained closed to the presence of others. Jacob sat down at the child size table strategically placed in front of the one-way mirror and started a construction project with the Legos. Jared threw down the 'See and Say' in lieu of masturbating on a large stuffed animal in a corner of the room opposite of the lit corner.

Awkwardly, Sam and I sat down in the little chairs across from Jacob at the little table. After a few minutes I said to Jacob that I thought he could build well with Legos. This compliment brought a shy smile to his lips and a tilt of his head in the direction of my voice. When his Uncle Sam chimed

Jared (left) and Jacob come into care. Ages 22 and 36 months.

in with more praise, Jacob's little hands started working faster. A yellow tower on red wheels came to be and lots of complimentary "oh's" and "aaaas" for a job well done from Sam and I followed. That did it. Jacob finally raised his head and with an expression on his face that seemed to be saying "Who are you guys?" he looked ever so briefly into my eyes and then Sam's. His cheeks had turned a rosy "happy kid" color and the blue eyes were sparkling. Following this exchange, Sam moved his chair next to Jacob's and asked enthusiastically and in a child-like way if he could try his hand at building with those Legos too. This delighted Jacob and he smiled broadly. "Sure! Would you like to try the blue ones?" he said, chuckling to himself and already engaged in another construction. He seemed like a sweet child.

Jared and his Aunt Jenny had been exploring his new toy. Jared would pull the string and Aunt Jenny would provide the giggles. A rotation eventually took place with Sam playing with Jared and Jenny playing with Jacob. They had to start all over again with each child of course. As I watched aunt and uncle attempting to connect with their kin, I suddenly felt like a stranger looking in.

The hour went by quickly and it was soon time to go. While Sam and I helped Jacob put his Legos away, Sam told him how much fun he had playing with him. I didn't know what to say in terms of a closing statement. *Maybe we'll see you again* didn't seem right; a child in his position didn't need false promises. Jenny seemed to be at a loss for words too. So we just stood there in awkward silence watching the foster mother pick up the 'See-and-Say,' take Jared's hand in hers and start walking toward the door, motioning for Jacob to follow. With his Lego bucket in hand, Jacob followed dutifully but mechanically. His eyes fixed to the floor as if determined he wasn't going to look back. We adults said our good-byes, though they went unacknowledged, with pretend cheerful smiles to mask the sadness that had invaded the room. And then as Jacob passed through the doorway and rounded the corner into the hallway, I saw something that touched my soul.

In the smallest increments of seconds, I watched the little boy Jacob transform into an old man. His head fell forward, his shoulders slumped, and he suddenly looked weary, aged, and tired. The bucket of plastic Legos, the gift of love offered in celebration of his birth, suddenly looked too heavy to carry. The rosy cheeks of the child momentarily happy at play were gone, having been replaced by a sickly wanting gray. It was like watching the human aging process via computer animation except the marvel was missing. Twisted was the imagery on a little four-year-old child. Old age is the point at which we ask ourselves if our lives were meaningful and the point at which death becomes more than just a concept in waiting. Was this transformation a figment of my imagination? I wondered. Perhaps. But it wasn't with imagination that I felt the child's pain. His spirit wasn't free to explore the wonders of childhood. How could it be? Children aren't suppose to celebrate their birthdays in child welfare offices. And now his future was uncertain. Uncertainty is a heavy burden for any child to bear.

"Why don't we go find a place to talk," the caseworker said once Jacob was out of sight. Then she led us down to the cafeteria which was a huge room, and at that hour of the day, void of people and activity. The smell of the day's lunch still lingered in the stale air. Fluorescent lights stretched across the ceiling, exposing all the nasty little stains in the commercial carpeting. It was a place well traveled.

"Now that you have all had the opportunity to visit with Jacob and Jared, I would like to tell you about the behaviors we have seen in the boys," the worker began. "When they came to us initially, they smeared and ate their own feces and drank water from the toilet. We think they nearly starved to death while with Julie." Her voice was forceful and scolding, like a judge finally being able to call attention to an evil deed. I thought she was just embellishing the truth until I looked over at Jenny and Sam. They knew something I didn't because though they looked sorrowful and bowed their heads in shame, they didn't necessarily look surprised.

The worker continued on. "The boys are what psychologists call *unattached children* and we don't know what to expect in terms of their being able to bond with an adult or adjust to an adoptive placement. They are *severely emotionally disturbed* and we may see fire setting or animal killing. These are the behaviors often observed in *unattached children.*" Her eyes fixed on each of us at random, including me. I kept waiting for her to wag a pointed finger in an attempt to draw out the guilty one. "While they have come a long way, they are significantly *damaged.* Jacob appears to be the more *damaged* of the two, since he was neglected the longest. And he may have a seizure disorder. It's just too early to tell what to expect from Jared. He's still so young yet."

The words seizure disorder sounded like cause for alarm but it was the word *damaged* that kept ringing in my brain. It sounded so permanent, like there was no chance for improvement and never would be. I sensed the woman was only trying to be honest but I found this approach distressing. She was Jacob's and Jared's State appointed caretaker; the one to speak on their behalf. Yet it was as if she was saying: *You can try some fertilizer but I think these flowers are dead all ready.* She was introducing us to the world of the welfare child; a world in which there is so much bad that it's probably hard to remember to look for the good. But I was someone who believed strongly in the resiliency of the young child and the power of the human spirit to overcome. Jacob and Jared were still just little children; only three and four years old.

To label young children *severely emotionally disturbed* seemed like such an injustice. I hated that label. I had always equated the word disturbed with people who murder, maim and rape. To mental health professionals disturbed means unbalanced or disordered. I had just learned about the different meanings of such labels to different people when I went to work at a private psychiatric hospital following graduation from college. Unbalanced and disordered were the people on the adult unit of the hospital who were being treated for mental illnesses, such as schizophrenia and manic depression. One of the staff therapists kept insisting there were clients at the hospital with multiple personality disorder, too. According to the psychiatrists, however, there was no such thing as multiple personalities.

The hospital was new and shiny and clean, a private facility. Insurance companies paid a lot of money to send a client there for three or four weeks. Shock therapy and/or medications were administered in an expedient manner. The sooner the client was mentally stabilized and out of there, the better. That was policy. I'd read about shock therapy in college but I didn't think it was actually being used any place. I couldn't get used to the idea of electrically shocking someone into sanity. Every time I saw a client being wheeled into the shock therapy room, the room without windows and marked "Keep Out," I'd look away and pretend I didn't see anything.

Fortunately, I didn't work on the adult side of the hospital. I worked on the adolescent unit with teenagers diagnosed emotionally disturbed. They were kids from middle class families with two parents at home. Most of them lived in the state of Washington. Their parents brought them into Oregon to that hospital in particular because it was a locked facility. Once in, the kids stayed for thirty days, at least. They were tough and rebellious kids but I met very few who I thought were unbalanced or disordered based on the standards of the time: runaways, delinquency, anger problems (rages when provoked), and drug use were the common behaviors. One boy at the hospital was a child molester and in a class of his own but I'd never heard the term "unattached child" and I'd not met a fire setter or an animal killer yet. For the majority of cases, it seemed more like an issue of coping. The parents weren't coping well with adolescence and the youth weren't coping well with it either. Thirty days, locked in, and supposedly safe, allowed for a nice break for both parties.

But being in the hospital meant something had to be wrong, that was the nature of the setting, so all negative aspects of the individual's personality were called attention to, studied, and analyzed. And although research has yet to determine the direct cause of emotional disturbances — heredity, brain disorder, diet, stress, and family functioning are thought to be contributing factors — at that hospital the cause of any given problem was believed to rest with the family unit. "This is a dysfunctional family," is how the professional team meetings typically began.

Jacob and Jared were under the care of the Child Welfare system. The negative aspects of their personalities were being paid attention to, studied, and analyzed. They were declared *severely emotionally disturbed unattached children*. Fire setting and animal killing were predicted.

"And they *could* be cruel to adoptive siblings," the worker concluded, bringing me back to the present.

With this comment, Tom's body language said *I've heard enough, I'm ready to go*. Jenny picked up on her husband's form of communication and took the initiative to bring the meeting to a close. The worker looked surprised. "We'll be in touch," Jenny said. Then like a Boy Scout leader, she marched our little group to the elevator. The seemingly endless moments waiting for the elevator were filled with forced small talk.

On the way back to the car Jenny started crying. In between sobs she said, "I knew there was something wrong with Jacob and Jared, they didn't seem to be developing the way I remembered our girls' development. Julie liked keeping them in the playpen. I told her she should let them out once in a while. I told her they needed things to play with, too. But she wouldn't listen to me. She'd fly off the handle and yell at me: 'You telling me I don't know what to do with my own kids?!' I didn't know she wasn't feeding them! I only saw the boys a couple of times before they were taken away. Julie was always moving and never had a phone so it was hard to keep in touch with her. She probably wouldn't have called me anyway because we've always had a hard time relating. Haven't we Sam?," she asked, although it didn't sound like she was really talking to Sam or to anybody else. Poor Jenny, she was grappling with her own: *What should I have done?* It was too late and the remorse was tearing her apart. I was hearing the story finally.

Several days passed and as could be predicted, Tom wasn't up to the challenge of parenting one or both of his wife's nephews when he had his own little girls to think of. After all, their safety could be at stake. Jenny was broken hearted. Prior to the visit, she talked about putting the girls together in Kristin's room and painting Emily's room blue for the boys. "Right now it's pink with ballerinas on the border," she had said. Another aunt was asking about adopting Jared and visitations were being arranged. Nobody asked about Jacob, "the more damaged of the two." But Sam wanted to see him again and so did I.

I had not been able to stop thinking about the little boy. I was drawn to him as if he was somebody I knew in the past but couldn't remember when or where. There was a sense of urgency about the whole affair, too, which gnawed at me uneasily.

Despite my failed parental efforts, I still liked kids. I had always liked kids. Especially the elementary school age. While in college I did volunteer work with children of that age group in addition to working with them through the Parks and Recreation Department.

So Sam and I decided to have Jacob over for a weekend visit. Because Sam was the biological uncle, visits were approved and we were given the telephone number of the foster home where he lived.

Chapter 2
Is This What Damaged Looks Like?

J acob called his foster mother "Mommy Sherrie." Sherrie was a tiny little woman, five-feet-two maybe, small boned, and very quiet. She seemed pleased someone was taking an interest in her little charge. "I think this will be so good for Jacob," she said while gathering his things for the weekend visit. I only half listened while she recited his likes and dislikes because I couldn't help being distracted — her house was a very busy place. There was a baby in a high-chair, four preschoolers including Jacob and Jared, and an older child. There was a seemingly delayed much older child and another adult woman, who Sherrie introduced as her daughter. All total, counting Sherrie's husband, ten people lived in that house. And everybody was doing something: cooking, eating, pounding, running, jumping, hitting, screaming, crying.

After zipping an overnight bag and giving it a final pat, Sherrie handed it to me along with a bottle of liquid medication. "You may need this. It's sleep medication. Jacob has a hard time sleeping at night. Just follow the directions on the label," she stated matter-of-factly. I didn't think to ask for the details.

Sam voiced his reluctance to using drugs to induce sleep. "Have you ever tried herb teas?," he asked Sherrie.

"No. But you can give those a try, too," was Sherrie's

response. An odd expression came over her face and a small elfish but knowing grin crossed her lips. I didn't think anything about her comment and just assumed the grin meant she didn't believe in alternative medicine. A lot of people don't. I didn't at the time, but Sam did. He believed alternative medicine and organic foods were the key to a healthy mind as well as longevity.

Sam and I were different in a lot of ways. He was the introverted intellectual type and non-traditional to a degree. I was more conventional and considered an extrovert in social settings. Sam watched NOVA. I watched sitcoms. He thought me foolish to believe in a Creator, yet he revered nature and sought always to live in harmony with it's creatures. The fish in our mountain streams deserved to be left alone, ants were admired because they could carry twenty times their own body weight, and he wouldn't disturb a spider's web unless it was absolutely necessary. I liked Sam's quiet demeanor. But mostly I liked Sam because he was kind and trustworthy. I valued these qualities in another more than anything else. Now as far as our eating preferences went — MSG was good enough for me. I didn't even like to cook. At least not on a regular basis because I hated all that menu planning. Chinese take-out was my style — a box of shrimp with snow peas could make two meals.

For money Sam worked as a maintenance man and manager of the apartment complex. The senior citizens loved him and he them; his casual pace was just right for them. Managing the apartment wasn't necessarily his strong suit however. Paper work and record keeping made him nervous — too tedious and mundane for him. He liked it when I offered to take that part of the job over for him.

There was no indication that Jacob remembered either Sam or I. Even when Sherrie told him he would be staying with his

"Uncle Sam" and "Aunt Donna," implying there was a connection I guess, he still made no eye contact with us. Yet he came gladly, which surprised me. I thought he might cry or at least fuss a little. In the mental health field the willingness to go with a person whom the child doesn't really know is called "a lack of stranger anxiety."

When we reached our apartment it was the dinner hour, so I asked Jacob what he would like to eat. Sherrie said he liked soft foods — scrambled eggs, jello, peanut butter without nuts on white bread. I thought he said "scrambled eggs" but I couldn't be sure, his words were muffled and he kept his head down. Abused and abandoned children tend to have speech problems which are thought to be linked to emotional problems. I had to ask Jacob to repeat himself a couple of times. Finally I decided it was scrambled eggs all right and started walking toward the refrigerator, grateful he didn't ask for jello or white bread because I had neither in the cupboards. "Okay, I'll get the eggs and cook them for you," I said as I opened the refrigerator door. I thought we were getting off to a good start — I had eggs. Then suddenly, there was this little person pulling my arms from the refrigerator with a mighty force and screaming at me.

"No! Jacob do it, Jacob take care of Jacob!" he said. I was so taken by surprise all I could do was stand there and stare at him for a few seconds. Finally I told him he could scramble the eggs but that I should manage the stove. "No! Jacob cook for Jacob!" he screamed and ran for the refrigerator again. I cut in front of him and stopped him short. Then he started running through the apartment, screaming something I couldn't understand. He didn't go to the apartment door like I thought he might, but kept running and running from room to room, frantically, reminding me of a laboratory rat trying to make its way through a maze.

Sam was in the basement in a room directly below our apartment, he'd gone down to put some things away before dinner. He came upstairs right away when he heard the commotion. Jacob was passing through the living room again as Sam was opening the apartment door. When Jacob saw the door open, he lunged for it, almost managing to slip through Sam's legs. Sam picked him up and cupped him tight to his chest, face to face. Jacob's arms and legs were flailing, and he was screaming. Finally he stopped flailing and started crying, deep heartfelt sobs, stopping every so often to catch his breath. Sam sat down in the rocking chair next to the couch and holding Jacob close to his chest, he started rocking him. Jacob struggled at first but then he finally relaxed. In time his sobs were replaced with soft crying. Sam continued to rock him ever so gently. Finally, like an exhausted toddler, his face streaked with tears, Jacob fell into a restless sleep. None of us ate that night.

Sherrie had sent a playpen for Jacob to sleep in and we set it up in the bedroom so Sam or I could keep an eye on him. Jacob woke up when I was getting him ready for bed but went right back to sleep when I put him in the playpen. I slept on the couch, but not very soundly because the playpen creaked as Jacob tossed and turned all night. He also whimpered a lot. Then he awoke before dawn Saturday morning, screaming and shaking the bars of the playpen like an angry gorilla shakes the bars of his cage at the zoo.

Jacob still wore diapers, so I was surprised to find he could dress himself, brush his teeth and wash his hands independently. There was something eerie about his hand washing however that made me uncomfortable. He wanted to scrub and rinse them over and over again. When I asked him to stop, his hands only moved that much faster in order to get to the next cycle. When I raised my voice and commanded him to stop, he looked up at me with an agony in his eyes that seemed to be saying: *Please help me for I cannot stop myself.* I couldn't stand this display of obsessive-compulsive behavior — it falls under the category of severely emotionally disturbed — and I didn't want to think he was disturbed. So I hurriedly grabbed a towel and dried his hands.

Other than building with Legos, Jacob didn't seem to know how to play with toys, which is typical of children with emotional problems. Sherrie had sent some toys with Jacob but he couldn't sit down and engage himself, he had to be in motion. Around and around in circles he would go in the living room, alternating between walking and running, with elbows bent and hands in a fist. The movement was constant until I placed my hands on his shoulders and asked him to sit down. If I forced him to sit down for any length of time, he would scream and throw the toys. Inadvertently, I found soft music seemed to slow him down somewhat so I kept tapes playing on the stereo. When I took Jacob to the park he was even more energetic. Around and around he would run. When he passed by me he said, "Aren't I a good runner?"

"You sure are," I responded, nodding in disbelief. He ran for a solid fifteen minutes, never slowing down. It made me dizzy just to watch him. When we headed back to the apartment, which was just two blocks away and visible from the park, I took his hand to guide him. He had to be guided, seemingly more so than most four-year olds. Even though I told him where we were going and what we were doing, he still acted as if he had no idea where it was he was going, where he had been, or where he was at. He was "spacey" — for the lack of a better word to describe it.

I took Jacob to the store with me in the afternoon, which was a mistake. It was one of those big concrete warehouse stores with wide isles, bright lights and a lot of people. We were hardly down two isles when he started crying and screaming and kicking at me from his seat in the shopping cart. I had no idea what set him off. I didn't know what he wanted or what to do to calm him either and everybody was staring at us. Finally I approached him from behind and took him out of the cart. I knew I didn't dare let go of him or he'd surely take off running, so I left the grocery chart and its contents standing where it was, and with Jacob on my right hip like a sack of potatoes, his legs flailing behind us, I made for the door. Once outside he seemed a little calmer but as soon as I strapped him into the seat belt of the car he started screaming again and kicking the seat.

On the drive back to the apartment, Jacob unbuckled his seat belt twice. At first, I yelled at him "Don't do that. That seat belt is to protect you!" He just looked at me in a spaced-out way and did it again two blocks further down the road. Then he tried to open the door. I panicked, pulled the car to the side of the road, and gave him a swat on his little bottom. There were no further episodes the rest of the way home but I was still a bundle of nervous and exhausted energy by the time we reached the apartment. I let Sam know I would never go anyplace alone in the car with the child again.

I never thought I would welcome the sun going down as much as I did that day. I had given Jacob a bath after scrambled eggs for dinner. He wouldn't eat anything else. He liked the bath and played contentedly in the water for quite a while. All was quiet while I dried him and put his diaper on. But when I got his pajamas out, chaos erupted. As soon as he saw them, he started running around again but this time it looked like he was trying to find someplace to hide. He went under the bed, behind the couch, and into the closet. When I finally got my hands on him, he started kicking and screaming and spitting at me. He was just a little guy but a powerhouse of energy and I couldn't hold him. Once free from my grip, he ran to a corner, threw himself on the floor, and got into a fetal position. There he started rocking back and forth with his arms wrapped around himself and sobbing deeply, he buried his face into the carpet. I wanted to pick him up to comfort, but I didn't for fear I might be intruding on what seemed to be a space for him alone. I sat down on the couch instead and watched him for almost half-an-hour, until he fell asleep. I picked him up and put him in the bed instead of the playpen, thinking it might be more comfortable for him. I was so tired myself, that I laid down next to him and fell asleep with my clothes and shoes still on.

When I was abruptly awakened a couple of hours later by a blood curdling scream, I thought I was dreaming. But I wasn't. It was Jacob. He was sitting up in the bed wide awake screaming and staring into space. I put my arm around him in an effort to bring him close to me, but he jerked away and started crying and hitting himself in the face. Then he flew from the bed and started running around the apartment again. Sam had been asleep on the couch until Jacob woke him. With a stunned look on his face, he sat and watched his nephew for a few minutes. Then suddenly, he stood up and, rather nervously, announced, "I'm making some chamomile tea."

Jacob finally came to a halt and sat down on the floor in the living room. Slowly then I approached him and started gently rubbing his back which seemed to soothe him a little. When I asked him if I could rock him in the rocking chair, he didn't say anything nor did he look at me, but nodded his head yes. So I rocked him slowly and rhythmically. All was calm and quiet then while we awaited the tea water to come to a boil.

Every light in the apartment was on by then including the lamp next to the rocker. Sam thought it might help to turn it off so that Jacob could go back to sleep, but as soon as he did, Jacob bolted and started screaming again. So I had Sam turn the lamp back on, and I continued with the rocking. I thought Jacob was just afraid of the dark, but it was more than that. He had been staring into the light evidently, and wanted to continue to do so. Some people stare into lights, but it's not considered normal and I was feeling uncomfortable.

Sam got Jacob to drink a little chamomile tea, but it didn't seem to help because he still had enough reserve to fight sleep. Finally after about an hour and just before Sam went to bed, I had him give Jacob some of the sleep medication Sherrie had sent. Eventually, his little body went limp in my arms and he fell asleep.

It was 2:00 in the morning when I laid Jacob down on the bed next to Sam. I laid down on the other side of him and folded my body around his so that he was wedged between Sam and I in a sort of human cocoon. Exhausted but unable to sleep, I found myself thinking: Is this what damaged looks like? What could make a child scream like that?, I wondered. It wasn't a normal scream and he wasn't suffering from the night terrors typical to young children, I could tell. It was the kind of scream a wounded animal might make when it's caught in a trap. It sent chills up my spine. What really happened to this child to terrify him so?, I wondered. Monday morning I would call the child welfare worker, I decided. I needed information. Something must have gone terribly wrong someplace along the way.

I don't remember Sunday other than that Jacob was awake and moving at the crack of dawn, less than five hours later. We didn't leave the apartment until it was time to take him back to his foster home.

"We have a pretty clear history of what happened to Jacob," the worker began when I called her the next day. "We have records that go back four years and that is why this case is in 'permanent planning' already. Julie has proven to us that she is clearly unable to parent at this time."

Evidently, when Julie was about three months pregnant with Jacob she sought medical care for an ulcer from a community health clinic. She was living in a hotel room without a refrigerator and not eating well. A referral was made to community health nursing for prenatal care, counseling on alcohol consumption while pregnant, counseling on personal medical care, and breast feeding. When she didn't keep the follow-up appointment because someone beat her up, forcing her to move to another part of town, her case was transferred. After the move she was stable and followed through with appointments, so things seemed fine. Then her father died and she became depressed. Then she moved again and was living alone for a while. Jacob was born two months later at which time his father moved into the home. Because Jacob was born in fetal distress, which means he had an urgent need to be taken out of the womb, follow-up nursing in the home was necessary in order to monitor his health. The nurses visited the home twice monthly.

When Jared was born 14 months later, Julie expressed difficulty coping with two little ones. Individual therapy and group therapy were recommended in the home and at a mental health clinic, to teach her coping strategies for managing stress. Infant stimulation was encouraged by the community health nursing staff. Often when a nurse arrived at 3:00 in the afternoon Julie had to be awakened. The boys would be in their cribs in a room upstairs wet with urine and unclothed. Julie would retrieve them and get them cleaned up then place them in the playpen in the downstairs part of the house. There was little talking to the children on her part nor did she touch or cuddle them, outside of the diaper and clothing changes. The nurses encouraged her to talk to the babies and hold them. They even demonstrated for her how it is done.

Julie tried hard and did make some changes, so things were better for a while. But by age two Jacob was diagnosed with Autism because he suddenly stopped talking and he wouldn't interact with people. Autism is a serious brain disorder that impedes the child's ability to function in all activities of living — communication, social interaction, even play. There might also be repetitive actions, head banging, and body rocking. Sameness in routine and environment are critical in managing the behaviors. Sometimes, as in Jacob's case, any language the child had suddenly stops at about two years of age. Once diagnosed with Autism, the nurses stopped encouraging Julie to touch Jacob because children with Autism often dislike being touched.

At 13 months, Jared was diagnosed "failure to thrive" because he was so listless and apathetic. Julie was provided training on proper nutrition for babies. A housekeeper aide and transportation in order to keep medical appointments was also provided. But things kept getting worse. The children weren't being immunized accordingly and Julie would put them on water fasts when they had diarrhea. When they began to lose weight rapidly the Children's Services Division entered the picture and removed them from the home. Jacob was almost three by then and Jared almost two.

"Some say it is one of the most severe cases of emotional and physical neglect they had ever seen," the worker said.

"But why the screaming at night and all the running around in circles?" I asked. I was an information seeker — the more I knew about something, the better able I was to approach the situation successfully.

"We know what the nurses' notes tell us but we don't know what happened to the boys otherwise. We know the father had poor coping skills and a hot temper; he lived in the home off-and-on evidently. He had substance abuse problems, too, and wouldn't go to parenting classes or drug and alcohol treatment either. In fact, he refused to claim paternity even though Jacob looks just like him," the worker responded.

I knew a little about the father already from Sam so this part of the conversation was not enlightening me about Jacob's behaviors. I wanted more details. "What about a possible seizure disorder?" I prodded on.

"Well we haven't explored it thoroughly yet but Jacob seems to get terribly out of control physically and emotionally at times," the worker explained. "And apparently for no reason. It's hard to know what given situations might trigger memories for him. Sherrie says he has always had problems sleeping and eating too, evidently," she finished up.

If he was physically abused maybe he relives the abuse in his dreams and that is why he fights going to sleep, I ventured on in my own thoughts. Since he was confined and imprisoned in a crib or playpen, those items are probably not symbols of comfort or joy. It was like putting together a jigsaw puzzle with the imagination taking responsibility for what the missing pieces might hold.

"I think Jacob is pretty damaged, Donna," Sherrie said. I called her after talking with the worker. There's that word *damaged* again, I thought to myself. It seemed common practice among the child welfare people to use the word. I still didn't like it, though. *Damaged* according to the American Heritage Dictionary means: *Impairment of the usefulness or value of person or property.*

"He acts frightened all the time," Sherrie went on. "When he first came to us he didn't know his own name. It was just luck that I found him an Early Intervention placement right away."

Early Intervention programs are effective government funded programs for young children from low-income (poverty level) families or in Jacob's case, foster children, who need extra intellectual and social stimulation in order to enhance their overall development so that they are more ready for meeting the demands of a regular school. It was fortunate Sherrie knew what Jacob needed. It was fortunate also that there was a slot. In Oregon, at that time, only 3,303 children of the 14,848 in need of help were being served because the federal government didn't want to provide anymore money to help children.

"Every day for the longest time Jacob would sit with his hands over his ears when he first came home from school," Sherrie said. "He would come off the bus repeating what people had said to him throughout the day — like 'good morning Jake', 'nice shirt Jake.' He talked in a high pitched voice too for the first three months with us. He has always had eating problems and sleep problems. There for a while he banged his head every night for about a half-an-hour before going to sleep. One night he crawled out of the upstairs bedroom window at 3:00 in the morning. When I found him, he was running down the side walk headed for a busy street. He had a crazed look in his eyes, if you know what I mean."

"He walked with a hitch in his leg too. I thought he had a bone deformity but the x-rays were normal. The only thing the doctor and I could conclude was that he wasn't used to walking. I thought I would never get him to stop eating his feces. I even turned his jammies around so that the zipper was in the back, then I pinned it. And do you know what that child did? He chewed the feet out of the jammies and got to it that way! He's *emotionally disturbed*. The psychiatrist wanted to institutionalize him at first. She also thought he was probably borderline mentally retarded. But I don't think he's mentally retarded because he's made great strides in the Early Intervention program. The child development center I took him to six months after coming to me said he wasn't autistic, but that his behaviors were likely the result of the severe emotional and physical neglect he suffered. He was so deprived. Jake and Jared both ate dirt from my potted house plants and drank water from the toilet. I'm telling you, they were like little animals!"

As Sherrie described the bizarre behaviors, I couldn't help but think of the time I went with Sam to Julie's apartment shortly after meeting her. I had to use the bathroom and naturally helped myself once she pointed the way. Upon opening the bathroom door I found two crazed-eyed cats staring at me. It looked as if they'd been in there for days, maybe even weeks. There were animal droppings all over and no sign of food. When one of the cats raised to its haunches and began hissing, I sensed I was going to be attacked, but I couldn't move for a moment because I was paralyzed with fear. It wasn't until I heard a growl and felt a thump where my hand rested on the door knob, that I realized I was safe on the other side.

I needed no further descriptions or explanation about behaviors, calling up this horrifying image was enough. Julie had starved and confined her babies just like she had done to her cats.

I was very upset after talking with Sherrie. I had no idea things like that could go on for so long. A terrible injustice had occurred and my heart went out to those poor little children.

Needing to hear something that made sense, I lashed out at Sam. "Why didn't you go over and try to help the boys?" I asked. "Did you know Julie wasn't feeding them?" My voice was loud.

"I didn't know that," he said. "But I did know she was having a hard time coping. She called me one day and said she was going crazy being cooped up in the house all the time. I told her to get out and take the kids to the park or something. She said she'd already tried going someplace with them on the bus, but that she ended up dropping Jared because she couldn't manage Jacob and him too," Sam answered in an apprehensive tone. Then cautiously, seeming to weigh his words, he preceded on: "Julie is an alcoholic, Donna." In a more light hearted tone, he added; "I have to hand it to her though, she's been trying for years to stop drinking. She'll sober up, find some minimum wage job and not drink for quite a while, sometimes months. But something always happens — she can't handle stress — and she'll binge drink for days on end until she loses her job. Then the cycle starts all over again. I think one of these days she'll make it and stay sober," he said in her defense, obviously satisfied with his perception.

"How can you defend her?" I asked, the impatience in my voice so obvious. I felt no mercy for Julie and it was obvious. Sam shot me a look of contempt and opened his mouth to say more in her defense but I stopped him. I knew there was no point in continuing the discussion. There were no easy answers and the downfall of the human race isn't an uplifting subject. Besides, Sam had been rescuing his youngest sister most of her adult life, that was the basis of their relationship. It was either that or abandon her, which wouldn't help anything because she was obviously enslaved to alcohol. Sam was doing the best he could and I was wrong to think he had the power to do more.

I was going to tell Sam I didn't want to have Jacob over again after talking with Sherrie and remembering Julie's cats. I wanted to pretend I had never heard about any of it and forget all about the unwanted child. I didn't want to get involved. He wasn't my responsibility. I just wanted to get back to the activities of my own safe world. Child welfare takes care of children like him, I kept telling myself.

But the more I thought about the little boy, the more uncomfortable I became. Was his future one without hope? What would happen to him if he wasn't adopted? If he exhausted Sherrie to the point of rejection, would the next foster parent be as knowledgeable, tolerant, and hard working as she seemed to be? Foster children get moved around a lot. I couldn't imagine a child in Jacob's condition being able to endure more disruption or, heaven forbid, any more abuse and neglect without his behaviors worsening. I had heard horror stories of children suffering from sexual abuse in foster homes.

Jacob's beginning was more than just a sad story, it was a nightmare. It seemed to me that permanency through adoption was his only hope or the nightmare would surely continue. But who would knowingly adopt a child labeled *severely emotionally disturbed?* I wouldn't. Some of the behaviors and characteristics seen in children with emotional disturbances are: hyperactivity, short-attention span, self-injurious behaviors, the failure to initiate interaction with others or social isolation, excessive fear or anxiety, inappropriate crying, temper tantrums, and poor coping skills. Jacob's behaviors seemed to fit all of the above.

I felt sorry for Jacob. He was a lost little soul who had never known love. I thought if he could be reached, his behaviors changed, and that terrible label removed, his chances for adoption might increase. But he needed one-on-one attention, intense individual help. I wanted to help him. Otherwise institutionalization might still be a possibility while foster care was surely the reality for the unwanted and seemingly undesirable child.

So I suggested to Sam that we continue to have Jacob over for weekend visits to try to change his behaviors based on what I knew about personality development and with some of the techniques I had learned at the hospital. Jacob wasn't a teenager but the American Psychiatric Association suggests there

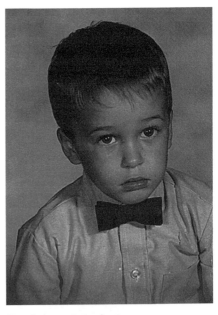

Jacob, age 4, in foster care.

isn't a "clear distinction between childhood and adult disorders." Sam thought this a great plan. "With you knowing what to do, I think we can help him," he said. Working at the hospital did give me a sense of competency. The job was my first in its capacity but being fresh out of college, I was very enthusiastic and so sure therapy could fix anything.

Chapter 3
"Someday Jacob will be a Real Boy"

I n the field of psychology there are many personality theories that attempt to explain why we humans think, feel,
and behave as we do. The ego and its defense mechanisms
operating at a subconscious level in order to reduce anxiety, is a
popular theory. The theory of personal unconscious, collective
unconscious, extroversion, and introversion, works for some.
Then there is the idea that we are all striving for superiority
and self-realization while struggling with feelings of inferiority
at the same time. The humanists see each of us a being unique,
set apart, and above all other life forms. Some people think most
human beings are innately psychologically healthy provided
the basic needs of food, shelter, safety, and love are met. Others
believe social environments play a critical role in the development of personality. Then there is social conditioning, cultural
influences, biology, and genetics. Now, the behaviorists, they
tend to reject theorizing altogether and believe human behavior is lawful and thus predictable.

At the psychiatric hospital psycho-therapy and discussion
around social conflict was used to address the defense mechanisms. Behavior modification, because of its predictability, and
a lot structure was being used to change behaviors. So each time
Jacob came to visit, I structured the days and evenings in every

way possible. I forced myself to cook and meals were placed on the table at the same time each day. I decided on a set bed time and established a routine which consisted of a bath followed by a story. If Jacob didn't scream he earned stickers. He seemed to take great pride in earning rewards, or "tokens," as they were called at the psychiatric hospital.

Occupational therapists work with all people — children, teenagers, adults, the elderly — using an activity that has purpose to the individual to promote mental and physical wellness. So in between meals Jacob and I did various hands-on projects. I would have him engage in a task of some sort while I worked beside him, or I would set up an activity so he could work at it independently with me in the same room. The tasks had to be the simplest in nature because his attention span was short. He liked coloring, building with blocks, and stringing beads. Work type activities seemed to have purpose for him, too, because he liked to stack the dishes from the dishwasher, clean the bathroom sink, and wash woodwork. With each task completion he would earn a sticker or a cookie. With exception to the screaming, he was seldom unsuccessful.

Jacob was interested, motivated, and easy to engage in activity; a therapist's dream. Once engaged he would become earnest and diligent, often talking to himself and smiling while he worked. Things were to be kept in a precise order however or he could become quite upset. The blue color crayon had to be placed next to the yellow, for example, and the glasses could be placed in one spot only on the shelf. I let him work at this sense of order. And I strived to maintain his comfort level by keeping the environment orderly and quiet at all times with the exception of soft music playing in the background.

Structure, purposeful activity, and rewards for appropriate

behaviors were working but I knew there was more to Jacob's wellness than just external controls. He had suffered severe physical and emotional abuse and neglect and it all started in infancy — the beginning and a critical time for human emotional development.

All human beings are suppose to develop the emotion of trust during infancy. If we don't, we might carry suspicion and doubt of others through the rest of our lives. This idea comes from a man by the name of Erikson, a psycho-analyst, who believed that the type of society a person grows up in with all of its interpersonal relationships with others, is just as important as the person's instinctual drives. He theorized that a person's personality develops around those interpersonal relationships as they relate to childhood experiences and then unfolds throughout the life span, passing through eight developmental stages in the process. At each stage of one's psychosocial development — as Erikson called it — there is a natural emotional issue or conflict that has to be resolved. If it is not, it will trouble the person and perhaps hold him back in achieving his goals throughout life.

The development of trust — trust in a parent, trust in a sibling, trust in another human being — is the emotional stage for infants through three. It is believed that through this early development of trust, a child will be able to learn how to depend on others later in life. And depending on others fosters teamwork, harmonious marriages, and loving parent-child relationships.

In order to develop the emotion of trust which also leads to a sense of self, which in turn influences one's moral development, a baby must experience what it feels like to get his needs met. When he cries he learns someone will come. When he is hungry he learns someone will feed him. If nobody comes when he cries, if he cannot be comforted, or if he doesn't get fed when he is hungry, trust in another cannot develop and the world is perceived as an unfriendly, perhaps even hostile, place.

There is nothing simple about human development — environments, culture, genetics — each are contributing factors. Even the body makes a contribution to the growth and development of personality as babies need touching and holding, too, as well as food and comfort. Touching and holding is "contact comfort" and it provides the sensory stimulation necessary for the infant's brain to develop all the dendrites needed to make strong interconnections between nerve cells. Sensory stimulation also promotes bonding and attachment between parent and child. Some people believe children who are deprived of sensory stimulation during the first two years of life will grow up to be violent, aggressive, drug abusers, and alcoholics.

Jacob was not fed, held, or comforted, and he likely didn't bond with Julie — thus the label "unattached child." That didn't mean there wasn't hope, though.

Years ago a study was done with some young male monkeys who were isolated and deprived of contact comfort since birth. They were withdrawn, fearful, hostile, and aggressive. But once they were placed with normal infant monkeys who naturally wanted contact comfort and sought it out, crawling all over them, the abnormal behaviors eventually disappeared.

So I started touching Jacob as much as I possibly could. I hugged him. I held his hand. I put him in my lap and tickled him. We wrestled and rough-housed, which he absolutely loved; lapping it up little a hungry kitten with a bowl of cream. I became his playmate basically. I also modeled for him imaginative play with toys by getting down on the floor and playing with them myself. I showed him how the animals can talk if we let them.

Childhood is also the time of gross motor development, something that is as critical to intellectual development as trust is to emotional development. A famous psychologist named Piaget discovered years ago that in order to obtain the higher level intelligence necessary to learn in school and function independently in the world, a youngster must be allowed to run and jump and move. The reason for this is because movement, with its sensory feedback, helps the child to know his body in a concrete way and the brain can't process abstractions until is has this knowledge of the body. This is why kids are little motor machines and always busy during the early years from birth to seven. There is a sequence to gross motor development, too: babies sit up first, then they crawl for a while, then they stand up with the help of the coffee table, and pretty soon they are walking; getting where they think they need to go. When they start running, every environment becomes a playground and mommy and daddy have their hands full.

Although Jacob wasn't a toddler anymore, I started thinking of him as one in relation to all that energy — he needed to run it seemed. I had always thought toddlers shouldn't be pinned in, it's not natural, and Sam agreed with me. "Yep, he's like a pup," he said, "and we can't keep him pinned in. Pinned puppies usually grow up to be untrustworthy adult dogs, you know." So, in addition to taking Jacob to the park when the weather permitted, I brought his Big-Wheels from Sherrie's so he could ride it in the basement.

The basement of the apartment complex was almost half-of-a-block long. Jacob loved his Big-Wheels and would peddle back and forth for sometimes up to an hour. One afternoon he fell asleep over the handle bars: exhausted, satisfied, content, too tired to fight the demons that awaited him in his sleep. The physical freedom to move seemed to help him sleep more soundly than the sleep medication so we stopped using it. But still, he was always awake by 5:30 or 6:00 am and ready to run.

Pretty soon I was able to make the distinction between Jacob's raging and temper tantruming. There was a difference and I didn't make this discovery because of clinical abilities. When he temper tantrumed, he cried and kicked as any young child with low frustration tolerance and an inability to communicate would. If I could figure out what he wanted, I would give it to him if it was reasonable. His tears would subside then and he was content. When he tantrumed I registered feelings of sympathy and sometimes frustration because I wanted to support him even though it was difficult to understand his wants. However, if I couldn't discern correctly or if I denied him because a given request was unsafe or unreasonable, the situation could escalate to raging status. When he raged, I registered feelings of fear — fear for his safety, fear for my own, and fear for anyone else caught in his wake. That is how I came to know the difference between raging and tantruming — by my own feelings.

Therapeutic hugs, which entail criss-crossing the child's arms in front of his chest then holding them from behind, is a way of containing a child. It was the technique suggested to us by the Jacob's worker. Sam and I had been using it fairly successfully. Sam likened it to a straight jacket but he didn't have any qualms about using it. I found it humanly ungratifying because I could not look into Jacob's face to let him know I was friend and not foe. The hug had to be administered in precisely the right moment, too, in order to be effective. A few seconds of hesitation could mean the difference between managing a tantruming child or managing a physical being of mountainous strength.

Such was the case one day when Jacob wanted to go home with a friend of mine whom he had never met before. When I said no he started screaming and running for the door. Gearing myself up to initiate a therapeutic hug, I lost the moment and Jacob slipped through the open door. He was so fast. Within seconds he had run into the lobby of the apartment complex and was banging his head on the glass of the entrance door. I knew he had to be stopped but I was so overcome with fear that I couldn't move, I was paralyzed.

Sam had his wits about him though and pulled Jacob away from the door. Jacob must have been frightened too because he was still screaming. Then he started crying and kicking Sam. Sam wasn't able to do the therapeutic hug. Exasperated, but not angry — Sam didn't get angry — he then did something "creative." He scooped Jacob up, carried him back into the apartment, turned on the cold water in the shower and with Jacob screaming, kicking and hitting him in the face, he stepped into it. Clothes, shoes, his watch; everything they had on was drenched. Jacob calmed down immediately. The contrast between a heated rage and a cold shower was probably shocking to Jacob, but keeping him safe was a serious undertaking.

I found Jacob's screaming and rages unnerving and not being able to anticipate what would set him off kept me on edge. The stickers, cookies, and time-outs worked well most of the time to keep things under control. But sometimes when I wasn't prepared, I resorted to a very human tactic: yelling. Some times it was a swat on the bottom. These were gut reactions on my part and not helpful to me or Jacob. So I sought to keep myself out of tight corners and Jacob happy, safe, and successful by tracking his likes and dislikes. Eventually I came to recognize situations and environments to avoid. Brightly lit supermarkets, crowds and noisy settings consistently upset him. So we stayed in the apartment or went only to the park. Sam would watch him when I went grocery shopping; I refused to take him in the car alone. We stopped having company over when Jacob was with us, too.

Weekend after weekend, Friday evening through Sunday evenings, Jacob came to visit. I kept trying different things, throwing out what didn't work and keeping what did. With each visit Jacob became more and more responsive to me, his behaviors seeming to change rapidly. Within two months, the compulsive hand washing and staring into lights had ceased completely. Though he was still physically active, he wasn't running around in endless circles; he had slowed down just enough to relate socially. His speech had improved or maybe I just got used to it, so the temper tantrums had been reduced somewhat. He was finally potty trained, an important psychosocial milestone. The emotional conflict for the child between ages one and three is autonomy, or control, over his own bodily functions. Erikson said if the child is unsuccessful in learning autonomy in this stage of his psychosocial development, he will develop shame and doubt about his own abilities. Jacob was late, but late was better than never.

Jacob's eye contact, something which is thought by some to be an indicator of one's honesty and aggressiveness, was markedly improved with Sam and I, though not with others. The rage lived inside of him restlessly, always ready to rear its ugly head if need be, but he wasn't scaring me anymore. The nightmares I decided to qualify as a given but they were fewer and farther between. He was playing independently and would spend time manipulating toy figures and talking to them imaginatively like little children do. Never was he cruel to the cat. In fact, he was naturally kind and gentle with her. I had thought a child so young who had experienced cruelty would need to be taught gentle behavior.

During the week days, when Jacob wasn't with us, I found myself thinking about him a lot and wondering how he was getting along in the world. I liked the little boy. There was something awakening in me but I wasn't sure what it was. Then one day I found myself missing Jacob and looking forward to the next time I would see him again. We extended the visits through Monday evenings after that. Pretty soon it was his questionable future that weighed heavy on my mind. He was certainly a complex child and anger perhaps his only outlet for the pain and suffering he had been brought to bear, but he was responsive and learning quickly. And his future emotional development was dependent on one factor: people.

As a way of keeping Jacob structured up and having contact comfort with him too, I read to him a lot. He loved stories and would sit in my lap to see the pictures. When he started sounding out words, I introduced him to phonics. Then one day, to my surprise, he started reading to me! The books were simple little children's books but his words flowed smoothly. He seemed to love books in general because he'd climb into the little bed Sam had made for him by now, and place several of my college text books strategically on his lap, thighs, and lower legs, as if they were a lap blanket. Then he would sit looking at pictures pretending to read. From reading he went to writing. "I'm going to write today!" he announced one morning. And he did, from that day on. He'd ask for paper and pencil and sit down to his work independently. With the single mindedness of a scientist or scholar, he would attend for long periods of time, taking great pride in every letter he printed. It was as if he was hungry for learning or perhaps just in love with learning itself.

Jacob was obviously not mentally retarded, or even slow, but rather quite bright. Everyone likes working with bright children — they make the job easier. I liked Jacob because he was smart, this is true, but it was his kindness that kept drawing me in to him emotionally. He was a little sweetheart. If he had two cookies he'd want to give me one. When he saw a little girl in a wheelchair on television he talked about how he would help her. "I would push that wheelchair for her if I was there," he said. When the cat contracted an eye infection he gently helped me nurse her back to health. I personally believe kindness is a mark of wisdom but it can't be measured in an IQ test. If it could be, then maybe adults would be more comfortable with outward demonstrations of concern, sympathy, and understanding.

Jacob continued to come for visits. With each visit, his true nature continued to show itself. When he walked around the apartment one day saying to himself "Someday Jacob will be a real boy," I felt it wasn't just a line from the Pinocchio story we were reading, but his own personal goal. Then one day he announced boldly: "I'm not going to suck my thumb anymore," and he never did from that moment on. He had a self-determination or inner strength about him which couldn't be ignored and I admired him for it. He was what a mental health therapist would call a "survivor;" the new word today is the "invulnerable." He suffered horrendous circumstances yet survived with a desire to learn and to love. There was still a lot of emotional healing to do but he was receptive; without willingness and receptivity change can be nearly impossible. He was beating the odds, too. Deprived environments can affect children intellectually, but true to what studies demonstrated decades ago, Jacob was showing remarkable improvements once placed in an intellectually stimulating environment. Studies have also shown that the earlier a child is adopted the higher its later IQ scores tend to be.

I'm not sure where time went. I had been so engrossed in Jacob's care that when I stopped to take account, nearly four months had slipped by. While thinking about his successes one day, I realized my own life was now bursting with a fullness I had never known before. The idea of watching Jacob become a "real boy" — brave, truthful and unselfish — was inviting, calling me to join in and believe. There was a newness in the air which filled me with excited anticipation. I knew I could never turn the child out to strangers now; I loved him. When I shared this discovery with Sam and then voiced my desire to adopt Jacob with him, he smiled and let out a long sigh. "Thank you, Donna," he said.

My friends and especially my co-workers opposed the adoption. "Why would you want to do this?" they kept asking. "You're playing with fire!," someone said. I understood their doubts and concerns but I couldn't begin to explain what was in my heart; everything was too personal now. Some professionals who are fresh out of college think they are going to save the world but this wasn't about saving the world for me and it wasn't about being a professional anymore either. It was about love and hope. I liked Jacob, too. He was good and kind and smart — a 'diamond in the rough' — with a tremendous amount of potential. I refused to let words of doubts dampen my spirits or my hopes for him. Even when the child welfare worker said Medicaid insurance, the federally funded insurance for the poor, would be provided because "Children with a history like Jacob's often need residential treatment when they reach adolescence," I closed my ears.

Residential treatment centers are government funded psychiatric facilities for children and youth considered disturbed. The worker was referring to Jacob likely acting out in adolescence when he would be struggling with identity issues. Finding one's identity — which is to determine who and what one wants to be in relation to society — is the emotional conflict for the adolescent in his psychosocial development. Unresolved conflicts with identity issues can result in role confusion for the teenager which might then carry over into adulthood. For the adopted child, identity issues can be especially difficult if the earlier emotional stages continue to need resolution. But Jacob was catching up and I refused to think love wouldn't make the difference.

The worker was happy for Jacob, though, and said permanent placement stories like ours made her job rewarding. To my surprise, Julie was amicable to the adoption. Knowing Jacob was with her brother, she voluntarily relinquished her parental rights instead of having them terminated, thus saving the court system a great deal of money. And though I vowed I would refuse to see Julie again after meeting Jacob and his brother, I never had to test this resolution because she graciously removed herself from the picture once Sam and I became involved in Jacob's care and we never heard from her again. Technically, because ours was to be considered an "open adoption," she had the right to pictures of Jacob yearly. But as the adoptive parents, Sam and I had the control and I didn't want to give her anything.

Sherrie was overjoyed with the adoption. "Bless your heart. Jacob has come to care about you and Sam and he talks about you guys all the time," she said as we gathered Jacob's things. "You tell him not to worry about Jared. We'll keep him here with us," she said sincerely. If Sherrie had her doubts, she never said so.

Sherrie and Jacob's early intervention teacher were very supportive during this time. They brought me in as a member of the team and kept me well informed. Jacob carried a notebook to and from school where his behaviors and emotional state, in general, were logged faithfully on a daily basis. I would receive the notebook on Fridays and send it back to school with Jacob on Mondays.

In addition to information, the teacher was always filling the pages of the notebook with words of hope and affirmation. She too believed in the resiliency of children and was an adoptive parent of four children herself. "Jacob is a smart boy and he's come so far. He's good and kind and he adores you Donna. You are an angel! Keep up the good work!" Her husband was a pediatrician and he orchestrated a complete metabolic work-up and a 'head-to-toe' physical on Jacob in order to rule out a "seizure disorder." A seizure disorder was not found although Jacob did have a weak immune system which meant he wouldn't be able to handle a lot of stress. "That is why you're seeing upper respiratory problems — running nose and coughing," the doctor said. A vaccine was administered in order to give his immune system a boost and vitamins to supplement his diet were recommended. I didn't ask the doctor if Jacob was born with a weak immune system or if it was something that had developed due to the stress he had endured for so long.

On St. Patrick's day 1989 Jacob came to live with us. While those watching us were shaking their heads, making remarks about the future, I was busy strategizing and problem solving the demands of the day. Caring for Jacob on a daily basis meant changes in the daily and nightly routines, consistent meal preparation, a refrigerator and cupboards stocked with milk, white bread, peanut butter and of course, eggs. There were toys to pick up, extra laundry to do, little shoes to buy, haircuts, and trips to the drug store for cough syrup. My previous life style as I'd known it, coming and going as I pleased, lounging on the couch with something to read, or napping on a Sunday afternoon, was no more. I missed those naps. But since Jacob didn't nap, I didn't either. There was the housekeeping and laundry, too. Sam wasn't one to help with such tasks. He never said it outright but they were considered "woman's work." Until this point it had not mattered, but now that his nephew lived with us, I felt he should take some responsibility too. He promised to help and as proof, he started helping with meal preparation.

Parenting also meant scheduling and transportation issues: dental appointments, visits to the doctor, parent-teacher conferences. I was working forty hours a week, too. Fortunately, Jacob was picked-up in front of the apartment by a school bus and transported to the Early Intervention program so I didn't have to worry about that. Then at noon he was transported to the day care center Sherrie had enrolled him in where he stayed until I picked him up at 5:30, after I got off work. I was working at the hospital from 8:30 until 5:00. Sam couldn't help with transportation because he didn't drive, a bicycle was his sole means of transportation. He refused to drive a car or obtain a license. He didn't want to contribute to pollution, he always told people but I knew it was likely an excuse to live a healthier life. His father died relatively young from a heart attack so as long as Sam didn't have license to drive, he was forced to exercise.

We were happy, though, in spite of such seemingly small conflicts. Those first couple of months after Jacob came to live with us Sam and I laughed a lot and made plans for the future. He saw nothing "out of place" now as far as his nephew was concerned and like an unspoken truce, we didn't talk about Jacob's past. He and Jacob related in a way that perhaps only kinship males can do: cuddling when watching television together and chatting in such a familiar way, like people do at family reunions. Sam had a gift for explaining the abstracts of science and nature in the simplest of terms, capturing Jacob's attention as well as his imagination. Jacob often tagged along after him on building maintenance projects or assessments. Chatting as they roamed the halls, I'd hear Jacob saying, "But *why* Uncle Sam?" He emulated his uncle, eventually taking on some of his mannerisms and body posturing; he was bonding.

Jacob emulated me too, copying my verbal expressions mostly. Like an echo in a canyon, I'd hear him repeat what I said to Sam or someone else. The extra work and longer days that parenting demanded required more energy and a concentrated effort on my part. I felt young again, though, and would seem to catch a second wind the moment I saw Jacob at the end of the work day. He was a pleasure, seemingly so grateful and appreciative to have someone who loved him. "I'm so happy you came to see me!" he'd exclaim, once we were situated in the car. The day his teacher said "Jacob refers to you as '*My Donna*,'" I thought my heart would burst from joy. I'd never known such a feeling before and I too was grateful. In the evenings we rough-housed and played. Never knowing when I was going to turn into the tickle monster, Jacob would watch me, and wonder, then squeal with delight when I caught him coming around a corner.

Then one sunny late spring morning, almost three months after Jacob came to stay, my world was shattered. It was a Saturday morning and as usual, Jacob was awake at 5:30. A calmness had settled over him in the previous weeks and he seldom awoke ready to run but would play quietly with his toys until I was fully awake within the hour. But this particular morning he awoke screaming and then running through the apartment. He wouldn't eat his favorite breakfast of scrambled eggs. Instead he pushed the bowl off the table and screamed at me, "Jacob take care of Jacob!" I had forgotten the worker said there would be a "honeymoon" period where adopted children act on their best behavior out of fear of being sent back. I was devastated. Had I done something wrong?, I wondered. It was confusing. Time had turned itself around and we were heading backward instead of forward.

I finally collected myself only to be overcome by the sense of a great sadness for this child whom life had forsaken at birth. Jacob couldn't disguise his deeply seated fear that people might in fact, be untrustworthy. It wasn't his fault he harbored feelings of suspicion and doubt. As a helpless infant he wanted to trust someone would come when he cried but nobody came. He wanted to trust that his hunger would go away but it never did. He had had to face the darkness all alone. Powerless to withstand its pull, and too young to endure the pain of knowing that the world can be a tricky place, he forfeited his right to safekeeping. Unknown to him was the vow of parental love. It's a guardianship that promises "You before me," at least for a while. Without faith, Jacob could not know his uncle and I would take care of him. Or, perhaps more importantly, that we *wanted* to take care of him.

After discussing Jacob's regressive behavior with the worker, I never hesitated to call her when faced with a dilemma, I was relieved to discover maybe time wasn't working against us after all. "It's normal behavior for the child who has suffered emotional and physical abuse and neglect," she said. Jacob's spirit was calling out helplessly from the void of distrust, desperately longing to believe in another human being before it was too late. Life was thrusting him forward but without resolution of the emotional conflict, he was forced to revisit the past and all its emptiness. I had to help him; he had to know I could be trusted. But he had to be shown, I felt, as words alone cannot penetrate the darkness.

So, I ran out to the store and bought a baby bottle, the symbol of love and survival to the young. After filling it with milk and asking Sam to leave the room, I sat down in the rocker and wrestled Jacob to my lap; he wouldn't submit willingly. Then I pinned his feet under my right thigh to keep him from kicking and I wrapped my left arm around his chest to hold his arms. It was hope alone that sanctioned this act and pushed me forward. When Jacob opened his mouth to scream and spit, I filled its emptiness with the nipple of the bottle, inviting him to suck. When faced with his adamant refusal to suck, I rested the nipple on his lower lip and watched as the milk dripped slowly yet knowingly, coating his tongue with its sweetness. When he spit it out, I put it back in. Will against will, I kept putting the nipple in his mouth and he kept spitting it out. He wouldn't let me see into his eyes. In a very quiet voice I told him I wanted to feed him because I loved him. He wouldn't respond. I could feel the rage in his body and was forced to hold him tight, my arms aching from the tension running through my veins. Time crawled at an agonizingly slow pace. Moment by moment, it robbed me of my strength. I was nearly defeated when suddenly, something amazing happened. The rage in Jacob's body subsided and in the instant it disappeared, his little body melded into mine giving me the impression of a newborn who has finally been delivered to the bosom of it's mother. His eyes were filled with anticipation when he asked me to feed him. There was an urgency in his suck when he drank from the bottle and his eyes never left mine throughout the entire "feeding time." Afterwards, he rested peacefully in my arms for the longest time, looking up at me with shining eyes and a tender smile. He eventually jumped down from my lap, ran to his collection of toys and picked one out just for me. "Here's a present for you," he said with a smile, and handed me a pink teddy bear. When I held out my arms for a hug, he said, "You can kiss me if you want to."

The sun burned brightly that day, enveloping Jacob and I in its warmth. We weren't genetically bonded and I hadn't given birth to him, but now I felt as if he had always been a part of me. My heart was filled with a wholeness; so complete and reassuring. I became a mother that day in every sense of the word. It's not a position that bears prestige or even merit by modern day standards or priorities, but for me it was an honor to be called upon to guide this child on his journey to adulthood. It was a calling, too. One in which I was compelled to answer, for I felt that if I could raise just one healthy child in a world filled with strife, I might then be able to look back one day and think my life more meaningful.

Chapter 4
What About My Brother?

Prior to Jacob coming to stay permanently a child welfare worker visited our apartment in order to certify Sam and I as special foster parents until the adoption was final, a process that could take up to a year. This was following face to face interviews, and several phone conversations with the caseworker, Jacob's second by this time. The first worker had been with us such a short amount of time that all I can remember about her was that she really did seem like a caring person who just happened to get stuck with the rotten job of "introductions."

It was the second worker who told us about the "special needs adoption subsidy." Evidently most people who adopt America's children have moderate incomes. The adoption subsidy, which is a certain amount of money sent monthly, is meant to meet any extra costs should the child need special therapy. In addition to the psychological trauma they suffer, some children who are adopted have serious physical handicaps, too. Some can't walk, talk, or feed themselves. They are either beaten into such a state or born that way. Sam and I didn't even know we could get financial help with Jacob before we decided to adopt him. I suppose some people might adopt just to get the money, but the worker never made us feel like we were receiving a handout. In fact, she seemed like someone who was glad she could offer something. She moved on too, but I never forgot her smile and the kindness in her eyes.

With the certification out of the way, the subsidy and Medicaid insurance in place, and a new worker named Barbara, we were now ready for Phase II: seven weeks of pre-adoption training classes, one night a week for three hours. Phase III would be: the completion of a personal history questionnaire, called a "home study". Phase IV: if determined worthy candidates, our names and our situation, along with two other interested adoptive parties, would be set before an adoption committee, who would then make the final decision. And then Phase V: the acquisition of a lawyer. And finally, Phase VI: the judge's chamber — legal declaration. It was all a little bit like a nine month gestation and then birthing, except that biological parents aren't psychologically scrutinized.

It would have helped if Sam could have attended the pre-adoption parent training classes too but someone had to stay home with Jacob. We didn't trust anyone else to care for him. How could we? Jacob wasn't a child who was seen and not heard and he couldn't be pinned in or forced to sit still. He had to be in control of certain things too, like: opening the doors, combing his own hair, carrying his things when going someplace. He stopped doing something when it suited him to do so rather than when we adults asked him to, and he had to touch everything. He still raged too. There was only one way to best manage a rage, I had concluded, and it wasn't a cold shower: anticipate and head-off in order to avoid if possible.

Jacob wasn't easy to second guess though and his temper tantrums could be easily interpreted as rages and then become rages. In order to obtain care for him I needed to be able to trust in another's ability to observe, anticipate, and make the distinction between a rage and a tantrum — not attributes typical to the untrained eye. And I had little faith that the critical moment essential to the effectiveness of a therapeutic hug wouldn't be lost to the natural tendency of human beings to protect self in light of fear and thus flee or fight. If a sitter were to flee and step back for safety, Jacob would then be a side show to gawk at: a freak filled with rage. If a sitter chose to fight, the potential for harm to them both was certainly a possibility.

According to the pre-adoption training classes, Jacob's need for control was a symptom of his past. Control and who has it becomes an issue for children who have suffered physical and emotional abuse and neglect. The severity of the circumstances only compound the issue of course. Anger is a symptom of the abused child's past too, especially the physically abused. It is believed that when children have experienced abuse and neglect, an internal chaos haunts them. When placed in stable situations, they may battle for control and try to sabotage the placement in order to make it fit with their already shaky self-image and internal chaos. External structure and consistency within the environment helps to decrease the child's need to sabotage because it imposes self-control and introduces a more grounded reality.

My being aware of the abandoned and abused child's need for control was helpful but I knew too that it really wasn't so atypical of all children in Jacob's age group. The preschool age child is supposed to strive to develop his own way of asserting his needs and gaining rewards all the while battling with the conflict from within of inner desires versus society's demands. Erikson said that if unsuccessful at this stage, the child will internalize feelings of guilt rather than the desire to take some initiative, so I purposely gave Jacob a lot of opportunity for some control. I wanted him to find his own way in the world eventually.

Some of my apprehensive feelings about sending Jacob to a sitter were due to my own need for control as well. He and I were still bonding, knitting together our parent-child relationship of interdependence. Together we were facing his trust versus mistrust issues. For awhile he had allowed himself to be my baby by virtue of regression. If he was moving into the stage when the fears of separation-anxiety become real for the child, I didn't want to be insensitive to its call; he was attached to me. It was the newness of it all too, I suppose. I wanted everything for Jacob to be done just right, much like the way a first time mom will insist on the application of baby powder with each and every diaper change.

That spring we moved into a three bedroom house. Moving required Sam having to give up his managerial job, but I was optimistic he would find another avenue of employment right away. We had to move. Jacob needed his own room and a real bed, responsible and successful parenting dictated this. The house was a charming English Tudor in a quiet neighborhood and logistically conducive to the needs of a child: an elementary school two blocks away and a small park with a slide, swings, teeter totters and a merry-go-round right next door. The back yard was partially fenced and a beautiful mimosa tree stood over a two foot deep home-made pond. It was also just six blocks from my new job. I had been laid off at the hospital and went to work for a community mental health clinic serving chronically mentally ill adults.

We moved into our "new blue house" as Jacob called it, in the middle of June, after school was out. Jacob loved the house.

The entry-ways between the kitchen, the dinning room, the living room, and the hallway, marked off the "island" he informed us. The challenge was to see how many times he could run around the island before he was gobbled-up by the tickle monster.

Jacob regressed following the move: temper tantruming and flying into rages. But once things were quiet again and the structure and routine put back into place, his anxieties subsided. He was like the "boy in the bubble," I often thought; insulation and sameness were his lifeline. On the days when I couldn't find the time or energy to rough house with him, he was most content to play by himself or sit and read. When I worked in the yard, he would play in the pond under the mimosa tree. He continued three days a week at the daycare center he had attended previously, which was now just three miles from our home. I tried taking him to a children's play and an art show, but he was too active for such environments and called undesirable attention to himself. To get out of the house we took walks in the neighborhood or went to the park next door. A learning type activity with him after dinner, which was our "special time" together, followed by a bath and a story before bed, was the extent of our nightly routine. Every once in a while, when he wasn't busy setting up his new shop in the garage, Sam would join us for "special time." Jacob never had an issue around food again following our "feeding" session and his food preferences were expanding. Life was good, though simple, and it was to my advantage that I was a "homebody" by nature.

I'd always been a "homebody" more or less. I didn't care for being on the go all the time and I liked things nice and quiet around my house. Environments and how they can influence a person being successful or not was something I learned about in college, but for me personally, they had always had an incredible influence on my moods. My home was my haven. I could create a cozy and warm atmosphere in my home, conducive to my inside self, by way of homemade curtains, refurbished second hand furniture, and assorted "art" hung on every wall. Flea markets, garage sales, junk stores and antique stores were my favorite haunts.

I had fun decorating Jacob's room. I found a bed and a little desk for him at a garage sale and gave each item new life with a fresh coat of paint. I made curtains and a bedspread using fabric of bright red, green, yellow and blue; the primary colors thought to be so good for children. Jacob became so excited when he saw his room, that he zipped around and over the furniture a few times to make his happiness known. I made school clothes for him and curtains for the living room and dinning room that summer, too. I loved to sew, primarily because I liked the soft steady hum of the machine. I did my best thinking when I was sewing.

I did a lot of reading about parenting that summer too. I learned about various parenting styles; an important issue having never been a real parent myself. I learned how to talk to a child so he will listen and how to listen so he will talk. I read about dysfunctional families because I knew what I didn't want us to be. Self-esteem is thought to be a "family affair" another book said; if parents don't feel good about themselves it will impact how the child feels about himself. I also attended three workshops specific to adoptive children and adopting the older child where I learned that adoptive children need help grieving for the loss of birth parents, separations from siblings, and the break-up of friendships made while in various foster homes. I read because I wanted to be a good mom.

During Jacob's weekend visits he didn't talk about his brother, but after he came to live permanently he did. "Is Jared at Mommy Sherrie's?" he would ask time and time again. Every once in a while I'd hear him say to his toys, "How you doin' Jared?" He missed Jared. So for Jacob's sake, I thought it a good idea that we have Jared over to the apartment from time to time, especially since I had learned about children needing to come to terms with separation and loss issues. Jared had been the one constant in Jacob's life and he was going to lose him. Sam appreciated my willingness to do this and he was always available when Jared spent the day or an afternoon. After we moved into the house we increased the visits to over night.

Jacob loved it when Jared spent the night. The first time I told him Jared would be staying over he squealed with delight. "If Jared sleeps here, will he get to hear stories too?," he asked. It surprised me he would think of that. When I told him that yes, I would read to Jared too, he became very excited and clapped his hands. "Good! I bet he will like them too." Jacob was his little brother's keeper. Unfortunately, I didn't know stories can be as treacherous to the wounds of the young as asphalt can be to their knees. I found this out the hard way while reading to the boys one night when Jared stayed over.

It was a story about a little bear that had been sent as a gift to the King. His human parents put a name tag around his neck and sent him to the king by himself. He was late getting to the palace and didn't make it in time for the King's birthday because he had stopped along the way to help those in need. The King's guards were very angry with him for arriving late, so they locked him in the dungeon instead of presenting him to the King. Many weeks went by and in his loneliness and despair, the little bear sang a song of his plight in order to pass the hours. The birds heard his song and took his words back to the people he had helped along the way. His friends then went to the King and told him why the little bear was late for his birthday. The King was overjoyed to know he had been sent such a good little helpful gift bear and had him released from the dungeon immediately. Jacob and Jared took each others' hands and cried when I sang the little bear's song. The happy ending wasn't enough to keep their tears from flowing. I just sat there and watched them cry. I didn't know what to say. They were suffering from the pain of the knowing between them — abuse through imprisonment was one of the links to their brotherhood — comfort was found in holding hands.

Having Jared over was demanding for me because he required so much physical care. Still in diapers and totally dependent for dressing and bathing, he was like a toddler, and seemingly quite delayed in all areas of development. Although he was three-and-a-half by now, he was little and scrawny and his arms and leg muscles still had that mushy two-year-old feel to them. He didn't run and jump like other children his age do: he preferred sitting on the floor. His thumbs bent backward and his hands were so weak he couldn't hold or carry things very well. He was always dropping sandwiches and toys. Rather than pick them up or come and get another sandwich, he would cry until someone retrieved the items for him. I felt sorry for him. It was as if he didn't have enough sense of self to know he had the power to pick things up. He drooled, sucked his thumb, and mouthed objects constantly like an infant. When eating he bit his tongue and the insides of his cheeks. He talked very little even though his language skills seemed fine. Crying was his primary form of communication. When he wanted something he would point and cry. He was helpless in so many ways and people didn't seem to expect much from him, myself included. Some of the helplessness was no doubt learned I thought, but still, the child needed help.

Sherrie had been "clucking like a mother hen," as she put it, to get Jared into an Early Intervention program since he came into her care, but there were no slots. So she placed him in a childcare center but she wasn't pleased with it. "The staff just aren't trained to work with his special needs and Lord knows they've got their own troubles. The center is about ready to close because they don't have enough money and it's located right smack-dab in the middle of gangs. A drug house across the street was cleared out and boarded up last week. But, it's better than nothing."

Sam's other sister Linda had looked into adopting Jared and had had him to her home for a visit. Evidently when he smeared feces all over her walls, she brought him back to Sherrie's two days early and had not been heard from since. The maternal grandmother's health was failing so she couldn't take him. There wasn't anybody else left to ask. I wasn't surprised when Sam asked me if I would consider adopting him too. "No" — was my empathic response. It was too soon for me. I was still adjusting to juggling work and parenting as well as the seriousness of raising just one child. Plus I wasn't drawn to Jared like I had been to Jacob; he wasn't at all like his brother.

In the beginning I watched Jared a lot when I went to Sherrie's to pick up Jacob. He often played alone, seemingly out of choice. A mean spirited child by all appearances, he would grab whatever he wanted from the other children, then scurry off to a corner and sit grinning when they cried. He was mean-spirited with Jacob too, but Jacob would readily give him whatever he wanted even at the expense of denying himself. I'd encourage him not to but he'd say "I don't mind," in the sweetest tone of voice while scooting off to find himself something else to play with. He acted as if that was the way it was supposed to be. Sadly though, whatever Jacob gave, Jared wanted more. If Jacob had three toys and was willing to give Jared two of them that wasn't good enough, Jared would want the third one too. He was greedy.

Was he damaged? I didn't think so — he was still so young. However, his eyes were dull and his skin lifeless, the telltale signs of emotional neglect. But then, life had yet to give him something to feel happy about. There was something ever so lonely about the way he kept to himself. When I talked to him or attempted to interact with him, other than to take care of his needs, he would stare at my hair or my mouth making me feel as if I didn't exist.

Jared didn't rage like Jacob did but he had his little control issues too, particularly around food. When the food was served he had to be first or he would cry. The biggest portions had to go to him or he'd reach for Jacob's helping and shove it, sometimes spilling, all the while paying close attention to making sure nothing happened to his own. And oh was he oppositional. Getting ready to go in the car was opposed. Having his diaper changed, clothes changed, or hair brushed was opposed. Transitions from play activity to bathing was difficult. To make his opposition known, he would throw himself to the ground and kick and scream. The opposition was due to a lack of trust, I knew that, for he too had been forsaken at birth. Sherrie kept saying he was tough, but I wasn't so sure about that; he seemed rather fragile to me.

Despite his negative behaviors though, Jared had a way about him that could melt even the coldest heart. He sought affection from all adults, especially women. It didn't matter if he knew the person or not; everyone was seemingly a long lost friend. He'd crawl into someone's lap and with his thumb in his mouth, plant himself like an embryo egg attaches itself to the uterine wall. When he wanted my attention specifically he'd grab my thigh and step all over my feet to make his presence known. This behavior was most annoying but when I'd look down and see those big brown eyes looking up at me with the anticipation of a puppy, I'd pick him up and hold him for awhile.

It was a strain to hold Jared sometimes because there was a foul odor coming from his skin and his mouth, a nauseating smell like that of rotted meat. Unfortunately, he liked to kiss and be kissed. I felt this was a positive quality to his nature and I didn't want to discourage him, so I'd bend down and offer my cheek. He'd deliver a sloppy kiss and I'd return a kiss in kind, then I'd go to the bathroom and wash the putrid saliva off. At night when I tucked him into bed he'd want a kiss on the mouth. "Would you kiss me on the lips?" he'd say, but I just couldn't. Sherrie thought he might have an endocrine problem but it turned out to be much simpler than that. He was always getting ear infections. As soon as one was cleared up with antibiotics, another would take hold. So finally Sherrie took him to an ear, nose and throat specialist. Two small objects were found in each nostril of his nose. The items were wedged so high that only a specialist could have discovered the condition. When a rigid plastic toy car wheel was pulled out, a thick substance of green and black coloring oozed from the orifice. The doctor said that judging from the amount of decay, it was the antibiotics for the ear infections that had kept the poison from reaching Jared's brain.

Poor Jared. He was a little boy waiting to be loved and

wanted and there was no hope in sight yet. He belonged to the child welfare system: nobody's child. Time would likely work against him as it had already. As an infant time held him in an existence of nothingness. Love and trust were not his to know and thus the training in suspicion and doubt made complete. Time was working against him now when at three-and-a-half, he was already too late. There would be no early intervention for stimulation in order to make up for what he had missed. He was safe with Sherrie but I felt sorry for him and wondered where he'd end up and if it would be any place like where he started from.

Jared seemed to have a hold on Jacob. A hold that felt intrinsically unhealthy to me and I didn't know why. Sometimes I wondered if it would be best if I kept Jacob from Jared completely, knowing full well it was erroneous thinking. If I kept Jacob from seeing Jared he might never resolve his grief for the brother he was now separated from and would be further separated from in the years forthcoming. A birth family is a child's roots. We can no more cut those roots away without providing support and not expect consequences than we can cut away the roots of a tree and not expect it to topple over. Someday Jacob would ask: "What about my brother?" Then what? There would undoubtedly have to be contact. And if Jared wasn't adopted — the older a child becomes, the less likely adoption — would he grow up harboring feelings of resentment toward Jacob because he was adopted? It was a most difficult situation and hard to know what was best for everyone. I was trying to predict the future, which was absurd, but planning was a part of my nature. So we continued with the visits. I didn't know what else to do. It seemed that to care for one child, was to also care for the other.

Then something incredible happened one day to shed some light on Jared's true nature. He too was a complex child and highly skilled at keeping his guard up.

It was the beginning of August and the days were hot, 90 and above. Jared was staying over for the whole weekend and we had plans to spend all day Saturday at the beach. The day began the way it usually did with Jared: he was slow moving in the mornings and he hated having his pajamas taken off. So I would sit him in my lap to dress him. Sometimes he'd cry and kick me. This particular day he cried at the breakfast nook because his cereal was supposedly too hot even though I tested it and it felt lukewarm to me. He insisted on having Jacob's cup but rather than ask he grabbed and spilled cereal all over. He cried when I washed his face and hands and screamed when I combed his hair. Just when we were about to leave I had to dress him again because he soiled his diaper and clothing. By the time I got the car loaded and Jared seated and belted in, I was exhausted. I almost shut the car door on his little leg because it flopped out when I wasn't looking.

When we got to the beach I thought the fresh sea air might serve to bring Jared out of himself but as soon as we piled out of the car he made for a spot underneath the picnic table and refused to come out. After coaxing and pleading with him for the longest time to join us, I finally gave up. Nearly an hour had passed when he finally emerged. But the boy who came out from under the table wasn't the same one who had gone under. The new boy's eyes were shining bright and his cheeks had taken on that rosy "happy kid" color. He looked long into my eyes and for the first time it felt like he was actually seeing me. When I offered him food he didn't scrutinize the portions and said "please" and "thank-you" which he had never done before. By his own initiation he shared his potato chips with Jacob. I watched in wonder as he helped feed the seagulls.

There were no tears that sunny afternoon and while the boys scooped sand together in harmony, I was afforded the luxury of a nap. On the way back home, listening to his Uncle Sam's silly jokes and funny stories, Jared laughed for the first time. He was a belly laugher — laughing from the heart. A precious sound, the laughter of a child, and it made all the work that day worthwhile.

I was completely surprised at this change in Jared's attitude. I thought certainly it wouldn't last but it did. Once home we played peek-a-boo around corners and rough housed. Exhausted, we both fell to the couch and cuddled mutually. Then I turned into the tickle monster and gobbled up his belly laughs. Beaming, he cupped my face in his hands and declared, "You're beautiful!" From the way he said it, I felt like I was. He was the story book description of "little boy charm" and I was hooked. Then he surprised me again when he sat down on the kitchen floor and cuddled and kissed the cat ever so gently. Occasionally he'd look up and flash me a big smile. When I looked at him I saw a glow illuminating his being, a glow as radiant as that of a firefly illuminating the dark of the night. Wanting to capture the light burning bright within him, I retrieved the camera and took a picture.

In the days that followed I found myself studying that picture, wondering who the little boy in the picture was compared to the Jared who acted mean-spirited and greedy. I was drawn to him now, curious and wanting to know what he was made up of. Jacob and I were watching Star Trek one evening, right about this time, while I was busy thinking, and the episode was relevant to our situation. It was story about a group of children who had survived the cruelest of circumstances and yet remained loving, pure, and innocent of spirit. The story ended with a question — something to the effect — "What is the special ingredient that sustains the human spirit?" I was deep in

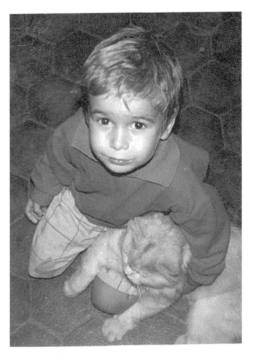

thought pondering the question when Jacob looked up at me and said "It's the heart isn't it?." Is it the heart?, I wondered. Is the heart the secret weapon of the survivor, or is it merely the key to unlocking the power of the spirit itself, wherein lies the desire to learn and to love?

Did Jared have the heart? I couldn't be sure. If so, he was going to need people bigger and stronger than him to shelter the heart's flame. And who would do it — fight the darkness on his behalf? Could it be his uncle and me? Could we adopt him too? Could we take on such a responsibility — parenting both of the boys? Parenting wasn't paradise, it was work, sprinkled with moments of joy like a stretch of beach is strewn with an occasional treasure. And Jared was behind. He would need a lot of extra attention to make up for the early neglect and abuse and lost time. Adopting Jared would definitely serve to map out the future somewhat for Jacob. But lets wait and see, I told myself.

Chapter 5
The Bureaucracy

Shortly after the beach trip, Jared opened up, like a flower in the spring, and began speaking in complete sentences. To everyone's surprise, he could articulate his words as well as any public speaker which was promising because a child's prognosis is typically thought to be subject to his language development.

Trucks, planes, trains, and cranes were Jared's favorite topics of conversation — he wanted to know how those man made machines worked. He was all boy and going to be an airplane pilot someday he said. He had a sense of humor too, the mark of intelligence some say. He would make jokes about people and their idiosyncrasies using bits and pieces of television commercials for punch lines. When Jacob would fly though the house, screech to a halt then pounce on a pile of Legos to begin a light speed construction, Jared would chuckle and say "Jake, Jake, he's a Lego maniac." To himself he was always saying softly, "Stay calm." He was mimicking the Nike commercial so popular at the time, but for some reason I got the feeling it held a very personal meaning for him.

The depth to Jared's character fueled further my thoughts regarding his potential — the dark and it's opposite, the light, the future and the fight. He was still oppositional and clingy,

but seemingly more aware of others. With a very real hunger
for contact comfort, he would crawl into my lap and say, "I'm
cozy now" when I put my arms around him. Endearing was
the way he said, "Do you think you like my new shoes?" or
"Will your camera take a picture of me today?"

The unlayering of the many facets to Jared's personality
were preparation of the soil: he too had the heart and it was
tender, he just didn't want anyone to know it — it wasn't safe.
A seed was planted when I wasn't looking, and love found it's
way into my heart for the little boy. The roots were already there
— his brother was the apple of my eye. But there was plenty of
room in my heart for him too — he belonged with us. Sam and
I discussed it and decided we would adopt Jared, too. Jacob
smiled big and clapped his hands with delight when we told
him. We started making plans. Then suddenly, everybody else
wanted Jared too.

It was the first of September and the nights were just beginning to get cooler. Nearly a year had passed since that fate-
ful day when I met Jacob — the boy who liked Legos — and his
little brother. Sam and I had already told Sherrie that we wanted
to adopt Jared too, and we were just about to tell Barbara, she
was his worker also, when Sherrie received word that he was to
be moved from her home so he could attend a day treatment
program for children diagnosed *severely emotionally disturbed.*

Day treatment programs are basically the mental health
system's contribution to early intervention for children, except
that the focus is on the modeling of appropriate behaviors as
opposed to academic learning. Sherrie became very upset with
this decision. She felt strongly it wasn't the time to uproot Jared
and place him with strangers. "He's just beginning to trust,"
she said. "A move will set him back." Sherrie knew Jared better

than anybody yet her opinion was not sought after. I never forgot the way her voice sounded of impending doom when she said, "And once they start moving him it won't stop."

Over the course of time and visitation pick-ups and deliveries, Sherrie and I had become friends. Just knowing her and the children she cared for was educational for me. Until I met Sherrie, I didn't know there was such a high need for foster homes. Babies in America today are being born drug and alcohol effected at incredible rates. Crack cocaine, heroin, methamphetamine, alcohol — whatever mom is taking, smoking, shooting, drinking, baby is too. Sherrie had been a pediatric nurse at one time and was medically trained in the special care the babies require when they're going through withdrawals from those life sapping drugs. A good proportion of the babies are often times adopted by their foster families while at the same time more babies in need of care keep coming. Sometimes it will be a sibling, a testimony to the repeated offenses, and the foster family will adopt that child as well. Sherrie and her family were adopting the baby and the two toddlers already in their care.

It took time to get to know Sherrie. Few people, from what I could tell, impressed her, myself included, and she wasn't one for small talk. She was a woman of vision though, and I learned to listen when she did speak. Usually we sat at the kitchen table and talked — the kitchen was the hub of the house. Or I would follow her from room to room as she made her rounds: into one of the bedrooms to change a diaper; the bathroom to toilet a little one; the back yard to make sure everybody was still there; then back to the kitchen to make sandwiches, pour glasses of milk or pass out cookies. I don't know how she kept up with it all, she was in her middle forties.

Sherrie wasn't what I would call patient with children, but

she was extremely tolerant and accepting. The hum of the background noise, or more realistically the roar, of children running, jumping, screaming, crying, fighting, didn't seem to faze her. Seldom did she raise her voice. And she had an almost uncanny ability for summing up a child's insecurities in three words or less. "Jake comes undone," she had said while watching us load his things into the car the day he came to live with us. Then as nonchalantly as a doctor might say go home and take an aspirin, she offered a prescription for his well being: "You just keep him wrapped up tight with lots of structure and he'll be okay."

It bothered me at first the way Sherrie always talked about Jacob in terms of his past, forcing me to remember that word *damaged*. But I soon learned this was Sherrie's reality base — all the children who came to her had a past. Her home wasn't one of those gloomy places where foster children were housed but not loved, either — she cared for the broken and wounded unconditionally. Religious devotion motivated her and her husband while their upbringing in Canada taught them that children with handicapping conditions were no less important than anyone else. As an advocate for the child, Sherrie had little faith in birth parents. She had seen too many six-week old babies with broken arms and bashed in heads to believe parent training classes were going to transform the cruelties of the "human condition" and make such homes safe once more for children.

Sherrie was well aware of the constraints of her job but that didn't stop her from speaking out for children. For eight years children had been coming and going from her home and she knew the child welfare system well. "The system isn't about helping kids," she said, "It's about pushing paper." If she suspected a child's best interest was being overshadowed by an agency's need to make money, she would say so openly. I had never known anybody as frank as she was. She didn't like the idea of Jared going to strangers. "What on earth do they think they're doing?" she said as if thinking out loud. "He's just coming out of his shell for goodness sake. Of course it's to their advantage if he goes under again." When she asked that he stay with her and attend the day treatment program, her request was denied. Her home was considered too busy and understandably so. The plan was in motion and Jared was to be moved in two weeks.

I had learned at a workshop that moving children around is emotionally damaging to them. In fact, some experts believe such moves are causing attachment disorders. But I thought this would be a good move for Jared. He would be one of only ten children chosen to participate in the program and he would live in what was called a "therapeutic foster home" where he would get a lot of attention. The foster parents had received special training and they would work closely with the professionals of the program. Jared would be taught appropriate social skills, self-help skills, and his motor development would be addressed too. This was reassuring to me — he needed a lot of extra stimulation. I had a lot of faith in the helping professions and likened the intensity of the program to a staged and concentrated front designed to shelter Jared's flame from the strong winds.

While the arrangements were being made to move Jared, I let Barbara know Sam and I wanted to adopt him. Oddly, she didn't respond to what I said, but I let it go thinking that as soon as things settled down, we would discuss the particulars. I didn't know Barbara like I had known the other workers. She was a very quiet person, by nature, it seemed. I knew she was fresh out of college, just like me, but other than that, we didn't talk a lot.

I envisioned Jared living with the new foster family for about six months and then transitioning to us. Meanwhile we would continue having him for visits on a regular basis. Sam and I would be asked to become a part of the team in order to insure that the same techniques were being used across all environments. Jared would be the healthier for it and the transition to us later on made easier. Hopefully he would be able to stay in the treatment program for a while after coming to us. I actually thought it the ideal situation and that with everybody working together, Jared was sure to succeed.

I said gingerly to Sherrie that I thought the program might be good for Jared. She was over reacting, I felt. She didn't want to let go. I understood her pain. She had cared for Jared for nearly two years by now, doing the day-to-day work on the front lines and she was very much invested in his well-being. In all fairness, she seemed to be the only one who had invested in him. But she was being too hard on the professionals, I felt. "You don't get it, do you," she said, as if I was stupid or something.

Sherrie fought, and admirably, to keep Jared. She knocked on "political doors" and "rattled cages," as she put it. She even asked for legal guardianship until he turned 18, the woman was that committed. All to no avail. Julie's parental rights had been terminated, Jared was a ward of the State. Being a child, he had no legal rights. Being a ward of the State, Sherrie could not get him a lawyer for legal representation either. Shamefully, Sherrie was declared "too emotionally involved," and the only recourse with her employer was to let Jared go. He was moved a week later according to plan.

I had wanted to support Sherrie, but after that first week I didn't see her again until the day Jared was being picked up by the new foster mom when Jacob and I went over to Sherrie's to see him off. His things had already been loaded into the car by the time we got there. He didn't have much. A few clothes and a well used Hot Wheels, that's all. Following a wave of hugs and kisses, we all stood there at the driveway — Sherrie and her kids, Sherrie's best friend who was a foster mother also, and four of the eight children she cared for, and Jacob and I — watching the car roll out and waving good-bye. Jared was barely tall enough see out of the window but he waved back. Sherrie was crying. And then he was gone. It all happened so fast. Like a tornado that found a spot to attach it's tail to, it circled around for a while and then swish, it was gone, taking Jared with it.

I tried comforting Sherrie and told her not to worry, that Sam and I would be taking Jared soon. She looked at me like I was crazy. "You watch and see. I bet you won't get him until they're through with him." Then she went into the house and brought out a small cotton blanket with pictures of rocking horses on it and a matching pillow. "Here, I made these for Jared. You keep them with you so they don't get lost." Then she excused herself, it was time to fix lunch, and went inside. I would see Sherrie from time to time in the years to follow but our relationship was never the same after that.

I called Barbara right away after Jared was moved to set up visitations. She was so agreeable to Sam and I being involved in Jared's care and the visits continuing, that I thought she was in support of us adopting him too. We were getting off to a good start after all, I thought, even if we weren't talking very much. It was decided I would pick Jared up late Friday afternoon and take him back Sunday evening every-other-weekend. The phone number of the new foster home was provided.

The following weekend, Jacob and I went out to pick Jared

up. The place was in the suburbs, a forty-five minute drive one way from our house. Jared seemed happy to see us. But once we got home he started crying. "Aren't we going to Mommy Sherrie's?" he asked. I told him no but that we would go and visit her soon. It didn't help. He cried even more and said in between sobs, "I want to go home." When I heard this a sick feeling lodged itself in the pit of my stomach and a little voice called out: *Oh, oh, this whole thing could be damaging to him.* Sherrie wasn't home that weekend so all I could do was try to reassure him everything was going to be okay.

Jared finally made the adjustment to the new foster home and did quite well for a while. His skin coloring changed and his eyes found something to sparkle about. He was jubilant and boastful when he spoke of the change of events in his life: "I'm going to school now," "My daddy has a truck!" and "And we have a little dog named Sugar;" the fondness in his voice for the critter was so precious. The oppositional behaviors decreased somewhat and he stopped crying so readily. The foster family seemed like caring people. My apprehensions subsided then and I regained my optimism: Jared was going to benefit from all of this.

As time went by however, I kept meeting with an uncomfortable silence when I called Barbara, and I started getting worried. We didn't talk about planning for Jared. Two months passed and I didn't hear from the mental health professionals either. Then one day, Barbara called and reprimanded me for allowing Jared to call me mommy. Jared called everybody mommy. "We just don't want you encouraging him," Barbara said. When she said this I realized then that we were not communicating. So I brought up the subject of adoption again and asked her if she had any idea when Jared would transition to

Sam and I. "Oh, he'll stay in the program until he's considered adoptable or until he turns six, whichever comes first," she said.

I didn't like that word "adoptable," it reminded me of the word damaged and I didn't see Jared that way. I felt he was fragile but that he was going to make it; we just had to be careful with him. "He's already 'adoptable,' as far as we're concerned, Barbara," I responded.

"Oh no, Jared has multiple special needs and I don't want him to be a failed adoption," she said. I was surprised by the finality of her words and a bit insulted by the condescending tone. It wasn't as if Jared was a "poster child" whom Sam and I had never met but fell in love with because he was cute or something. We wanted Jared because he was Jared; problems and all. We knew he was behind and that he would need a lot of extra attention and stimulation and I shared this acknowledgment with Barbara. I thought maybe it was just a matter of words so I asked her to define for me, in her terms, 'multiple special needs.' She responded with "emotional and developmental problems" and suggested I do some reading.

I thought Barbara might be concerned Sam and I wouldn't work with the professionals so I spoke to this issue as well. I wanted to work with the day treatment staff because I knew we couldn't do it all by ourselves. I was even hoping Jared could stay in the program until he turned six. But Barbara didn't respond to these comments either. This was frustrating for me. I wanted her to openly voice her concerns so that we could discuss them. I wanted her concerns to be reasonable, too, though. When she said "Jacob and Jared are too needy to be placed in the same home," I actually thought she was excuse making. The boys had been placed together with Sherrie and her house was full when they got there. Jared wasn't receiving all of the therapeutic foster parents' attention either because they had two children of their own — two adopted teenagers. Jared slept in a crib in the corner of the older son's bedroom.

At this point I was feeling like Barbara wasn't being fair with us. She had never met Sam or spoken with him. She had Jacob's file but she had never met him either. He was a nice boy and a loving brother. He had stabilized so well and was no longer out of control. Play therapy at the community mental health clinic seemed to be helping. In fact, Jacob was chosen that fall as the model child for the Early Intervention program. Our home life was stable; the house was nice; I managed to maintain a well kept yard. Sam hadn't found gainful employment yet but he was looking.

Barbara did finally come to our home once, for an hour, when Jared was there. It was our only chance to make a "showing" and as luck would have it, things didn't go well. Now Jacob wasn't a grabber, Jared was. But that particular day, at that particular hour, Jacob decided to take the toy that Jared had in his hands. I was completely surprised and almost proud of him for defending his territory, it was his toy and Jared had taken it from him beforehand, so I didn't intervene immediately, although I was going to. I sensed Barbara thought I should react right away. But then Jared took care of it, and very appropriately I thought. "It's not nice to grab, Jake," he said assertively. I was pleased, he was obviously benefiting from therapy.

Unfortunately, the next time I spoke with Barbara over the phone she said she was convinced Jared needed to be an only child. She was right — that was probably the ideal — as an only child Jared could get a lot of attention. But God didn't make him an only child, he already had a brother, and Barbara was crossing a line.

After three months at the therapeutic foster home, Jared didn't want to go back on Sundays. "Please let me live at Jacob's house!" he'd wail, hanging onto my legs and refusing to get into the car. Then things started to deteriorate at a seemingly rapid rate. Jared was back to crying a lot and extremely fearful, thinking there were monsters in our basement even though he'd never been down there alone. He was potty trained shortly after going to the therapeutic foster home but soon went back to wetting his pants. Gone was the shine in his eyes. He was slapping himself and saying "I'm weird." Sometimes he would say "I slap my face off." He was hitting Jacob and scratching him for no apparent reason. When I talked to him about hurting his brother, his response was "So." He had never been shy about hitting Jacob or any other child when he didn't get what he wanted, but now his aggression seemed to be taking on a violent quality which alarmed me. It was as if he was angry at everyone now, especially his brother. Barbara said it was normal for a "child like Jared" to regress for a while.

"A child like Jared" — that comment bothered me. Up until this point I did not feel Barbara was perceiving Jared as disturbed. That was one thing I liked about her. She knew Jared had emotional and developmental problems but I always felt she thought a little bit like me: that he needed love more than he needed anything, and lots of it. I don't think she would have been so protective of him otherwise. But she was changing. I suppose people do when they work in a job like hers, witnessing the ugly abuses of children day after day and then having to make life altering decisions for those children and their families from the remaining shattered pieces.

But Jared was being treated by the mental health professionals, so Barbara didn't have to work alone. They were acting as her advisors, so-to-speak, on emotional problems in children. So I called the mental health folks to see what they thought about Jared coming to Sam and I and to get an idea of the depth of Jared's problems. The family therapist expressed his favoritism toward Jared and he didn't talk as if he or the other folks were opposed to Sam and I adopting him. It would be in their time though, I realized, because he said, "The system functions around crisis situations and Jared is not in crisis." Sherrie words came back to me then — *I bet you won't get him until their through with him* — and I shuddered. I didn't think it was a matter of anybody taking advantage of Jared, but obviously, finding him a permanent family was not their focus or concern.

Everybody thinks they know best when it comes to children and I was no exception. I wasn't going to wait until Jared was six years old to adopt him. At six his formative years would be nearly spent. The formative years are the impressionable years when a parent can have the greatest influence on a child's personality development. I personally believed that the power to influence was in the relationship itself, between parent and child. Well, I wasn't going to wait, and I wasn't going to take no for an answer either. So I spoke with Jared's Court Appointed Child Advocate. Children with histories like Jacob and Jared's and nobody to look after them, are appointed a child advocate after entering the system. Working on a volunteer basis, with nothing to be gained politically or financially, the advocate oversees the plans being made for the child and speaks on his behalf if he or she feels the best interest on the child is not being taken into account. Jared's advocate was a very caring person but she said very little and wouldn't make a commitment. I got the feeling that she too thought Jared should be an only child but I felt even more strongly that she really didn't understand the situation; her conversations were primarily with Barbara.

Then in the middle of January, Barbara called at 10 minutes before 5:00 on a Friday afternoon to ask me if Jacob had been molesting Jared. Evidently when Jared returned from staying at our house for a week during the holidays, he had a red and swollen anus and blood in his stools. These symptoms sounded serious to me and yet he had not been examined by a doctor even though the symptoms were well over three weeks old, Barbara said. I had not seen inappropriate behavior between the boys and I seriously doubted that Jacob would do something like that, but I wasn't an expert. So I suggested to Barbara that she have Jared evaluated. At the height of my concern was his physical health so I pleaded with her to have him taken to a doctor as soon as possible. She thanked me and hung up.

With the click of the receiver I felt as if the line had been cut. Although I knew I needed to stay calm and not worry, it wasn't that easy. Jared wasn't a foster child to me and I didn't work for the child welfare system. I had never received money to care for him; love was at the heart of what was going on between us. When I thought about Jared being sexually violated, I wanted to cry — such a blow to his fragile ego and poor self-concept would only serve to compound his problems. And when I thought of him possibly being physically ill and needing help, I felt incredibly powerless.

A complete physical found Jared had an oral-fecal parasite living in his intestines. It had been there for quite some time. No one knew for certain if he was molested because the third piece of the evaluation with anatomically correct dolls was not given. "Jared will always be a victim and we didn't want to influence a future evaluation," Barbara relayed to me. I didn't ask why she thought he would always be a victim. All I could think about was: How can his future be predicted with such certainty? And that his emotional well-being as well as his physical health were at the mercy of many — too many.

It's a dirty world — child molestation, drug abuse, rape, poverty, corruption, human degradation, spiritual emptiness, pollution, crime — who was to protect Jared from the predators supposedly awaiting?

After this incident, I contacted a lawyer regarding legal action in order to obtain parental rights of Jared. Like a mama bear, I was prepared to fight for my cub if I had to. I wouldn't be the only one. Evidently, there were a lot of others ahead of us. The lawyer was nice to talk with and he wanted to take our case, but when he quoted his fees, and said it could takes years, I had to give the idea up — we couldn't even afford the retainer. "You know, if I were you, I'd start looking at protecting myself, child molestation is a serious accusation," he said just before hanging up.

He was right. Innocent people get blamed all the time if there is need for a scapegoat. I wanted no part of any of it. I didn't want to stop seeing Jared but under the circumstances I thought it best for everyone's sake that he not come to our home to visit for a while. On a personal level, I needed a break from the stress of trying to communicate with Barbara when her mind was so closed. I wasn't giving up though and thought I would go back at it once things settled down a little. The boys had to see each other, though, so we set up visits for them at the welfare office. And then everything changed.

Chapter 6
"Jared Needs Me"

J acob was hospitalized for an abscessed tonsil in late February, shortly after I stopped Jared's visits. He was terribly sick and couldn't move his head due to swelling in his neck. Surgery was recommended to lance the tonsil in order to drain the infection, but when I informed the doctor's of his weak immune system, a more conservative approach was taken. Antibiotics administered intravenously became the treatment of choice. Then came the wait. It would be five days before he was well enough to go home, and I was so grateful for the medical insurance.

I had been up with Jacob all night for two nights prior to the hospitalization. Out of sheer exhaustion, I went home the first night after getting him tucked in. When I returned early the next morning I discovered leaving him had been a terrible mistake. The nursing staff reported he cried all night for me. After that I stayed by his side the entire time except for when I would dash home to shower and change clothes. The nurses set up a cot for me to sleep on and faithfully, between the hours of midnight and dawn, Jacob would crawl into the cot. His little body would meld into mine as if the warmth of human contact was as essential to his wellness as the antibiotics were to his bloodstream.

I couldn't sleep much in the hospital with bells dinging and lights flashing all night. My exhaustion continued to mount. After two days, I asked Sam to relieve me for a night or a few hours during the day so I could go home and get some sleep, but he resisted. He had other priorities. Over nine months had elapsed since we left the apartments and he still had not found gainful employment. Why he chose to suddenly look for a job with such diligence at a time when I needed him emotionally, I couldn't understand. While Jacob slept in my arms, I searched the past to determine were it was that things had gone wrong.

I had always thought Sam would eventually put as much energy into building a future for the boys as I was, but he didn't think in terms of tomorrow; he lived for the day. And he never did quite make the shift as far as parenting was concerned. He was a good uncle, always chatting with the boys about various things and discussing with me their strengths and weaknesses on a regular basis. He cared about them a lot and they adored him. He had a special way with Jared. When Jared became distressed, Sam could light up his spirit and dry his tears simply by telling silly stories in a highly imaginative and childlike way. But when it came to the actual physical care that young children require — well — that was "woman's work" too. Whenever Jacob was sick in the night, I was the one up with him. The laundry, the cooking, and the housework, were my jobs as well. If I wasn't working, it wouldn't have mattered. But I did work and I did all the driving too. I was tired of doing it all by myself.

As I laid there in the hospital, sleep eluding me and daylight beginning to peer through the drawn curtains to mark the passing of day three and lay claim to day four, wondering what was coming next, a small voice suddenly called out, "Jared needs me!"

It was Jacob. He was asleep but the panic in his voice told me he too was struggling with private thoughts. It wasn't the time for him to be worrying about Jared and I felt bad. I know he had heard me talking about Jared on the phone and I wondered if the stress of his situation had affected Jacob, contributing to his illness. His body couldn't handle stress. Whenever he had an especially hard day at school or a couple of sleepless nights, the result was often a running nose and cough.

I pulled Jacob closer to me. I wanted to transfer to him what strength I had left. He needed it for the restoration of his health. I had become consumed with Jared's situation, proclaiming myself the only qualified keeper of the flame. I couldn't sit Jacob down and explain to him why things were the way they were. The adult world is a mixture of riddles and inequities, and I didn't have the words to justify the means. Jacob knew already though, in his own way. To live is to struggle with the contradictions in human nature, including our own. I wanted so to take Jacob home where we could snuggle on the couch, cozy and warm, while the sun gave new life to our souls. I was thinking about our home and the morning's dawning casting its light on the philodendrum sitting on a bookcase in the corner, when my mind drifted peacefully into sleep.

When I awoke, I felt as if I had slept for days even though it had only been a few hours. The chaos was gone. In its place was a calming truth, standing as boldly as the crocus amidst the dormant undergrowth in early spring: I was going to break up with Sam. We were truly too different. I needed someone who would work as hard as I did to be a parent and maintain a home. Sam wasn't a bad person. Quite the contrary. He just wasn't cut out for parenting. Some people aren't.

Jacob and I left the hospital two days later, by ourselves,

hand in hand. As we passed through the automatic doors of the hospital entrance and the fresh air blasted my cheeks, I savored its coolness. When I looked up and saw the winter sky, I gave thanks that it was still there. I squeezed Jacob's hand to make sure he was real and I gave thanks again: for the privilege of purpose and the clarity of meaning.

Sam moved out three weeks later. We decided mutually that it was best Jacob stay with me. But I decided against taking Jared even if Barbara were to let him go. I was alone — a single woman in charge of growing a man. Just one person with time, little money, and my own set of human shortcomings. Besides, Jacob had his problems, and had been my first priority. It wouldn't be fair to deprive him in any way. I had been content basking in the warmth of our unity and paving the way for my child of promise. I should not have tried to take on Jared's troubles too. A little voice kept telling me it was essential the boys be together but what else could I do? I had to let go.

Poor Jared. His future was already predicted really. Thousands of dollars would be spent on his therapy but there was nobody making a long term commitment to him; he would eventually move on as he had before. At age two he came into care with a brother. At age four he was with strangers. An adoptive placement was planned for after age six. Then he could join with the thousands and thousands of other children in the child welfare system waiting for something that lasts. For the adoptive child it's the "forever" family.

The child welfare system is a social attempt at doing the right thing, but if Jared was moved around his life with child welfare likely wouldn't be any more safe or loving than his life with Julie. So I wrote a letter to the Citizen Review Board, another body of people who try to act in the best interest of the child, on his behalf.

Writing was something I could do in the quiet of the night after Jacob was in bed and I could reflect and find the words that hopefully would deliver my true meaning. I explained Jared's situation, all the time hoping he might become real to somebody like he was to Jacob and I. I also explained my situation and why it was that I was removing myself from his life. I asked for a good-bye visit with him. Then I pleaded for someone to look after his safety and well-being. I made copies of the letter for Barbara, the mental health people, and the child advocate. As I sealed the envelopes, I wondered if anybody knew Jared wanted to be an airplane pilot someday.

At the last minute I remembered another layer of the bureaucracy: the elected officials, and sent copies of the letter to my district representatives as well. I don't know what possessed me to do that — I wasn't an advocate. Quite frankly, a part of me wanted to let Barbara know she wasn't an all powerful entity within herself, but mostly, I sent it because I wanted to think somebody might care.

Within the week, Barbara called to tell me I was now being considered as an adoptive resource for Jared. I was completely surprised and elated too — it felt as if I had been in a race and won. I didn't ask what happened to change her mind. I didn't want her to spoil my illusion that heart's might still be open in the world and that little children were still cherished. Then she said, "The adoption worker will be getting in contact with you," and hung up, abruptly.

"We don't think you are being realistic and we don't typically place children like Jacob and Jared with a single parent, but we'll have some evaluations done and if the results are good you can have Jared," the adoption worker began. I asked her for details on parenting both boys. What was "realistic," I wanted to know. I asked for concrete information, observations, and feedback, but she wasn't able to qualify anything. There would be a parent-child interaction evaluation which entailed me interacting with both boys at the same time and a separate evaluation with just the boys interacting together in order to determine if they were bonded. And I would have to take a personality profile evaluation as per Barbara's requirement. I was also being asked to pay for it myself.

I had already completed and sent in the adoption home study questionnaire which consisted of open ended questions regarding my history, past relationships, coping strategies, own childhood, ways of handling stress, expectations, and discipline techniques. I shared that I was the oldest girl raised in a single parent family — I knew responsibility — and I answered the questions regarding my parenting style based on my ideals and what little experience I had had with Jacob to act as a spring board.

I had heard that personality profiles could be asked of potential adoptive parents, however, it wasn't a requirement of either Sam or I when we took Jacob — the more "damaged of the two." In fact, the home study and pre-adoption training classes arrived after he did. I knew Barbara wasn't happy with me for questioning her authority so I assumed she was either getting back at me by requesting the evaluation or else she thought there was something wrong with me for wanting to adopt Jared. If the latter was the case, Jared's future was indeed bleak because that meant anybody who would want to adopt him would likely be suspect.

I was so tired of it all and just wanted to get on with my life. Defensive and filled with a nameless anxiety, I asked

Barbara's supervisor what would happen if I refused to cooperate with those evaluations and if I stuck with my decision to not take Jared. "If we find the boys to be bonded, and you refuse to take Jared, then you will force us to place Jacob in a home where they will be together." This is when I realized how serious things were. Jacob's adoption wasn't final yet and it wouldn't be for quite some time. Technically, I was only his special certified "foster mom." Like him, I had no legal rights.

We had to move on from the situation and I knew now that I couldn't leave Jared behind to fend for himself. So I agreed to the evaluation and adoption if granted. I was alone but I wasn't going to forsake Jared. I still loved him, although, I too, crossed a line at this point — it wasn't just about love anymore, it was about right and wrong, too.

As I contemplated the upcoming trek into the paper jungle of the bureaucracy I wondered if Jacob, Jared, or I, would be able to perform. I knew love likely wouldn't show itself on paper. Not wanting to subject Jared to anymore uncertainty, I thought it best I not see him again until this process was well underway and it appeared something definite would be decided. I really didn't think it would take very long.

By this time it was the middle of March and I was glad to see the sun coming out. That previous three months had been the worst time of my life. On top of it all, my new job was not going well. The pay was lousy, I broke my foot stepping out of the agency van and I was reprimanded for talking on the phone too much. It was the calls to Barbara, the family therapist, the child advocates, the lawyer, Jacob's therapist and teacher — all the people I couldn't always get with one call on a Friday afternoon. About the only thing nice that happened to me during this time was when my little sister sent us a box of food goodies marked "CARE PACKAGE."

Chapter 7
Welcome Home Jared

I n June we were called in for the evaluations. On the drive to the psychiatrist's office I thought about Jared and wondered what it was going to be like to see him again. I had not seen him in over five months. For all I knew he might not recognize me. Such was a possibly since I never knew if I was significant to him or if it was just my house and the brother who lived in it that he had a longing for. It was like going to the airport to meet an old friend -- I was excited but wondering if we had anything in common anymore.

When Jared walked through the clinic door and lit up like a Christmas tree when he saw me, running past Jacob to wrap his little arms around my neck, I knew then that I was real to him and had to choke back my tears. In the moment I held him close I realized I had caused him pain when I stopped the visitations, undermining the value of my presence as a constant within the uncertainties of his child welfare life.

The uncertainties were the reality too. Sherrie's predictions and the future itself, had in fact, come true. Jared had just been moved to another therapeutic foster home because the first one couldn't tolerate his behaviors any longer. Saddened by regret for leaving him alone, I was wishing I could go back to do it differently when I suddenly remembered the evaluations. We were people to be classified according to evaluation standards and our weaknesses subject to individual interpretation. I felt powerless. The testing took four hours total. Then came the wait.

While waiting to know if I would be the parent of one child or two, I went to work for an agency that provided rehabilitation therapy to the elderly in their homes. It was a job without benefits of any kind but flexible hours, something I deemed now to be as valuable as gold, and the pay was double.

Jacob didn't get upset about Sam leaving like I thought he might. "I know I'll see him again," he said. And he did. Sam was very good about calling or coming to visit Jacob. A couple of times he took him for an afternoon. This is when Jacob's relationship with his uncle was at its best. Jacob cherished his Uncle Sam's undivided attention. Sam was grateful to me for trying to keep the boys together, he said one day. He called me "Mommy Most Donna," which was his way of saying "Thank you." He kept in touch with us fairly regularly there for a while.

My dad came to live with us shortly after Sam left, which was a blessing. He had just retired and his lady friend of thirteen years had just died. These were big changes for him and I didn't want him to be alone. Plus, I needed help and some company since all my single friends had moved on. Even my best friend was gone. She moved to Mt. Shasta, California, that spring; somebody told her the air was much cleaner down there.

My dad liked Jacob a lot. Like Sam, he had a special way with him. He and Jacob had already met the year before when I asked my dad to pick Jacob up from school for me for a week until school busing could be arranged. Jacob called him Mr. Rogers. "I saw you on TV yesterday," he would say, so innocently and trustingly, as if a man on television could actually be in his own living room. I think it was my dad's plain attire and old bill cap that fostered the association, as well as his patience and simplistic view of the world. Unlike me, my dad was able to take Jacob's rages in stride. He'd sit quietly and patiently, like a monk waiting out a war, until Jacob was finished. "You must be a little tired today Son," he'd say, then take his guitar in hand and start strumming and singing — he was a self-taught musician. Jesus Loves Me or Puff the Magic Dragon were Jacob's favorite songs. This was a great help. He helped with the chores around the house too. Although he was generous and kind spirited, a deeply religious man, he couldn't quite understand why I wanted to adopt Jared too. "I don't know why you think you need another child to look after," he said. But he accepted the fact nevertheless.

Then one day I was introduced by a co-worker to a man named Joe. Joe asked me for a date, but the timing was terrible; I didn't want to date anyone yet. Joe was a persistent man and he kept calling. I finally said yes simply because I was impressed with that fact that he wouldn't take no for an answer; it seemed he thought he had something to offer. He worked as a first mate for an ocean going tug boat company, an industry he had been in for over 17 years, and he was out at sea six to seven weeks at a time which made it hard to get to know him. When he was around however, he was extremely generous with his time and very good with Jacob — tolerant and nurturing — and I liked that. Plus, he drove a car, paid his own way (and mine too), and he didn't think too much about things like MSG, which I found refreshing. When I told him about Jared and that I wanted to adopt him too, a funny expression came over his face and he said, "You've got moxie kid."

In August Barbara called to tell me the evaluations "found the boys to be bonded" and that I could pick Jared up at any time. Finally, we could get on with our lives. I asked to wait until September for Jared to come because I needed time to prepare myself mentally. I was adopting finally, venturing out on a journey in which there was no turning back as far as I was concerned. I wanted to get excited, to feel my heart pound with anticipation, but I had to be cautious with my caring now; Jared wasn't with us yet. I likened the struggle for parental rights — the laborious birthing — to a difficult pregnancy; it wouldn't be over until the baby was delivered and all fingers and toes accounted for. I wondered if it was a bad omen, too, having to work so hard for something that might have otherwise been blessed.

I wanted to think I still knew the "baby," too, so in order to do this I went back to the day at the beach when a piece of me bonded with the sweet little boy yet undeveloped in Jared. There I saw his eyes smiling as the sand slipped through his fingers. I saw the apprehension in his face when he fed the seagulls. I heard him laugh. I saw the sun work its wonder on his soul. Then I saw him grown up and working as an airplane pilot. This image of Jared becoming an airplane pilot was dear to me because it gave me permission to weave dreams and dare aspirations the way most parents do when they give birth to a child.

Arrival day was set for September 15, 1990. Jacob and I would drive across the Columbia River into Washington to pick Jared up. Ironically, the fifteenth of September was the exact same day he was moved from Sherrie's one year prior. It was hard to believe a whole year had passed and that it actually could have been even longer.

As arrival day approached, a gladness filled my heart which left little room for the wanting already past. With gladness I could dream of the day itself... Jared would run to me and wrap his arms around my neck just the way he had done at the psychiatrist's office. Then he would look straight into my eyes, for a second, just before planting a sloppy kiss. He and Jacob would hug. We'd eat cake and ice cream. Afterwards, I'd turn into the tickle monster and chase the boys around the house. I'd tickle Jared until a belly laugh erupted, then we'd kiss and hug some more. It would be a glorious day. My dream was perfect, and in its entirety, as fine as a freshly painted nursery with everything in its place.

With the cake baked, ice cream waiting in the freezer, and a banner that read WELCOME HOME JARED taped to the wall, Jacob and I piled into our old oxidized blue Datsun, and landed on Jared's doorstep forty-five minutes later. But the moment I saw him and he looked past me, I knew my perfect dream was mine alone and would forever remain locked up inside of me. He didn't run to wrap his arms around my neck and there were no hugs or sloppy kisses. The drive home was quiet and somber. When we walked into the house, I felt a shadow creep in behind us and cover the room the way a rain cloud creeps in and covers the sun. Jared wouldn't eat the cake and ice cream. He chose hiding under the big chair instead. When I tried to hug him he said "Don't, that hurts." There was no tickling or a chase. It wasn't a day of celebration but rather like a gloomy Monday and the disappointment filled my heart with sadness.

When Jared finally came out from under the chair and started following the cat around the house, my hopes rose. But in the moment he picked up the cat and brought her to his chest, he abruptly threw her down again because she scratched him for holding her too tight. Teary eyed he shouted, "You're a bad cat. We'll have to send you to another home." His words rudely awakened me then to the harshness of reality and all its cruelties once more. He wasn't a baby or even a toddler anymore — he was three months shy of turning five years old and now in his fifth home. I told him he would never have to leave again but I don't think my words were enough to convince him his little human journey, the search for a group in which to belong, was really over.

In the weeks that followed, Jared's favorite places came to be underneath the big chair or the table. Occasionally, he'd take a toy along for company. I wanted him to come out into the light where love was waiting for him but he wouldn't come. I needed to believe the light inside of him was still burning yet I feared it wasn't so. Watching him crouch under the chair, I detected something very different in his presence now. It was as if he had come "home" in body but not in soul. He sought isolation and yet he had a profound fear of being in a room by himself — "Then I'll be alone!" — he'd wail. *Home Alone*, my brother tagged him, which I hated. It was too descriptive of the Jared seemingly caught prisoner to himself. And like one who is depressed, he welcomed sleep at any hour. Yet once asleep, he would toss, turn, and flail his arms and legs like a fish trying to survive out of water.

I had to watch Jared carefully now because his play had taken on a calculating sadistic quality. In the moment Jacob was experiencing pleasure with a toy, Jared would grab it. Then he'd throw it aside in dissatisfaction awaiting the next opportunity when he could again rob the joy. Sometimes he was more sophisticated in his dealings. With an air of illusion, he'd ask in a gentle tone, "Can I see that Jake?" leading anyone to believe he just wanted a look and would give the object right back. But it would go into his pockets instead or get stashed somewhere when Jacob wasn't looking. Once in a while Jacob would ask timidly for a like exchange. "Can I see that Jared?" he would ask sweetly. "No, it's MINE!" would be Jared's response as he grasped the object tighter or brought it in closer to his space. Jacob didn't have the will to pursue even when I coached him.

Yet it was Jacob who brought Jared out of himself, somewhat. Jacob was someone Jared seemingly trusted and he had a way of engaging his spirit through imaginative play. As long as there were no toys or material objects between them, there was little conflict that I could tell. Jacob had the kindness and wisdom to look beyond self in order to understand his little brother's frailties. He would carry the make-believe story line for Jared and wielding the spiritual shield for both of them, guide him through the mine fields of suspicion, intimidation, and manipulation — enemy ammunition strategically placed in order to instill fear, the ultimate power hold. Jared liked to think of himself as the bad guy but his brother never let him get hit; they always made it to the free zone together. I prayed that Jared's view of himself as "bad" wasn't to be his destiny.

In time the boys were able to sit on the floor and play together for longer periods. In fact, there was something peaceful about the way they related to each other through imaginative play; a togetherness which I couldn't define. Integral to the bigger picture, I suppose, was the fact that Jacob and his brother shared a past. It was a past marked with pain but it belonged only to Jacob and Jared and they liked talking to one another about it, especially at the dinner table. They were little chatterboxes at mealtime.

I was surprised the first time I heard the boys discuss the past. I thought them too young to hold the information and I thought Jared too confused to make the connections. Not only were they able to put words to the body of knowledge suggestive to who they were and the pain they suffered, complete with visual imagery and poignant emotional undercurrent, but Jared was often the one to initiate the dialogue.

"Our Mama drank beer," he said to Jacob one night from across the table. "We had to eat our poop, remember that?," Jacob responded. Then Jacob went on — rather matter-of-factly: "Julie wouldn't feed us" — he never called her "Mama". "Then Mommy Sherrie helped us," his voice trailing off. "And I waited for my best mom to come along," Jared interjected in a dream like tone as if he was still waiting. This topic of conversation came up often. Essential to the discussion itself seemed to be a need to keep the sequence of events in correct order as if being able to do so was permission to remember. I never interrupted when they talked like this. I was grateful they could talk. They were grieving for their losses and talking about it was the healthiest thing they could have done.

Some days Jared couldn't seem to track the once familiar environment of our home. When instructed to go into the bathroom from the kitchen to wash up, he'd head in the right direction then seem to get lost en route. I'd be right behind him, and watch him walk into the living room or dining room. I'd try to redirect him with verbal feedback. "Where are you going Jared?" He'd answer, "I don't know." When I tried to engage him more actively in the goal by saying, "Well why don't we finish what we started and go get washed up?," he would look at me bewildered and say in an exasperated tone, "Well how do I do that?" He cried when he couldn't find his way — frustrated lonely tears. My heart ached for him when he cried like that and I was constantly on watch to try to keep him from failing. When he was especially confused I would put my hands on his shoulders and guide him along, turning him to the right or to the left as we maneuvered from room to room. The source of this problem was a mystery to me. And since it changed from day to day, sometimes he could find his way and other times he couldn't, I couldn't get a clear picture of what was triggering it nor how to correct it.

I was shocked to find that even after a year of therapy, Jared was still unable to do the basics of dressing, toileting and washing his hands. It was as if time had moved forward but forgotten to take him with it. He was potty trained (if he could tell me in time when he needed to go) but he couldn't do the zippers and snaps on his jeans because his little fingers and thumbs were still too weak and uncoordinated. Even though he slept a lot, he was tired in the mornings and wouldn't stand up. So I had to dress him while he sat cross legged on the floor or the bed, whining or crying and fussing. He still screamed and cried when I washed his face and hands, and he ran when I got out the brush to brush his hair. Brushing his teeth was nearly impossible; he'd cry and pull at my hands trying to get me to stop. By the time I had him ready in the mornings, I'd feel like an ogre just for touching him. And even though I was getting up an hour earlier than usual in order to manage, I was getting to work late and already physically and emotionally spent. In the evenings, getting Jared ready for bed meant more chaos. Washing his hair was a major ordeal. He wouldn't close his eyes and he refused to tip his head back. I just wasn't prepared for the high level of physical care he still required.

Jared's physical care was demanding but it was his need for safety that I found overwhelming. I didn't dare leave him unsupervised. I told him several times not to go near a hole in the backyard because he might fall in but he went anyway and fell in, scraping his arm on the way down. And he liked to play with things that weren't toys, such as screwdrivers, pieces of metal, pieces of broken plastic, and knives. It didn't matter that I told him no and why we don't play with sharp things, or that I hid and locked up dangerous items, he had an uncanny ability for finding something that was either pointed or broken. Pretty soon it wasn't just pointed or broken objects that I had to watch for, he liked to tie things up too. Like a fixation, he tied up everything — chair legs to table legs, door knobs to bed frames, the cat to a laundry basket, his brother to the stove. He tied himself up too. Every time I found him or something tied up, my heart ached in despair; it wasn't normal behavior.

Jared was constantly putting things in his mouth. I explained to him why it wasn't a good idea to do that — that pieces of hose, toy blocks, and his hands were dirty — be did it anyway. I couldn't prevent it — everything went into his mouth. One day I was finishing up on some staining of a window sill when I had to leave the job for a few minutes to attend to something in the kitchen. I partitioned the area off and thought it would be okay, but when I returned he was sitting in a puddle of stain, licking it off his fingers. I simply couldn't do anything without having to keep an eye on him. I gave up trying to stain the windowsills and refurbishing old furniture was the farthest thing from my mind now. I couldn't even sew anymore.

Jared's oppositional behaviors seemed much more pronounced than before. He opposed just about everything: having to wear a hat or coat, having to change a dirty shirt, having to have his nose wiped, having to take my hand in public. I always explained the whys of things first but it didn't seem to matter. Like a toddler, he wanted what he wanted and I couldn't reason with him. Rather than throw himself to the ground to make his opposition known like he used to do, he used words now — big words, grown-up words: "I don't have to do that just because *you* want me to!" He had grown skillful at arguing. Sometimes it seemed he argued just for the sake of arguing. If I said the sky was blue, he'd say "No, it isn't." If I reminded him that he had a peanut butter sandwich for lunch he'd say, "No, I didn't." And he still had an obsession with food. Several times while I dished up the food, he would start crying, so sure he was going to be left out. "You're not going to feed me?" he'd wail. I didn't know now if such a perception — that he wasn't going to be fed — was the result of the hunger he suffered when with Julie, or if it was the result of a sick joke somebody had played on him along the way. It was pretty hard to know what-was-what when it came to his behaviors after so many people had handled him.

It was in the dead of winter when the days are dark and dreary naturally, and only three months after Jared came, when I awoke one Saturday tired and emotionally exhausted. I had a cup of coffee and made a list of the day's work ahead: laundry, floors, groceries, bills. All work would have to be done in between supervising the boys and keeping them structured up. If I kept organized I could get done and sit down and relax after dinner watching television; it was something to look forward to. Then something terrible happened.

Jacob jumped from his dresser, toppling it over and nearly falling into the window. At first I yelled at him, I was so startled and frightened. Then I gave him a swat as a consequence to such dangerous behavior. I don't know what happened but when he said "That didn't hurt," something inside of me snapped. I couldn't get control of myself. I gave him several swats and I hit too hard. He didn't cry during the act itself — his pain tolerance was high — which only fueled the flames.

He cried afterwards though when I was leaving the room. Once I calmed down and realized what I had done, I went back and sat him in my lap and apologized. I think he knew my remorse was genuine and he said he forgave me as young children like to do, but when he said, "You were like a beast in a rage," the disappointment in his voice told me, apology or not, damage was done.

Then Jared started crying. I felt so bad all ready, I didn't need him carrying on, too. Pretty soon I was yelling at him to be quiet. "Get a hold of yourself, Dear," my dad said, staring at me while Jacob and Jared watched on confused and bewildered. I couldn't get a hold of myself. I was trapped in a life of control battles, constant noise, endless laundry, "potty time," cooking, cleaning, and crying and fussing children with fears of harmful touch, imagined hunger, and sleepless nights. I wanted to walk out and not come back. I wasn't an "angel," screaming and yelling and hitting children isn't Godlike. I was ashamed of myself. "Maybe you've just taken on too much," my dad said, his gaze averting mine; he was ashamed of me too.

I went into the tv room where the curtains were still closed and curled up into a fetal position on the couch and slept. As morning changed to afternoon I continued to slumber, my awareness of the surroundings no more than a listless fog. A heaviness took over my body and weakened my legs so that I couldn't get up even though I knew I must, there was work to be done. I was ashamed of myself for hiding in the darkness of the room but I was so tired. And confusion and doubt, like the darkness, had a firm grip on me. Had I really taken on too much? I asked myself. Jacob and Jared were two very needy children. I couldn't stand the thought of Barbara being right. But maybe she was and maybe I should have stepped aside and allowed the boys to be separated. They didn't really need each other, a little voice called out from inside of me.....*Jared would have been all right by himself.....So what if he had continued to be moved around?.....If he wasn't tough enough not to grow up hateful of himself and others, that would be his problem; happiness and sorrow come from within.....You can't complain......You got what you asked for.* It was true. I got what I had asked for.

I don't know how long I would have stayed in that fetal state had it not been for Joe — he had just returned from six weeks at sea. I didn't want to have company that evening when he called. The house was a mess and so was my hair as well as my spirit. But he came over anyway and then kept at

Christmas morning.

me until I shared with him what had happened and my feelings of shame and doubt. I didn't tell him of my deepest fear — the fear that Jared's flame had been extinguished. I didn't want anybody to know this just in case negative thoughts really do come true.

"In the first place," Joe said, "Barbara has never been a parent, so what does she know? In the second place, the boys have to be together Donna, and you're all they have; you know that," he said with such certainty that I felt foolish for giving in to doubt. "You're just tired. Parenting is a lot of work." Joe was from a Catholic family of eleven.

"But do parents feel overwhelmed like I do? " I asked him. It didn't feel like a normal overworked feeling. "I feel like all of me is being consumed," I told him.

"Many parents feel all consumed at times when parenting young children; young children are all consuming," he said so matter-of-factly. "I'd help you with the boys if you'd let me," he said tenderly and so kindly, taking my hand in his. When I looked into his eyes I knew he was genuine and that compassion was alive in his soul.

Part II

Chapter 1
A Good Mom

I knew the truth in Joe's words. Jacob and Jared were not of my flesh but of my heart; they were my children. Nobody was going to knock on my door and tell me there had been a terrible mistake: that the system had suddenly been reformed; that somebody was waiting for Jacob and Jared, prepared to make all the sacrifices and concessions; that somebody loved them like I did. I refused to think I had taken on too much.

I was definitely tired, though, and I never could think straight when tired. I knew I just needed time to rest, then I would be able to problem solve how to go about reaching Jared; bring him out of his shell. Hope began to spring up inside of me and suddenly things made more sense — it was the newness of the situation; I was adjusting and so were the boys.

Joe did help too, he was a man of his word and willing to make sacrifices: we never went on a real date again. He was good at coming over in the evenings and helping out. He didn't know what to do at first. "You're going to have to tell me what you need help with and then you'll have to show me how you want it done. I can't read minds," he said straight-forwardly. So I told him: help with toileting, change wet pants when necessary, help with meal time problems, and supervise for safety. Joe liked kids too. "How can anybody not like a kid?" he asked me once.

I don't think my dad fully grasped the intensity of the situation, but he kept quiet and didn't say anymore about me taking on too much. He was able to babysit for short periods of time, managing behaviors and keeping the boys entertained at the same time by telling them Bible stories or playing his guitar. Many times I came home to find a child sitting on each knee, hanging on his every word, or dancing in the living room.

The support I received from Joe and my dad enabled me to regain my strength and within a relatively short amount of time I adjusted to the increased physical demands of parenting two young children. With renewed strength, the doubts and misgiving lifted from my spirit. Jared just needed love and attention in order to come out of himself. He needed to realize he wouldn't be going to "another home," too. Even the doctor I took him to see at this time for a complete evaluation at a child development center said things would take time.

I went to see the doctor in the hopes there might be a Head Start program Jared could attend in the afternoons for extra stimulation. He attended the day treatment program for only three hours in the mornings, while his afternoons were spent at a daycare center in our neighborhood. Even though the doctor found him to be one and two years delayed in all areas of development and "at high-risk for poor academic performance" he was too old for Head Start. There would be no help available until he entered the public school system where the doctor thought he should be "given the opportunity in a regular classroom with a learning resource center until such time as one is able to identify areas of weakness that might require more remediation." The doctor also said Jared had been previously diagnosed with Fetal Alcohol Syndrome.

Sherrie had said both Jacob and Jared were diagnosed with Fetal Alcohol Syndrome but I knew nothing about what that meant at the time. I had never before heard of Fetal Alcohol Syndrome; not even in college. I did notice though that whenever I mentioned it to Jacob's teachers or his therapist, they would suddenly change the subject. When I was struggling for parental rights of Jared, Barbara had suggested I read the *Broken Cord*, a book about a little boy so overexposed to alcohol in utero while his brain was developing, that he had to be cared for in a group home when he reached adolescence because he was mentally retarded and required so much help and supervision, but I wasn't sure how it was supposed to apply to us. Jared didn't seem to be mentally retarded and Jacob certainly wasn't. Barbara never actually said "Jared is Fetal Alcohol Syndrome" so I assumed she was saying that parenting a "special needs" child can be a disappointment. This was the case for the father who wrote the *Broken Cord*. I still wanted Jared even after reading the book and I shared that sentiment with Barbara as well as all the other professionals. But that must have been what she meant by "Jared has multiple special needs." Things were slowly beginning to make sense.

Now the doctor was saying "Fetal Alcohol Syndrome" loud and clear, but I didn't know what it meant in terms of Jared's overall development. I didn't even know how much importance to place on it. Jacob was thought to be mentally retarded and autistic at one time. Neither were correct. Once he was diagnosed autistic, Julie was no longer encouraged to touch him and hold him, which is what the child needed the most. And had he been treated as mentally retarded he might never have shown his true potential.

In fact, Jacob was doing quite well in school by now. After

Head Start, he was ready for a regular classroom so I enrolled him in an all day kindergarten class at the elementary school around the corner and down the hill from our house. He had a wonderful teacher who used his reading skills to boost his self-esteem by having him read to the class each week. He had taken an interest in math so she found him a fifth grade tutor to work with him daily in his math workbook.

"Continue to nurture" the doctor said, pulling me back to the present and the situation at hand. She encouraged me to call her at anytime. I left her office confused but she couldn't have known that because I didn't say anything. I was too busy trying to sort things out, put it all into proper perspective. It was going to be okay I told myself — Jared didn't have anything that love wasn't going to take care of and I was prepared — I knew about child and personality development.

J received a copy of the doctor's typed report a week later. In addition to the developmental problems we discussed, she wrote "Over and above these problems, Jared has had some emotional difficulties." With that, I decided nothing had changed. I would give Jared a lot of love and attention, plenty of contact comfort to promote trust and attachment, be sensitive to the losses he suffered, and help him catch up developmentally. So I stuck the report in a file where it was soon forgotten altogether and set to work on reaching Jared; pouring myself into his development and his every emotional need.

Jared had been through so much emotionally. Too much for a child with a beginning like his. I wanted desperately to make everything up to him. So I took care of him first always and catered to his every whim. The food was served to him first and I always made sure his portions were the biggest. I was there to wipe his every tear. I was there to ease the pain of his disappointments and shelter from the next. I let him suck his thumb and I quickly responded when he whined for his needs. He never had to go into a room alone if he didn't want to and he never had to pick something up when it fell because I did it for him. I couldn't say *no* — to deprive him anymore than he had already been deprived would be cruel. I bought him toys, a new Hot-Wheels, a cowboy outfit, stuffed animals. He bothered me when he said one day — "I want a house of my own" — but I bought him one anyway; the plastic type that snaps together. Joe helped me set it up in the living room and Jared would hide in it sometimes instead of under the chair or table. Anything Jared wanted I tried to give him. If he and I had a "honeymoon period" I suppose this was it.

I bought the boys Discovery toys — the learning toys made to stimulate the young mind. Jacob would become frustrated with them and Jared didn't like them at all. He would be interested at first but as soon as something required the slightest effort, he'd shut down and refuse to go on, throwing the item to the ground. "My brain tells me to play, play, play," he would say, but I didn't know what he meant. Eventually he destroyed all of those toys, taking them apart one piece at a time and playing with the broken pieces. He and Jacob never actually played with any toys the way they were meant to be played with.

Thinking I needed to use something less complicated, I bought Jared some Duplo Legos for building. Even though I coached and encouraged, he simply had no interest in a construction and would not engage in building or putting blocks together. I wanted to think it was because of the weakness in his fingers and thumbs, but these were the bigger Legos, the ones made for children who haven't developed fine motor dexterity so they are easier to manipulate. Young children love to put things together, it comes to them naturally. But it was as if Jared didn't want to do anything that had purpose to it. He preferred to play with one block at a time, pretending it to be a plane or a car. And even that was saying a lot. If left to his own doing, he'd wander back and forth through the house with his thumb in his mouth, touching the walls as he walked.

When Jared wandered he had a far away look in his eyes as if his own purpose or existence was in question. I'd watch him and think of the lonely tumbleweeds I see on the drive to my sister's house in eastern Washington. Babies don't cry without reason. Children don't typically wander without purpose. Even imaginative play, though seemingly void of purpose to an adult perhaps, is not without purpose to the young child.

It would have been easier for me to let Jared wander — less work, less arguments — but I couldn't bring myself to let him do that, he did have a purpose. He wasn't a weekend visitor anymore, he was an integral part of a family now and he didn't have to exist outside of our circle: he belonged. Little tasks such as putting the napkins on the table, carrying something for me, and helping pick up his toys were asked of him regularly. Instead of "I can't" like he used to do when I asked him to engage in little things, now, he simply refused. I'd put the objects in his hands and insist he do it anyway; he needed purposeful activity for his wellness.

I always praised Jared when he complied. "Oh, I liked the way you did that" — "Good job Jared" — "Thank-you Jared" — "Oh, what a big boy you're getting to be." I praised him even when it only looked like he might be trying — "Oh, I liked the way you tried" — "I'm so proud of you for giving it your best effort" — "You are such a hard worker aren't you!" I praised when he came when he was called. I especially praised when he occasionally offered to help voluntarily. I always said please and thank-you, too.

I finally gave up on Jared learning through play and went to the academics, the real stuff for school readiness. Naming colors, drawing, phonics, simple puzzles; the basics. I was as enthusiastic as a new teacher in her first classroom. I thought it was going to be easy, and that like his brother, Jared would cherish learning. But he didn't seem able to grasp phonics and I had to work so hard to get him to apply himself in the other activities. If he was learning at all, it was very inconsistent. Children between the ages of five and six can typically name basic colors and draw or paint in rudimentary fashion. One day Jared could name five colors but the next day list only two. Most of the time his drawings were compositions of broken lines with no shapes or form to them. Then one day he drew a picture of a "person" with a happy face. It didn't have arms or hands but at least there were three lines for a body. One day he could sing the a,b,c song. The next day, he'd act as if he'd never heard it before. Getting him to paint was most difficult and he hated to color. Simple puzzles were out of the question. He'd yell and scream at me in my attempts to get him to engage. "I hate you!" he'd say. Mostly it was "You hate me!" I was an awful teacher. Adamant that he at least try, I'd yell back at him. It didn't make a bit of difference, he would be that much more resistive. He was as "stubborn as a mule."

It wasn't the fact that Jared wasn't learning that bothered me. It was early yet, he was only five, and I wasn't skilled at teaching him. It was his lack of willingness to at least try that concerned me. I kept thinking this aspect to his nature would go away eventually. Instead, it became more and more pronounced. The more pronounced it became, the more anxious I

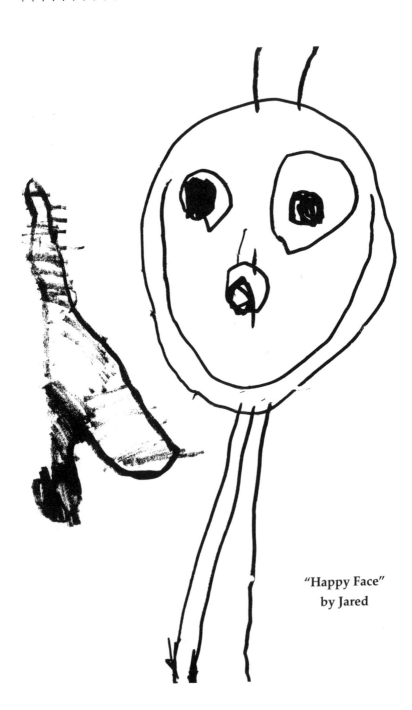

**"Happy Face"
by Jared**

got. I didn't know this trait in one's character was so important to me.

Every family has their own values and priorities. Some families value education; some value athletics; some the arts. Fun is a value, so is work. I valued learning and education. I valued common sense over a high IQ. I valued work and responsibility. I valued independence and the ability to meet challenges head on. Children are a reflection of their parent's values. Parenting Jared was forcing me to examine my values in a way I had never had to do before. I could drink from a chipped coffee mug, eat leftovers, and shop garage sales, but come to find out, I couldn't tolerate a child who wouldn't at least try.

Most discouraging was Jared's tearfulness — he was so quick to cry. When he was with Sherrie and while coming for visits, I thought they were frustrated toddler tears. But as he grew older they became "real" tears and flowed profusely like blood from a gaping wound. Even minor incidents like a toy not doing what he wanted it to, a ball falling from his hands or a trip of the foot resulted in uncontrollable tears. A tiny scratch, the poke of a fingernail, or an unexpected brush on the shoulder brought on tears of tremendous proportions. Other times, for seemingly no reason, he'd sit down on the floor and sob deep heartfelt sobs like one in mourning for his dead. It didn't matter how much Jacob and I reassured and nurtured him at times like this, it was like there was an emotional hole inside of him and love wasn't enough to fill it.

I was angry and bitter toward Barbara, blaming her for the depth of Jared's problems. If she would have let him come to us right away and given us some support, he might not have become so resistive and withdrawn. He wasn't about to trust anybody now. He likely received little or no human contact comfort when away from us because foster parents aren't allowed to encourage attachment. Now we needed to bond but I couldn't even touch him, hold him, or hug him unless it was his idea. "That hurts," he would say when I initiated physical contact. Secretly I worried that he had actually been sexually molested. Children who have been sexually abused will avoid touch supposedly. Time would eventually answer this question because children who have been molested will act out sexually, likely through masturbation or fondling of self or others. But the anxiety of not knowing for certain tossed restlessly amongst all my other worries for Jared's well being.

It was a difficult situation for me — trying to love someone with my hands tied. I had counted on using human contact to gain Jared's trust. Our relationship was superficial at best. I wanted to play with him as I had Jacob. But he didn't like roughhousing now and tickling brought on tears. I liked to use human contact to comfort too; sometimes a hug can make all the difference. Without the freedom of a spontaneous hug, I had to rely on words and finding the right words to comfort a child was not my strong suit. I felt I shouldn't force myself on Jared as I had done with Jacob just in case he had been sexually molested. Oddly though, Jared still liked to be cuddled and kissed as long as he did the initiating, as long as he was in control. So I cuddled and kissed only when he wanted me to.

While my relationship with Jared was anything but rewarding, my relationship with Jacob continued to blossom with each passing day. He changed after Jared came to live with us. At first, I thought they were good changes. With exception to getting himself ready independently in the mornings, he showed an increased ability to stay on task and even more willingness to take initiative. I'd be caught up in an argument with Jared and find Jacob busy taking care himself or already doing what it was I wanted Jared to do. With a keen eye for details, he never made a mistake and shined at moments like that. Compared to Jared, he was the perfect child. I appreciated his help but mostly I appreciated being able to count on him. Like me, he liked things neat and tidy too. The books on his shelf were stacked evenly, his stuffed animals were lined up in a row, and his Lego constructions were kept in special places.

United Way funded an aftercare program at Jacob's school which he attended until late afternoon. Whenever I could get off early enough from work, I would sit and watch him interact with others while at the aftercare program. It was the only way I could gauge how he was doing socially.

Though well regarded by peers and adults alike — he was always one of the first children asked to play a board game — Jacob wasn't necessarily social; he was a loner. He didn't pal up with anyone and he didn't tease and act silly like some little boys do. He was a thinker, studious and quiet, in love with learning. Faithfully, I'd find him absorbed in an activity at the end of the day, working diligently and conscientiously to bring it to completion. Getting him to stop even though the project looked finished to me was a never ending battle. He would inevitably want to add one more piece of macaroni, string, or sequin. Tired and anxious to get home, I would have to patiently direct him to closure and even at that, it had to be in his time.

At six-and-a-half Jacob seemed to have suddenly become conscious of his actions around other people. He was seemingly working very hard at maintaining control of himself, as if he didn't want to stand out in a crowd. Yet he was still fidgety, always moving fingers or feet and touching everything, especially electronic devices with buttons and lights. Store clerks were always yelling at him: "Don't touch that!" He wasn't screaming or having temper tantrums, though. Not publicly, that is. He still had difficulty stopping when he was asked to. Occasionally tiny sparks of anger flew through the air when he was frustrated. But for the most part, Jacob was trying to kept himself emotionally in check. His teacher and the staff at the aftercare program often mentioned how "anxious" he seemed.

At home, Jacob was less anxious and quite social in the evening hours. Still over active and always on the go, he liked to jump and run through the house after dinner. When in a carefree frame of mind, he'd laugh in route. I was still the tickle monster and waited to catch him coming around corners. Rough housing was the only 'kid thing' left we did together, but it was sometimes just enough. When I could make Jacob laugh, my anxieties about being overwhelmed would slip away for a short time. His hyperactivity could get on my nerves even easier now, what with all the chaos in our lives. He was always spilling his milk and bumping into things: the stove, refrigerator, walls, tables. If he got hurt, he'd strike out at the object with his fist or kick it in retaliation and get hurt again, acting as if the stationary and inanimate object was willfully choosing to hurt him.

Home was also the place where Jacob would unleash his anger. In this area, he was actually my most difficult child. He had a need to question authority — especially mine. I knew him well by now and his anger was just as much a part of him as was his kindness. He wanted reasons as to why he wasn't allowed to do something. If my reasons were deemed sound, he was usually compliant. But if I was feeling crabby and insisting on something "just because" he'd defy with a loud "NO!" then take on a defensive posture. With his fists clinched, he'd stand rigid and look at me with a steely gaze as if to say: I'll fight you if I have to! That was the look of a rage just waiting to happen and it kept me honest, so-to-speak, by forcing me to reflect on what it was I wanted from him and why.

It was about control and who had it. Jacob's life had been so out of control — he wasn't about to lose it again. The risk of replacing his unresolved anger with revenge was only one power play away. It was a most difficult challenge for me. I wanted to instill in him self-discipline, but at the same time I did not want to quash his spirit or even extinguish his anger completely. Anger and I had become intimate and I thought about it a lot. I had always thought feelings of anger were bad, and that a person certainly should never express them. I wasn't so sure about all that at this point though because, in a lot of respects, it was anger that was keeping me going. It wasn't a raging anger, but a subtle anger just below the surface, constantly moving me to action.

I wanted Jacob to know eventually that his anger could be used positively, too, but in the meantime I had to teach him how to express it in appropriate ways. At the psychiatric hospital the "appropriate" way to express anger was to process the conflict by discussing it calmly and rationally in a soft voice, never put another on the defensive by blaming, and ask that your rights, dignity, space, and differences be respected. And then keep asking. So I processed every little conflict with Jacob.

Jacob really wasn't the tower of strength he pretended to be. He was a friend to those perceived as weaker than he but he too was emotionally fragile and in many ways just as needy as Jared. Inside of Jacob was a little boy constantly looking for approval. If I complimented Jared without complimenting him too, his head would drop and his chest cave in. When an after-care staff person complimented the group rather than individuals, Jacob would scoot up next to the adult and ask in a rejected tone "Did I do a good job too?" Smiles, words of encouragement and a lot of compliments were Jacob's emotional staples. Criticism of any kind had the power to crush him. He also loved stickers and treats, the symbols qualifying a job completed or a job well done.

Jacob's mixture of needs was a most difficult combination. He needed nurturing and reassurance constantly but he needed equitable and firm guidance at the same time. He was a tough kid but he wasn't a bad kid. He just didn't trust adults. I don't think he liked them much either. He and Jared watched all adults out of the corners of their eyes. Jared hid behind doors in order to listen to adult conversation. "Adults can be tricky and we've got to watch them cause they're bigger than us," Jacob said to Jared during one of their chatter sessions at the dinner table one night. Jacob could get himself into some compromising situations too if I didn't watch him. With an unbridled passion for justice, he'd walk up to a stranger in the grocery store who had slapped a child's hands or told the child to "Shut-up!" and say things like, "Hey! You shouldn't treat your kid that way." It was a contradiction — Jacob wouldn't stand up to his brother or peers, but he'd take on a grown-up without reservation.

When Jared came to live with us, I anticipated Jacob would want to be the overseer of his affairs — he was the older brother — Jared's caretaker. And he did; he was always helping Jared. When Jared cried, he was right there to fix the problem. He answered questions for Jared and bandaged his owies. If I was busy with something and couldn't go into a room with Jared, it was Jacob who blazed the trail for him. Sometimes when I found him assisting Jared, especially if it was with things Jared could do for himself, I would intervene and make him stop. It was a difficult judgment call for me discerning how much was too much or too little. I didn't want Jacob taking responsibility that wasn't his to take; he was a child. I didn't want him being manipulated either. Yet it was plain to see, each child needed the other. Individually they brought to the relationship their own contributions. Though mired in the course of travel, those contributions were the binding holding the relationship together while it underwent repair.

Not only did Jacob bandage Jared's owies, but he bandaged his own as well. This bothered me for a long time — I wanted him to ask me to do it — most little children think only Mommy can make the hurt go away. And once when I saw a toddler halt at the landing of some steps simply because his mother said "No, that's dangerous," I felt sad inside. The toddler stopped without question because he knew instinctively that mommy loved him and wanted to protect him. I wasn't parenting children who would willingly comply without first questioning my intentions — their wounds wouldn't let them.

I never forgot the effect the bear story had on Jared's emotions so I took great care after that to watch what I read to him. I thought it important to stay away from anything having to do with abandonment, abuse or neglect. Then one day I read in a child development book that stories, if chosen wisely, can help children grieve and feel comfortable with their emotions. They can teach them about people and relationships too. I guess until that point, I'd not thought of books as really anything more than an avenue to 'reading readiness.' I knew I had to reach Jared somehow and since I didn't have words at my disposal, or human contact comfort, I decided to explore this idea of grief through stories and find out for myself if there was any validity to it.

Even though Jared seemed to hate learning, he loved being read to. Sometimes it seemed that was the only thing he enjoyed. The silly rhyming books that Jacob liked appealed to Jared's sense of humor, but when I began introducing stories with more depth about characters facing real trials and tribulations, his eyes would open wide, as if he'd spotted a friend in a room full of strangers. He particularly liked stories where acceptance by others is the theme, evidently finding kinship with those who had been left out too. The misfortune of another captured within the pages of a book brought tears to his eyes and from his lips, words of compassion and hope to the imaginary characters in support of their struggles. "That's okay boy," he'd say to the runt of the puppy litter. "Your mommy will find you, you'll see," to one of the lost. If it was a story he especially liked he'd ask for it every night for sometimes up to two weeks. That was something I noticed about Jared early on — he liked repetition.

Discovering what types of stories Jared responded to was helpful. I needed all the insight I could get into how he was perceiving himself in relation to the world around him. He was a most difficult child to understand and extremely moody. One day he could be cheerful, happy, and seemingly wanting to please. The next day, he was teary eyed, whiny, oppositional and fearful.

In a dark mood, Jared viewed things in absolutes with a gloom and doom attitude. If he had to take a time-out from riding his Hot-Wheels in the basement, he'd say: "I'll never get to ride my Hot-Wheels again." It didn't matter how much I tried to interject a brighter picture, nothing was ever going to turn out right according to Jared. In a good mood he bubbled over with love for his family, the cat, the house, the car — everything was wonderful according to Jared when he was in a good mood. "You are the best Mom in the world!" he would declare. "You are the best brother a boy could have Jake!" he would say in between hugs. "I love this cat soooo much." "This house is beautiful." His good moods were as extreme as his dark moods.

Jared charmed us with thoughtfulness when in a good mood. "These pictures are for you Mom." "I saved you a cookie from my lunch today Jake." It was the good moods that kept me going and gave me hope. Locked inside someplace was the Jared I knew and loved. In a dark mood he was self absorbed and everything was "That's MINE!" The dark moods always out-numbered the good ones, however, and I wasn't the "best Mom in the world," either.

Jared could frustrate me like I'd never been frustrated before. He hated change. He could become totally irrational and scream and cry at even the minutest changes. Things such as sitting him in a different spot at the table, moving the chair he hid under, making him wear different shoes, giving him a particular type of spoon, would bring on tears and screaming. Sometimes he cried over things he only thought had changed. Like his brother, sameness meant sanity. It meant my sanity too. We couldn't go anyplace now because Jared would throw himself to the ground and kick and scream in any congested environment. And poor Jacob, we couldn't do his beloved learning type activities in the evenings anymore. To do puzzles, draw, paint, or play Candyland meant chaos. When Jacob did activities, Jared would intentionally spill the paints or push the puzzle pieces off of the table. If Jacob or I moved our Candyland markers ahead of Jared's, he'd cry and scream, saying we were cheating him.

The mornings were becoming so strained. Dressing Jared

was such an ordeal. So I decided to give up on the academic learning activities for a while and concentrate on his self-help skills instead. According to an article I read in the paper, children at five can be expected to dress themselves and make their beds though the jobs will not be perfect and they need prompting. Asking a child to do such chores helps them to learn personal responsibility and self-discipline. I wasn't concerned with Jared making his bed yet but to master the basics of dressing independently would surely boost his self-esteem I thought.

I couldn't understand why the mental health professionals had not helped Jared in the area of dressing. I finally got to see the treatment plan. Self-help skills had been a goal all along. The treatment methods being used were verbal feedback along with natural and logical consequences set to create motivating situations for him. So I started working with him using these methods. I praised, pleaded, promised, and begged. It didn't work. For a natural consequence I told him he would have to go to school in his pajamas. It didn't work. I didn't think a natural consequence was going to work; it hadn't worked before. For example, I told him many times why he shouldn't play with the mace spray hanging from my car keys. When he sprayed it on his arm one day and cried when it stung, I thought that would help him to understand. But a few weeks later I found him playing with it again.

Every time I worked with Jared on dressing, I got angry at the mental health professionals. It seemed like nobody had taken the time to work with him. Or else they were using the wrong techniques. Well I was an occupational therapist and self-help skills training with my elderly clients was now my area of expertise. So I did all the things we occupational therapists do. I broke the task into steps. I bought clothes without buttons and snaps in order to remove the frustrations Jared encountered when manipulating small items. I put my hands over his for guidance. I encouraged him cheerfully. I offered rewards. Nothing was working. He pulled at the clothes or pushed my hands away. Finally, I took pictures of him trying for reinforcement which he did occasionally when it came to undressing rather than dressing. I even had him watch Jacob for the visualization. Nothing worked. This was my first bite of humble pie.

As much as I wanted Jared to be independent and feel better about himself, I decided I would continue to dress him for a while longer. He was young yet and emotionally unstable. It was a mystery to me as to why he couldn't do it himself, though. There was something odd about the way he fussed and whined when I dressed him. I wasn't rough with him. I didn't have to have things my own way either. He insisted on picking out his own clothes and I let him. Like his spoon and his spot at the table, the clothes had to be those already familiar to him and I accommodated. His socks had to be a specific type and the tops turned over just so; he didn't like the kind with thick seams. This too I accommodated. I really didn't mind dressing him except that there was nothing pleasant or enjoyable about this first interaction with him at the start of each day. It was putting a tremendous strain on the mother-child relationship I was trying to build.

Spring was upon us again but the sun didn't brighten my spirits. There was no joy in parenting. Up at 6:30, I had twenty minutes of quiet time to myself to indulge in a cup of coffee. I savored the moments because as soon as I woke the boys, the morning chaos would begin again. I would get myself ready first, then wake Jared, and while struggling with him, verbally direct and redirect Jacob to stay on task. Then came the breakfast chaos and the task of getting the boys to eat in a timely manner, followed by the bathroom chaos with each child taking off in a different direction. I had to repeat myself constantly — "Jacob get your teeth brushed," "Jared stand still," "Jacob stop talking and get on task," "Jared come back here," — it never stopped.

At 8:30 Jared was picked up by a cab and taken to the day treatment program out in the suburbs. Jacob was in school by 8:45. I worked 9 to 5, Monday through Friday. We were always late and I always arrived at work physically spent and emotionally exhausted. If there were no appointments to attend to we would get home by 5:30. Dinner was served between 6:00 and 6:30. The noise of children fussing, crying, whining, running, banging, throwing, tapping, touching, was always constant during this hour. Then it was bath time, followed by a story before bed. Every night the schedule was the same. If there was to be peace and harmony in the house — everything had to stay the same. Change brought on undesirable behaviors. I was constantly on edge trying to keep everything under control.

In the evenings I had from 8:00 until 11:00 to myself which I spent dozing on the couch or watching television. Once in a while I helped with fund raising activities for Jacob's aftercare program (it would be the first of many fund raisers), working with other moms in their homes or mine at night after Jacob and Jared were in bed. Before I went to bed I would take the boys to the bathroom because neither child could make it through the night without having to potty. On weekends we stayed around the house; it was too much work to take them out. I cleaned and cooked for the upcoming week, did the laundry, constantly rearranged furniture in order make the environment "child friendly," worked with Jared on applying himself, and in general, felt deprived. I had met a couple of nice women with "normal" children but after one or two visits to their houses we were never invited back. The women would call me to go to lunch or something, but whenever I suggested we "get the kids together," the subject was quickly changed. It didn't take long for those "friendships" to fizzle out. This was a lonely time for me.

Some days I didn't think life was even worth living; there was nothing to look forward to. I would have given anything to wake up just one morning and not have to wake Jared and get him dressed and going. I searched but I couldn't find anybody trained professionally to stay over and care for children with "emotional problems." So I just had to keep going. The boys and I were always sick with upper respiratory problems, fevers, and flu like symptoms. They were sickly in general it seemed — Jacob's mouth was often laced with canker sores, Jared was constantly getting ear infections, Jacob had had to have a hernia operation, and Jared always had a runny nose.

But no matter how tired I was, I couldn't rest peacefully at night. If I didn't wake up on my own from worry, wondering about what it was that I was doing wrong, or what it was that I could do better, I would be startled out of my sleep by Jacob's screams. The nightmares continued to torment him. I always went to him to comfort, holding him and rocking him for a few minutes. He never really woke up and I don't think he even knew I was there. Fully awake myself however, I would go back to bed only to lay there and listen to him whimper. Sometimes in a frightened yet forceful tone he would scream out "NO!" as if defending himself against demons; demons that only he could see. Sometimes I wondered if I was one of them — I was yelling at he and his brother a lot by now. And I was spanking Jared.

I had always thought a good mom is supposed to know what her child's capabilities are. And that if she doesn't know, she will find out because there is nothing more cruel than to ask something of a child that he cannot do. If she is confused as to whether or not it is a "can't do" as opposed to a "won't do," she will give him the benefit of the doubt, or at least she should. I wanted to be a good mom, but I couldn't get a clear sense of what Jared could or couldn't do as opposed to what he would or wouldn't do. By all outward appearances he was a "normal" child: he walked, he talked, he looked just fine. In fact, he could chat with anybody and adults liked him a lot because of this. He was as cute as could be and very charming. I wanted to give him the benefit of the doubt. I was trying very hard to give him the benefit of the doubt. But like his emotional moods, his capabilities and compliance was either up or down and changing all the time. The could or couldn't do coupled with the would or wouldn't do, muddied the water and I never knew what I should or shouldn't do.

Disciplining Jared with any kind of effectiveness was nearly impossible. Time-outs had no impact. Following a time-out, he'd return to the same undesired behavior; I would ask him specifically not to do something and he would do it anyway. Treats didn't seem to be enough motivation and half of the time he couldn't remember I had promised him one. Most frustrating were the times when I'd ask him to do something and he'd smile and say "okay" seemingly wanting to please, then he wouldn't move or simply walk off in another direction from the activity. I processed the conflicts, reasoned with him about the behaviors, talked him through what he shouldn't do. I tried to give him choices about things. Giving a child the opportunity to make choices is supposed to empower him. But reasoning and choices seemed to bring on mass confusion resulting in Jared arguing, screaming, or crying.

I vowed I would never spank Jared. That was the last thing he needed. But unfortunately, a swat was effective — too effective. A swat delivered to his bottom and he'd stop arguing. A swat could extinguish an unwanted behavior for a while. A swat could get him moving. I never went beyond a swat or two and I spanked only after I couldn't take anymore. I didn't like it when I lost control, but I knew that was what it was about: *control and who had it*. Jared was an abused and abandoned child — he was manipulating me in order to maintain control. Spanking him made me feel terrible inside. When I spanked, my hand was filled with anger and frustration, while my heart was momentarily filled with what felt like hate. Then I had to deal with feelings of guilt afterwards. My dad didn't think I had anything to feel bad about. "A spanking from time to time is just what that boy needs," he was always saying. "You spare the rod, you'll spoil the child."

The Children's Services Division offered parenting classes to adoptive and foster parents relevant to adoptive issues — specifically "attachment problems". I attended two classes, which was hard for me because I had such a sour taste in my mouth for the place. I didn't learn anything new either. Other than spanking I was doing things right, supposedly. I was consistent. I maintained structure; things were predictable. I encouraged and nurtured. I spent time with Jared. I listened when he talked. I set limits and stated the consequences to given behaviors. I processed every little conflict. I followed through. I praised. I rewarded appropriate behaviors. I was a good mom — or at least I was trying to be. So why wasn't any of it working? I wondered. Nothing was making sense. When the pre-adoption trainer said seeing me in the hallway at one of the classes — "You sure look good. Most of our adoptive parents don't look good when they come in for these classes" — I was surprised. I felt so awful inside that I thought surely it showed on the outside. I found myself wondering what she really meant by that comment, too. Were other adoptive parents feeling just as overwhelmed and as stressed as I was? I wondered. I thought it was just me.

Chapter 2
"Special Needs"

Within just a few weeks after Jared came to live with us, I had begun meeting weekly with the family therapist of the day treatment program. It took a lot of energy on my part to keep the appointments because the center was at best a 30-minute drive one way from my house. Since I went after work, I'd get caught in rush hour traffic after having spent an hour with the therapist. By the time I picked the boys up from aftercare they would be fussing, crying, tired and hungry. I never shared with the therapist my inner-most fears and anxieties or talked about the level of stress I was encountering for fear he would think I couldn't handle myself. After all, I did get what I asked for. I shared with him the different things I was trying and while he thought they were good, he kept insisting on the use of natural and logical consequences.

I had always intended to keep Jared in the treatment program as long as possible for the structure and mental health therapy. When I was invited to come and observe him in the program, I felt it a positive outreach effort to a working relationship, finally, between parent and professionals and I accepted the invitation gratefully.

The program was stationed in an old house. It was a warm and pleasant place with child size furniture, a sandbox, toys, and a water trough for making bubbles. Jared seemed very comfortable there. When he was asked by the staff to introduce me to his classmates, he did so readily. "This is my Donna but she's my Mom too," he declared, beaming at me. No one could have known how endearing this expression of love for me was, drawing out the sting of my suffering mother image.

Ignoring my fears of rejection, I reached out to give Jared a hug when a little boy suddenly leaped between us and stated in a taunting tone "She's not your real Mom!" Poor Jared. Tears swelled up in his eyes and he looked at me suspiciously, as if I had been lying to him about something. I put my arms around him and hugged him just the same. Then I whispered in his ear: "You didn't come from my tummy but God sent you to me so that makes me your real Mom." He recovered then and went on to play. He recovered but I didn't. The incident served to remind me of the many children waiting in limbo, just like Jared did. Their real mom is a loss they can never recoup and while her memory is perhaps a dull or painful ache, limbo in it's vast void of nothingness, pending the treatment that proposes to make everything all right, won't let them forget.

A few minutes later the child who teased Jared flew into a rage and slapping himself, stated over and over again, "I'm weird, I'm weird." With horror I realized where it was that Jared had learned that "I'm weird" business and that if those were the types of behaviors he had been seeing every day for over a year-and-a-half by now, how was he ever going to know what "normal" was? Since the day he was born, he had never been in a normal situation. So I removed him from the program that spring and placed him full time in the preschool he had been attending in the afternoons following the mornings at the day treatment program since the fall.

My removing Jared from the program was not easy to do. A meeting was called and I had to meet with all the treatment staff. I didn't go alone. I asked Jared's teacher at the preschool if she would go along with me and she was more than happy to help. She had observed how well Jared did with a little peer pressure and she thought it a good idea that he be "mainstreamed" with normal children. The day treatment staff had been planning to discharge him soon anyway. There was no mental health care follow-up upon discharge for Jared which I felt was probably just as well. It would have meant taking him into a mental health clinic at the end of the day for play therapy. I didn't need one more thing to do, especially at the end of the day. I would have been grateful if someone could have come to the house, but at that time mental health therapists didn't go into a family's home to work with a youngster.

Going from the quiet day treatment setting to the busy preschool was not easy for Jared, even from the beginning. I often found him at the end of the day peeking at the group from underneath tables and out of dark corners but at least he had a keyhole view of how things are supposed to be. The preschool staff made allowances for him and when they had the energy, they made extra efforts for him, too. They knew me all ready because Jacob had attended aftercare there when he was in Head Start the year before. Jacob had been well liked and in many respects he paved the way for Jared because of their behaviors being so similar — neither one did well with transitions and they had to be redirected constantly.

The teacher at the preschool seemed to like Jared. After the positive experience I had with Jacob's early intervention teacher, I valued the teacher-parent relationship and took great pains to talk with teachers daily to see how things went. I don't know that it helped anyone to better manage the boys' behaviors, but at least they knew I was available and that I cared. I always shared with anyone who worked with Jacob and Jared a little information about the early deprivation. I never told anyone they were labeled severely emotionally disturbed, however. I thought if I did then people would treat them as damaged and deranged. I wanted people to see Jacob and Jared as little children filled with promise; budding flowers in need of life's fertilizers — the sun, the earth, the moon, the stars, and human caring.

At the end of the school year I was called to bring Jared into the assessment center for the public school system in order to have him evaluated for the upcoming school year. I was quite surprised when they said he wasn't in need of special services; a regular classroom setting was recommended. I liked this outcome and thought maybe my hard work was actually having an effect. It was suggested I have Jared's hearing checked and that I enroll him in tumbling or gym classes during the summer months to improve his self-confidence in his motor skills.

I was just starting to breathe a little easier, feeling in control of the situation, when I was called by the child development specialist at Jacob's school to come and get him. It was just two weeks before the school year was to end. "Do you know your child has an anger problem?" she asked. Evidently she had not seen his file. The teacher didn't know what really happened. Jacob suddenly started screaming and raging, knocking books from the shelf. I guess he was pretty hard to get contained. I felt bad for him. He was so sensitive to people looking at him anyway and this must have really hurt his pride. Once home, we talked about the incident but he didn't know what happened. I told him not to worry, he had just had a bad day, and that pretty soon we would find someone who would help us with this problem.

The child development specialist recommended a particular counseling program for children that was having effective results in helping them to manage anger outbursts. I wanted to take Jacob there but the Medicaid insurance wasn't acceptable and I couldn't afford $80 an hour. I had his adoption subsidy but I was using it for enrollment in summer programs in order to keep him "wrapped up tight with lots of structure."

Life was so hard. I could never put a finger on what was going on with the boys or anticipate what was coming next. One day they would be fine, the next day, completely out of sorts. So the harder it got, the harder I got on them.

I kept tight parameters around Jacob constantly. This meant having to say no at times when he wanted something and he didn't like that. Sometimes I felt like I was still working in mental health at the psychiatric hospital. I didn't want to be manipulated. I had to maintain the control. If my reasons for saying no to Jacob were sound and he still wouldn't comply, I had to discipline. I never spanked him again after the dresser incident but disciplining him was hard work. I had to think through my every move in order to be effective. He was highly responsive to the earning and withholding of a treat so I used that strategy a lot. If I said I would withhold and he still didn't comply, I had to follow through. If I didn't, he would go out of his way to test the limits further. He didn't like losing a treat and would be grudgingly go to the upstairs stairwell where sound echoed to scream and cry loud enough for the neighbor's to think I was beating him. Or he would covertly bang his Lego buckets together because he knew it would annoy me. The dynamics were the same between us in relation to rewards, too. If

I promised him something and didn't follow through, he would hold me accountable by acting up again.

I was familiar with a clinic in another state that does what is called "rage therapy" for "unattached children." It entails the parent holding the child in a particular way while he rages. While raging there are several therapists hovered around him and his parent, coaching the parent in what to say. It is thought to be an effective way to promote attachment. But we couldn't afford it. With plane fare, hotel costs and food for several days, in addition to the fee for the treatment, such an intervention could cost well over $3,000 at that time. Even if we could have afforded it, I didn't think it was the way to go for us. I didn't like the idea of people staring at Jacob when he was in a troubled state.

There was nothing I could do. Play therapy was available through the community mental health clinic and I could use the Medicaid insurance for it, but Jacob had already had that for over six months, and he used the avenue of imaginative play a lot right at home. His frustrations and pent-up aggressions came out in his imaginative play; it was his favorite type of leisure activity. Always action oriented, it rang of territorial issues, war and power. He could sit for the longest time playing alone with action figures, defining each character's mission and giving voice to their individual ambitions and aggressions. I'd know contact with the enemy had been made when verbal monologue was replaced with the authentic sound effects of missiles firing and bombs exploding. I made it a point to give Jacob plenty of play time for this purpose, but it obviously wasn't enough. Clearly he had to find a way to express himself; his hurts were tormenting him, his anger was alienating him.

This is when I thought of the healing power of music. Music could serve as an avenue of expression for Jacob. Art therapists use art in much the same way when working with abandoned and abused children. So Joe lent us his portable electric piano, introduced us to a teacher (he was taking piano lessons from her himself), and for $25 a lesson, I started Jacob on learning to play the piano. To my surprise, he absolutely loved it. His ability to attend and concentrate when sitting at the piano was amazing. I had to guide him of course but I never had to make him practice; he did it willingly.

For Jared, I had an ear, nose and throat specialist remove his adenoids in order to decrease the probably of future ear infections — the Medicaid insurance was excellent when it came to medical care for the boys. I got Jacob started in summer activities, and I cut back on my work hours two days a week in order to take Jared to a tumbling class and a gym class on Tuesdays and Thursdays. I kept him in the preschool the other three days per week for socialization as well as learning. The adoption subsidies paid for everything and helped to compensate my lost wages.

Within just a few sessions I knew the tumbling and gym classes were a mistake for Jared. At the start, he ostracized himself socially by pushing and crying to be first in line. Then when he couldn't perform he'd throw himself to the ground and cry. I would nurture and try to redirect him but it was to no avail. In his frustration he couldn't see he was just learning and needed practice. Once frustrated, he wouldn't try anymore and refused to move yet would want to maintain being first in line. After several sessions of driving home with him in tears, I stopped taking him. He clearly wasn't ready for such activities. To keep taking him I felt was to hurt his self esteem rather than build it. I couldn't stand the other children and their parents staring at him anymore either.

Discouraged but determined to keep trying in order to enhance Jared's motor development, I decided to utilize the playground equipment at the park next door to our house. That too was most discouraging. Jared refused to go on most of the equipment. He liked the merry-go-round for very short periods but he cried on the swings. He wouldn't try going up the slide even when I was right behind him. The teeter-totter was something to run away from. Exasperated and thinking I might be intimidating him, I sat down on the grass to observe what he would do on his own. I learned a lot. He pushed a swing as if to examine how it worked and he sat down on the bottom of the slide and flung his feet into the air as if pretending he made it from the top. Mostly, he liked to wander around the grounds.

Jared was a difficult child to understand because at home he was climbing on the couch or hanging from door knobs all the time. I didn't mind if the boys ran in the house, but climbing on the couch was

Jared learns to ride his bike.

against the rules. I was aware that Jared probably couldn't remember the rule and I would patiently but constantly remind him. After hundreds of reminders, though, I had to wonder if he was doing it just to annoy me. I don't know how it was he came to learn how to ride a two wheel bike that summer given his fear of the playground equipment. But he did and he taught himself. I tried to help him. But like my hugs and kisses, my help was rejected.

Without the tumbling and gym classes to use as structured activity I had to find activities for Jared to do at home, which required work, patience and creativity on my part. It was pretty hard to keep a kid who didn't want to do anything structured up. Since I was trying to reach him emotionally I used things like bubble baths and water play at the kitchen sink. The activities worked well to keep him occupied for a while. For a little more structure and one-on-one attention from me, I read him stories. I did the grocery shopping and ran errands on the days he and I were home too; it was easier to take care of such business when I didn't have both of the boys to monitor. Jared liked to be the "pusher" of the grocery cart. His cart collided with aisle end displays and nipped the back of my heels all the time, but at least he was doing something constructive.

In spite of my goodwill and the freedom to attend to Jared individually, it was a long summer. Joe took us camping or on Sunday drives out into the country which helped to keep my spirits up. Once we went to an amusement park. It wasn't very fun for me because Jared fussed and whined the whole time. Jacob, on the other hand, had a great time and didn't want to stop. He was a thrill seeker; the faster the ride the better. "Meet your fun," he said to Jared as we passed through the entrance gates. This aspect to Jacob's nature concerned me.

By fall, it didn't seem like any gains were made in relation to Jared's emotional development. I knew he needed time and I was trying to be patient and give it to him. But a year had past by now and I was tired of catering to his every whim. The child's relentless demands were choking me. I felt constantly drained and exhausted as if something was sucking up the air I breathed. We were all catering to him. I dressed him, when Joe was around he carried things for him, Jacob answered questions for him and my dad had enough pity for him to last a lifetime. None of it seemed to be helping. It seemed like the more we gave, the more he wanted. He could never remember receiving a toy when he asked for another. He was still destroying them and playing with the broken pieces — trashed and broken bits and pieces of garbage — just as if they were still intact. And even though he would soon be six he still clinged, and sucked, and cried and whined. He still took what he wanted when he wanted it and he still guarded his position of being first as if his life depended on it.

It was at this time that I decided to attend a parent support group. It was a group specific to adoptive parents who had either parented or were parenting children with attachment disorders. I had to talk to other people. Jared and I weren't bonding. Some days I felt as if a stranger lived in my house. I tried to stay away from thinking he was an unattached child. The information I had on what to do in relation to attachment disorders was the most discouraging body of knowledge I had ever encountered. It is thought that there is not a lot which can be done for unattached children other than a lot of structure and the parent maintaining absolute control at all times. Even more discouraging for me was the fact that the unattached child is thought to be disturbed and non responsive to normal loving nurturance.

I couldn't tell if Jared was what the professionals would consider an unattached child or not. Like all disorders, there is a cluster of given characteristics and behaviors associated with attachment disorders. The unattached child is thought to be superficially engaging and "charming," lacks stranger anxiety, lacks the ability to maintain eye contact, isn't affectionate on the parents' terms, is destructive to self, others and material things, is cruel to animals, lies about the obvious, has no impulse control, has lags in learning, lacks cause and effect thinking, lacks a conscience, has abnormal eating patterns, has poor peer relationships, is preoccupied with fire, asks persistent nonsense questions and is an incessant chatterer, is inappropriately demanding and clingy, and has abnormal speech patterns.

Jared could be very charming and superficially engaging it seemed. His eye contact was poor. He wasn't affectionate with strangers anymore, but he didn't fear them either. I couldn't touch him unless he wanted me to and he definitely destroyed things, particularly his toys. He wasn't cruel to animals. He liked to tell us he had done something in the past, like own a horse for example when we knew he didn't, but that seemed more like wishful bragging as opposed to obvious lying. I didn't think he had an impulse control problem — he seemed to know perfectly well what he was doing at all times. He wasn't having learning lags — he wasn't learning at all. I equated the lack of cause and effect thinking to be like logical and natural consequences — Jared wasn't making those connections. I wasn't sure if his obsession with food would be qualified as an abnormal eating pattern. He had problems interacting with other children and he was demanding and clingy with me. I had not seen a preoccupation with fire, just tying things up. He had received speech therapy while at the day treatment program, but his speech was perfect — or so it seemed. He didn't ask persistent nonsense questions, but he chatted constantly with Jacob, to the point that it interfered with his listening.

I was optimistic on the drive to the house where the support group met. It was a Saturday afternoon and the boys were safe at home for a couple of hours with my dad. Free of worry, I was ready to absorb every piece of knowledge I could get. I thought the other parents might have come up with additional techniques besides just structure and control. As soon as I walked through the door my optimism vanished. The atmosphere was clearly not one of shared ideas or active problem solving. Rather, it was one of abrasive animosity toward the children buffered only by a sense of despair, which hung heavy in the air. Some parents gave testimony to their children stealing, lying, and hoarding food. The more seasoned parents testified to fire setting, animal killing, destruction of property, runaways and treatment centers. The stories were devastating and too much for my hopes to bear. It was like seeing the future already woven tightly as in a tapestry that can't be undone. Many of the people said mental health professionals were always blaming them. Others said there is no help. The fact that the people were well intentioned individuals just like myself, who had adopted for all the right reasons, only served to bring the bitterness of disappointment closer to home. I so wanted to stage a defense against the negativity but it would have been weak for I was haunted by uncomfortable feelings of animosity, too.

My spirits were at their lowest low and I was just about to leave when a guest speaker, a licensed therapist by the name of Diane Malbin, arrived to talk about the effects on a developing fetus when a woman drinks alcohol while pregnant. I wasn't interested. I wanted to slip out of there to be alone with my thoughts but I had to stay; it would have been rude to leave while she was talking.

So I listened half heartedly to her describe what happens physically to children with Fetal Alcohol Syndrome. They have a certain look about the the face, their growth is retarded, and there is organic brain damage. Then she started talking about how some children exposed to alcohol in utero might not be Fetal Alcohol Syndrome but rather Fetal Alcohol Effected. I had never heard this term "fetal alcohol effected" until that moment. I wasn't fully aroused either until she began talking about the cluster of behaviors typically seen in children with fetal alcohol effects. Then I went into shock; she was talking about Jared:

Young children with fetal alcohol effects are contradictory in their behaviors and at times most difficult to understand. No two are alike which only adds to the confusion. They are resistive to change in their environments, require considerable supervision for safety, can be demanding and relentlessly needy, are easily frustrated, have trouble with transitions or change of activity, are unable to grasp consequences, lack stranger anxiety, have short-term memory problems, have difficulty following through on tasks consistently, and they may have huge emotional responses to seemingly minor incidents.

Finally things started making sense. Jared wasn't like the little boy in the *Broken Cord* because he wasn't Fetal Alcohol Syndrome, he was Fetal Alcohol Effected! That's were the confusion was. Obviously Barbara didn't understand the differences between the two. The mental health therapists at the day treatment program must not have known he had been exposed to alcohol while in utero, that's why the natural and logical consequences they used didn't work. I forgot all about what the doctor had said. But I couldn't understand why the school assessment center didn't pick up on it. The folks there had said Jared didn't need help, yet I know the doctor sent a copy of her report to them stating he needed a learning resource center.

I felt terrible for ignoring the fetal alcohol. It was a classic case of denial. I didn't want to think there was something wrong with Jared that love couldn't fix. Now I wanted all the information I could get on fetal alcohol so I could parent him effectively.

I never went back to the attachment disorders parent support group. Instead I began attending the parent training/support group being offered by the therapist. She and a co-therapist were pioneers in the field, attempting to educate parents as well as professionals in unchartered waters; there was little published information available on the behaviors associated with exposure to alcohol while in utero or strategies for intervention. It was the first group of its kind to come to the Portland Metropolitan area. Because it was a parent training as well as a support group, a fee of $25 was charged weekly.

It was a lot of work for me to get out of the house in order to attend the group. I would have to get the boys dressed for bed and settled down somewhat before I left. Then I just kept my fingers crossed that my dad would take me seriously and actually get them to bed on time. He thought I was too fussy with their schedules. He thought I was "only imagining" that they were extra hard to manage the next day if not put to bed on time.

I learned a lot about the effects of alcohol on the human brain while it is developing and it's not good. The effects of alcohol on a developing fetus has been studied since the sixties with conclusive evidence to suggest alcohol permanently changes the brain. There is no cure or a way to reverse the damaging effects. The key to living in harmony with the fetal alcohol effected child is understanding. For some children, there is a hypersensitivity to sound which contributes to them becoming easily stressed in noisy arenas. Some can't maintain eye contact even if they wanted to. Some will look blank in their facial expressions. Among mental health professionals this is known as a "flat affect." Some can't distinguish fantasy from reality. Some have difficulty with verbal instructions even though their hearing acuity is fine. There are school problems. Some perseverate (pronounced: per-se-ver-ate) too, which means continued or repetitive actions, words, or thoughts. Once engaged in a task, for example, they don't want to be interrupted, completion is the goal. If interrupted before the task is completed they might become quite agitated, even rage. Even if the child is frustrated with a given task he may not be able to accept help from others, or stop and come back to the task later after calming down. Trying to reason with the him verbally is fruitless when he is in a perseverative state.

When I heard about the perseveration I wanted to scream, stomp my feet, and cry all at the same time. My Jacob was fetal alcohol effected too! He perseverated often around the house but I didn't know that was what I was seeing. I thought it was anger and the need for control in relation to his trust issues. When faced with a problem, rather than try different solutions, he'd insist on one particular way even though it wasn't working. His frustration would mount. I'd try to help him by explaining the alternatives but it was like he couldn't hear me. Sometimes he'd get that I'm possessed look in his eyes. He perseverated when he practiced the piano too. Every note had to be perfect. If it wasn't, he'd continue banging away at the keys determined he was going to get it right. The result would be total frustration with tears streaming down his cheeks but he still wouldn't stop. Not knowing it was perseveration, I was actually considering not having him take lessons anymore. I thought it was too much pressure for him. Now of course I wouldn't. Learning to play a musical instrument is also good for brain development. The piano, for example, utilizes mathematics and helps the child learn problem-solving skills.

Since Jared didn't like to do much of anything, I had not observed him perseverating. Once in the middle of the night however, something "odd" happened. It was perseverative behavior, I just didn't know it. I was awakened by a loud cry. I thought it was Jacob having a nightmare so I went up stairs to comfort him. The hall light was on and I found Jared up, walking back and forth from the rocking chair to the bed. I called his name but got no response. So I sat down in the rocking chair to act as a decoy and bring his attention to me. His eyes were open and he seemed awake, he even looked right at me, but he didn't acknowledge my presence. I sat there without saying anything more and watched him for nearly two minutes go back and forth, repetitively. He wasn't talking or touching anything, just going back and forth, back and forth.

It all added up. Now I had words for the behaviors. The hypersensitivity to sound was why Jacob covered his ears a lot when he first joined Sherrie at her busy household and why he and Jared didn't do well in congested environments. Now I knew why yelling at them was a sure way of getting their attention. Jacob and Jared were both effected but to different degrees. Like Jared, Jacob had the facial features associated with fetal alcohol effects. When he tipped his head a certain way they were obvious. He had the short term memory problem too. He was always saying "I forgot," "I forget," or "I don't remember." His difficulties weren't so obvious perhaps because he had received early intervention.

Sam had said Julie was a binge drinker. Binge drinking is now known to be extremely hard on the developing fetus. Julie probably drank more when pregnant with Jared. It stood to reason she would; caring for a new baby can be stressful for anyone. Jacob was probably not an easy infant to care for given his hyperactivity, and Julie had problems coping in general. Given the feelings of isolation she expressed to Sam, it wasn't hard to imagine her drinking, and drinking a lot when pregnant with Jared.

I had an incredible range of emotions to deal with upon making this discovery, that I was in fact, parenting two children with very "special needs." Now I knew what people meant when they said, "We don't think you're being realistic." Of course I wasn't being realistic. Nobody told me what parenting children with fetal alcohol effects was like. It wouldn't have mattered, though, I still would have taken the boys. I knew from the start I wasn't getting "perfect little babies." It's just that it would have been nice to have a real dialogue, a plan in place and some supports around us. But then maybe there was no such thing. According to our last adoption worker, there were no services for "post" adoptive families. Evidently a grant had just been received to study what our needs might be, but it would be three of four years before the program results were in.

To know that Jared was fetal alcohol effected was comforting in an unsettling kind of way. It was the lesser of two evils: a can't do, as opposed to a won't do. He wasn't an emotionally disturbed/unattached child, he was disabled. I would take that over emotionally disturbed or unattached — the tapestries of

despair — any day. I thought I could deal with just about anything as long as I could see it and face it head-on. Understanding Jared now meant I could help him and support him in appropriate ways. I needed to be more patient with him. It saddened me to think he wasn't going to be an airplane pilot someday, but that was all right. He wouldn't have to be an airplane
pilot, honor college graduate, or an over achiever to make me
proud, average or even below average intelligence was good
enough for me as long as he had the right attitude and was
willing to work for things. That is were the challenge was for
me: to bring forth in him a positive attitude and a work ethic.

Acknowledging that Jacob was fetal alcohol effected, on the
other hand, was extremely painful for me. It wouldn't be true if
I said I didn't take pride in his accomplishments. He loved learning. To parent a child who would have a lot of choices as an
adult was a source of pride as well as comfort for me. I thought
my job was to heal Jacob's heart so that his emotional problems
wouldn't hold him back. But to have a brain that plays tricks on
him, his struggles, and mine, were going to be that much harder.
It wasn't fair. He and his brother had been biologically ripped-
off.

I broke down and cried that evening right there in front of
the group. The tears poured out of me. In all of my life, I had
never done that before in the presence of others. I kept telling
myself: *Get a hold of yourself.* But I couldn't. It was all too much.
Too much pressure, too much confusion, too much isolation,
too much loss.

In the intensity of the moment I despised Julie again, heart-
lessly. I wanted to go to her and ask if she knew of the legacy of
confusion she left to her children. I wanted her to know her
babies weren't babies anymore but little people going out into a

world where survival of the fittest is the law of the land. I wanted her to know how hard I was working to provide for the children she brought into this world. I felt no compassion whatsoever for the woman. I would never be able to tell Jacob and Jared what she had done to them. When a child is born with water on the brain, a spinal cord that wasn't encased properly, Down's syndrome, or Cerebral Palsy; we may know how it happens but we may not know why. When we don't know the why, the disability is considered a birth defect. Fetal alcohol is classified as a birth defect. Fetal alcohol is also 100% preventable.

I attended the parent training/support group for a couple of months. It was so hard for me to get out of the house in order to attend. Plus the $25 a week, though it wasn't much, was adding up. It was the kind of group I needed to attend four to six months, possibly, because the information was so foreign to me. "Reframe, tolerate, accept," the therapists were advising. To integrate it entailed my looking at things from an entirely different perspective and then I had to get used to using it. I couldn't afford to continue paying cash and these therapists couldn't take the Medicaid insurance either. It was ironic, really. I was too proud at one time to even consider we would need mental health care with the Medicaid insurance. Now we needed it — the training/support group afford information as well as emotional support — and it was useless.

Before I left the training/support group, I made a list of some little things I could use at home to avoid conflict. It was always the little things that wore me down anyway. For example, when Jacob combed his hair he would get the top and the sides but never the back. The back hairs would be sticking straight up. This was because he couldn't see the back. I have no idea why, but if a child with fetal alcohol effects doesn't see something it literally ceases to exist. Jacob didn't like me combing his hair for him of course, but with this new piece of information, I could remind him to get the back by simply saying: "Remember to get the back. That's a blind spot." Now, when I didn't want Jared to play with certain things, all I had to do was slip the items under something so he couldn't see it. There was no argument and I had one less thing to worry about. This information also helped me to understand why it was the boys couldn't find something if it was covered up. Another helpful technique was to tell Jared 30 to 40 minutes ahead of time what was coming up when it was time to transition. The therapist also said don't give him a lot of choices about things. So I started giving him very concrete either/or choices which helped cut down on the opposition somewhat. All of this information was very valuable.

As much as I appreciated learning about fetal alcohol, it was depressing, too. I had a list now of the things that were wrong. The therapist was sensitive to the sorrow we parents were suffering so she gave us another list. It was a list of the positives traits often found in children with fetal alcohol effects. They are: cuddly, friendly, spontaneous, loving, determined, committed, caring, kind, helpful, curious, creative, artistic, musical, and sensitive; just to list a few. I've always thought these very fine qualities to find in a human being. Jacob already possessed a lot of them. Jared had them, too, but they had to be drawn out consistently. The therapists said that if not protected, these qualities could be eroded in the child by the middle school years. It was easy to lose sight of them, I'd already discovered, when I was so busy in life just trying to keep up with everything. So I posted the list on the refrigerator in the hopes that it would help me to think positively and remember to look for the good.

I learned that children with fetal alcohol effects do better in small groups. So instead of sending Jared to the elementary school around the corner from our house that fall, where the class size was at least 20, I enrolled him in a private kindergarten. The class size was only seven. After care in the afternoons was provided for too, so he didn't have to move around from one setting to another. The school was a quiet little place. Jared blossomed emotionally for a time. He blossomed at home too with his mother being more understanding and consequently more supportive. When he presented me with a picture he drew one day of "a boy having a dream," it was most encouraging. I loved Jared. To see him take an interest in things finally, feel better about himself, and show a creative side to his little personality, made life worth living for a change.

Jacob, on the other hand, wasn't doing so well. The further he moved into the elementary school years, the more complicated things became. Because he felt so comfortable in the area of music, I enrolled him in a public magnet school for his first grade year that had a performing arts program. Within the first month the teacher called to tell me how bright Jacob was because he could see patterns. He wanted me to move him up a grade. This I opposed. Jacob needed to be with his same age peers for socialization and I told the teacher why. Sharing even just a small amount of information about Jacob's past with this teacher was a terrible mistake, however. He called again a couple of weeks later. Not to tell me how bright my child was but rather to tell me how "obsessive-compulsive," resistive, and non-compliant he was. It was as if Jacob had suddenly become some sort of a social deviant; a bad boy bent on creating trouble for teacher.

I wasn't working anymore on Fridays by now; I changed

**"Boy having a dream" drawing
by Jared
10/24/91**

my work week to 32 hours as opposed to 40 in an effort to cut down on the stress. So I volunteered to help out in Jacob's classroom on Friday mornings in order to see for myself what was actually going on.

The room looked like a rat's nest with papers piled all over and every square inch of the walls tacked with more paper. The classroom was incredibly chaotic with the teacher the only adult to attend to 28 children; a number of whom didn't speak English. It was a joke to think the teacher could meet the individual needs of so many. The quiet children were forgotten, the needy ones ignored, the bright ones bored, and the demanding ones too all consuming. The noise volume was typically on high. To be engulfed in such chaos was too much for Jacob. He struggled for order in the best way he knew how by shuffling and reshuffling his papers and checking the sequence of his crayons often. I think it helped him emotionally to have me there on Friday mornings, but there was nothing I could do to assist him or the teacher; who seldom spoke to me. My jobs were to read to individual children in the corner or cut out symbols from construction paper. The children's jobs were to sit still, be quiet, and not ask for anything.

After a couple of months, during which time I was learning about the fetal alcohol, Jacob fell apart one night at bedtime and started slapping his face and crying. Fortunately, he was able to express himself when I asked what was wrong. "That school is too noisy for me. My ears hurt when I'm in the cafeteria and on the playground. In the classroom I just get settled and I have to go here and I have to go there. I don't like it!" he said between sobs. He was in his home room only a few hours a day, the rest of the time he went to various music and dance classes. I felt terrible. I made a mistake to think he was ready for such a program, but he was there and compensations needed to be made.

The therapists of the fetal alcohol parent training/support group, encouraged us parents to educate others regarding the behaviors associated with fetal alcohol effects for our children's sake. So after Jacob expressed to me where it was he was having difficulties, I shared with his teacher that he had been exposed to alcohol while in utero and what that meant in terms of his behaviors: the hypersensitivity to sound, perseveration, and the need for sameness. I asked that Jacob be allowed to go to the library following lunch for some quiet time; twenty minutes perhaps. I really didn't think it an unreasonable request. Jacob could sit and read at home for up to half-an-hour or more by himself; he loved to read. I didn't ask for help in relation to the schedule, moving around in the afternoons was core to the program. All I could ask of the teacher in relation to the perseveration was that he have an open mind to new knowledge.

"I can't let Jacob go to the library after lunch. That is isolative behavior and I will not allow it," the teacher replied. I tried, but couldn't reason with him. Jacob even wrote him a note expressing his feelings but it didn't matter. The teacher simply would not discuss it any further. Poor Jacob. The noise thrashed at his ear drums but he had to bear the pain and consequently the imposed isolation; how could he think about socializing when his ears hurt? My heart went out to him and for the first time in my life I envied children in wheelchairs; at least their disabilities are visible.

I didn't get far in educating the teacher about perseveration either. The only exposure he had had to the body of information specific to the effects of alcohol on the developing fetus was an article he read in *National Geographic* on Fetal Alcohol Syndrome. Because Jacob didn't "look" like the little boy pictured on the front page of the magazine, the knowledge I attempted to provide him on fetal alcohol effects simply didn't register. I could have challenged his resistance to Jacob having some quiet time and perhaps gotten support for Jacob through an individualized education plan, the public law designed to protect handicapped children from discrimination, but I didn't. Such a process can take months and I didn't have the time or the energy to go "begging" for some basic human rights or a little common courtesy either.

So in lieu of my time and energy, I decided to see if I could buy what it was I thought Jacob needed. I shopped around until I found a small private school. The classrooms were self-contained so Jacob could stay put all day. Lunch would be eaten at his own desk. The environment of the school was what one would call an "earthy" place, with huge plants, wooden toys, rabbits, fish, and hamsters housed in the classrooms. Based on the idea that children learn through their emotions, the curriculum consisted of art, music, poetry, drama, stories, hands-on experiences, and imaginative play. The children were not pushed or rushed and the first grade teacher would remain with the child through eighth grade. 75% of Jacob's adoption subsidy would go for transportation, tuition, and aftercare, which was provided for there at the school.

I really didn't want to leave the public school system, but Jacob was undone now and unless I wanted the hard work that so many others had put into his well-being to be wasted, I had to get him "wrapped-up" again fast. He wasn't the kind of child that I could stew about whether I should take action or not. Another explosion at school, another stressful setting, every blow to his fragile sense of self could have devastating effects on his future development I felt. And since his future meant my future too, I had to act. Without a supportive environment, I didn't stand a chance.

I had no way of knowing with any kind of certainty if such a school was going to work for Jacob. His teacher would be a man named Mr. Miller. I spoke openly with Mr. Miller regarding Jacob's early beginning; I still felt strongly that it was the best way to promote understanding and support for Jacob. Mr. Miller had been teaching children for over twenty-five years, several of which were spent working for the public school system with the "underprivileged" in the Bronx, New York. He felt Jacob's exposure to such a curriculum would be a healing experience. He spoke with passion when he talked about teaching children to learn with their hearts. It was comforting to meet someone with confidence and maturity, but it was with blind faith that I entrusted my child to Mr. Miller's care.

The immediate changes in Jacob's behaviors were proof that I made the right decision. After one week in his new school, he looked at me with stars in his eyes one night as I tucked him into bed and said, "This new school is just perfect for me Mom."

So Jacob was situated and things were quiet again. Adoption day came. After a child is placed in an adoptive home there is a waiting period required, about a year, before the adoption is finalized. This gives the adoptive parents some time to know if they really want to make it legal. Our year was up and we had an adoption ceremony in the judge's chambers. It was nice, I guess. Jacob chose to change his middle name. We celebrated at the ice-cream parlor with the adoption worker joining us.

The adoption worker was the last person I dealt with through Child Welfare. We actually became friends. It was too bad I didn't meet her first. She was a good listener I discovered by way of the "adoption presents" she brought for the boys. They were books; the boys loved books by now. They were special books, obviously purchased with them in mind. For Jacob it was: *Alexander And The No Good Very Bad Day.* For Jared: *The Little Engine That Could.* The worker had to discharge us and wrap-up our case but for the longest time she called me every once in a while to see how things were going. It helped to talk to her from time to time.

Joe asked me to marry him that year and I said yes. He wasn't at all like Sam; his feet were planted square on the ground. And he had the sunniest disposition, always focusing on the positive. No matter how discouraged I got, he could find something hopeful to say. He knew how to listen, too. Even when at work, standing in a cold phone booth, he listened. It would take a couple of days for a crew to unload the lumber or petroleum his barges carried, so he could call me while the tug was docked. I would talk and talk and talk and he would listen. He encouraged me to talk. I was constantly racking my brains trying to figure out positive ways in which to get Jared to respond; something that worked. In the course of my conversations with Joe I would think of new things to try. By the end of the conversation, I would feel much more optimistic and hopeful. Joe kept me going.

Joe's family was wonderfully accepting of the boys and me. Even when Joe was at work, we were invited for Christmas and birthday parties. Between Joe's eight brothers and sisters, their spouses or significant others, and several grandchildren, there was usually a full house. A house full of busy and sometimes loud people. The boys had a hard time with the noise level and so many people at first. Jared would cry when presents were given and food was served, sure he would be left out. One day he crawled under a coffee table and stayed there for quite a while. I thought somebody would insist he come out and then I would have to stage a defense on his behalf, but nobody said a word. It didn't bother Joe's family. They were comfortable with themselves so therefore they were comfortable with others.

Joe's family was united, too, and that was the difference between his and mine. They supported one another, quietly and respectfully; unity being the secret of their strength. They didn't always agree on various issues, but they knew when to let things go for the good of all, and they especially knew when to mind their own business. They were always doing something together. The uncles took their nieces and nephews to football and soccer games. Grandma and Grandad never missed a school play or a Boy Scout Blue and Gold Banquet.

I especially liked one of Joe's sisters. She was a therapist, also, so we had something in common. She and her husband had a "special needs" child too — their own. A boy, one year older than Jacob. I didn't know what his 'special need' was, and they didn't either. He was a little bit like Jacob and a little bit like Jared. He was driving his parents crazy with his hyperactivity, temper tantrums, and unreasonable demands. He wasn't fetal alcohol effected — his mother's body was a temple during the entire pregnancy — and he wasn't diagnosed emotionally disturbed either like Jacob and Jared had been.

It would be some time into the future before I would find out Joe had talked to his sister and asked her to call me from time to time while he was at work. "I know she has a hard time when I'm gone, but she would never tell anybody that," he told her.

So things weren't all bad. I was making women friends again. It helped to connect with people. I was understanding Jacob and Jared better and trying to come to terms with things in my own way. I even managed birthday parties for them that year and invited children from their schools.

Chapter 3
Expectations

A fter attending his little school for about four months, Jared's school work started coming home plastered with criticisms. His teacher kept saying "It's hard to know what Jared knows." He wouldn't attempt to draw anymore pictures. I explained to his teacher that he was exposed to alcohol while in utero, but she seemed to think that didn't matter. "I expect him to follow my instructions. I can't give him special privileges; it wouldn't be fair to the other children."

Based on the school work that followed, it didn't look like things were going to get any better. Jared slipped back in to "a mood" and whenever I picked him up early from the center he was playing by himself. The psychosocial stage of development for the school age child is that of industry — failure will result in feelings of inferiority, possibly for life. At home Jared was acting out. One night he strummed his child size guitar my dad bought for him and sang beautifully a child's song that he had learned at school. He seemed to take such pride and pleasure in being able to do this. A few days later he jumped on the guitar and broke it beyond repair. I was so mad at him. I was getting sick with worry, too.

Then Jacob started having problems in school. I stayed calm when he came home day after day telling me he had been to time-out several times. He didn't talk about the time-outs as if he was ashamed of himself, in big trouble with Mr. Miller, or even with a tone of disregard for Mr. Miller, so I didn't feel there was a reason to panic. I was still calm when I sat down to the first parent-teacher conference with Mr. Miller. It wasn't until he said "the damage might have been too severe" that my heart sank and panic swelled up in my throat.

It wasn't the perseveration, low frustration tolerance, or fidgeting that brought on the time-outs. It was Jacob's need to question Mr. Miller's authority. Mr. Miller was from the old school: "It is necessary that children respect authority." Evidently he and Jacob had been going around and around. When Jacob was asked not to do something, he did it anyway. "When I ask him to go to time-out, he clinches his fists, and with fire in his eyes says 'NO!'" Mr. Miller said. "You'd think I was asking him to give up his right arm," he went on. I liked the fact that Mr. Miller had a sense of humor, but this was not a good sign. If he was insisting on control for control's sake, that meant trouble ahead. He wouldn't win, and certainly, Jacob wouldn't either.

My thoughts started trailing off while Mr. Miller talked on. Oh how I had wanted him to see Jacob for who he was inside; to know the goodness so alive but in need of cultivation. Caught in my own feelings of isolation, I could not find the voice to speak in my child's defense. I was problem solving already as to where we would go next. *Could I find another school with self-contained classrooms? How far would this "just right" school be from home, once I found it? Would the hours coincide with my work schedule? With Jared's schedule? Was I up to the challenge of another adjustment, more information sharing, another attempt at educating the educator?* Consumed with my own need for order, I suddenly felt very tired. Then I heard words of hope.

"Jacob is a child who not only needs nurturing but he needs strong guidance too. All children respond to firm but gentle guidance. It may take a while but Jacob will eventually come around to my way of thinking," Mr. Miller said with confidence. "And I assure you I have no intention of breaking his spirit. The artistic work, music, literature and recitation we do here will strengthen his inner being, which is were the problem lies." My heart danced with joy and I silently gave thanks for Mr. Miller. He was taking an interest in my child's spirit; regarding him with respect and dignity. With the insight and sensitivity of a mental health professional, he wanted to strengthen Jacob's heart. He believed Jacob was good. In fact, he believed most children were good. "In all my twenty-five years of teaching, I've met only one child whom I thought was 'a bad seed,'" he said.

So Jacob was fine but I still had to solicit support for Jared. His teacher was frustrated with him by this time. I tried to help, but she wouldn't consider using the little tricks I was using at home to cut down on some of the opposition. I knew the opposition too. Like chronic back pain, it lived with me day in and day out. At the close of a day I'd put it to rest, then meet with it again faithfully every morning when waking Jared and getting him dressed. The teacher kept asking me if he was getting enough sleep. Our nightly routine was still the same. I made sure he got at least twelve hours of sleep every night. Faithfully I adhered to the schedule. I was even limiting his candy and withholding chocolate because it seemed to increase his lethargy and bring on a mood swing. He seemed to crave candy and would cry when I wouldn't let him have some. People thought this terrible, denying a child candy. I made the sacrifices that 'good moms' do and never went out in the evenings unless it was essential. I never answered the phone during the bedtime hour either. Day after day, things were always the same.

I was having a very difficult time thinking positively by now. I had to work at it constantly. I couldn't please Jared no matter how hard I tried. He didn't scream anymore, but he still whined and cried all the time. Every little "owie," every little bump and scratch, or just taking him by the arm, brought on tears. I never stopped hearing the cries, but I stopped responding after a while. He just wanted attention. I told him to buck up and stop acting like a baby.

Jared liked to blame me in particular for his problems. In fact, the older he became, the better he got at using his words to hurt. He was very smart when it came to making me feel terrible inside. "You're mean to me," he would say when I asked him to do things. "You never let me have anything!," was his typical comeback when I said no to candy before breakfast or cookies before dinner. "You just don't like me," he said when I removed a tire chain he had wrapped around his neck. The night he said, "You're just trying to kill me!" when I wanted to give him cough syrup for a cold, I sat down and cried. He was so negative and distrustful. It was amazing to me that a six year old child could be so negative. He reminded me of an old man claiming bitterly that life had cheated him.

Some eight weeks prior to this time, I made an appointment with a clinical psychologist at a Learning Clinic because I had heard that she was specialized in diagnosing children with alcohol effects. I wanted to make sure Jared was just Fetal Alcohol Effected and not Fetal Alcohol Syndrome. A little voice kept telling me there was something else wrong and I desperately needed it named and labeled.

The examination was very thorough with individual testing done by a pediatrician, an occupational therapist, a speech pathologist, a liaison educator, and the psychologist. It took from 9:00 in the morning until 4:00 in the afternoon. I was there all day speaking with each professional before they did their individual tests on Jared. The Medicaid insurance paid for the evaluation, fortunately, but my employer wouldn't let me make up for the day's lost wages.

The pediatrician thought Jared's head was too large in proportion to his body and that I should have it followed-up by our own pediatrician. He also suggested I have Jared's eyes tested; his vision wasn't within normal limits. The occupational therapist found Jared difficult to test because of his opposition and because *he was easily distracted and wandered throughout the room*. There were no specific recommendations for fine or gross motor development; each were thought to be fine. She thought he would benefit from a behavior management program, initiated both at school and at home. The speech pathologist found Jared's speech and language to be within normal limits, although he wondered what it was that Jared *couldn't do as opposed to what he wouldn't do*. He was especially impressed with Jared's ability to stay on task. The education liaison found Jared *difficult to test* and felt that his behaviors *were in many cases out of the ordinary — autistic like*. Academically Jared tested only six months behind.

With the psychologist Jared was almost completely non-compliant. In order to complete the testing, she had to *use several different strategies to coax him into participation*. He required *much more structure and variation than most children his age to complete test administration*. He was *easily frustrated and shut down when the items became difficult*. However, his intellectual functioning and cognitive abilities were *well within the average range*.

He was of normal intelligence. The only area in which the psychologist could find a problem was in his *adaptive skills*. He was functioning at 3 years, 8 months rather than 6 years, 1 month; his chronological age. "Adaptive skill acquisition is often indicative of emotional or behavioral issues," the psychologist said. I asked her if she knew why it was Jared couldn't dress himself. This skill was not tested. "You need to lower your expectations," she said. "Because of Jared's history he will probably always require help with dressing and hygiene."

I wanted to say: *No! You don't understand. I'll lower my expectations, but to what? What's realistic? He's all ready been declared too high functioning for special services through the public school system. He can't seem to use his body like other children do, though he's not physically handicapped. He's already flunking out of kindergarten, more-or-less. He argues like a defiant teenager yet cries like a baby. And he's making me crazy. I don't mind dressing him for now. It's the arguing and resistance that's so difficult. He won't accept my help. It's about our relationship! I want to look forward to seeing him in the mornings. I want the dread and ugliness between us to go away.* I wanted to say these things but of course I couldn't.

When the psychologist and all the others concluded Jared was neither Fetal Alcohol Syndrome or Fetal Alcohol Effected, I was completely stunned! He was found to have a mild Pervasive Development Disorder — which means severe impairment throughout all development — due to the early neglect. They thought he *would continue to stabilize and that he was showing every indication of responding to a nurturing environment.* So Jared supposedly wasn't disabled at all. He was of normal intelligence. He just had emotional problems.

I was so discouraged. His emotional problems weren't getting better, they were getting worse. Again I was reminded of his history. It was the introduction to every evaluation and with it came all the doubts. He missed out on so much those very early years. Those years were lost to us forever. Early Intervention and Head Start might have combated the delays and thus instilled in him a sense of competency as they had Jacob, but it was too late. His self concept was so poor and his sense of self-worth seemingly non-existent. Obviously, what difference did any label make when his true handicapping condition was that of a spirit with no desire?

Bewildered, confused, and even a little scared — I couldn't trust my own perceptions anymore — we headed home. For the first time I experienced a sense of hopelessness in regard to Jared's future. Hopelessness, the opposite of optimism and the destroyer of dreams. When we got home I laid down on the couch and called on sleep. I'll just close my eyes and go to Arizona were the sun is hot and the vegetation dry, I thought to myself. But I didn't go to Arizona that day or any other day in the chain of days that followed. I went to a place where there was no light to lead the way.

Maybe it was just plain stubbornness that drew me out of my depression. I refused to accept that I couldn't have expectations for Jared. If I didn't have expectations for him, who would? Expectations can send the message to a child that he is capable and some people succeed in spite of themselves just because someone else dared to have expectations. No, I wasn't going to lower my expectations and I wasn't going to give up on Jared's spirit either. I had to keep believing there was a tender heart inside. For all I knew, the opposition was his spirit, fighting to protect that tender heart so it wouldn't get hurt again.

A twenty-two page report from the center was sent to me via the mail. *Jared will need intensive intervention in order to maxi-*

mally achieve his potential as an adult, the psychologist wrote. I couldn't understand this comment. She had said Jared was of normal intelligence. This time I received a list of things to do to help him. It was recommended that: *Educators be aware Jared will have difficulty learning in a regular classroom without modified teaching strategies, he would need multi-sensory tactile and visual cues, music would be a good way to present information; that I and the educators begin work on functional skills such as time concepts, telephone use, using a calendar, money, etc.; that I structure positive social interactions with normally developing peers; that the educators and I structure social interactions complete with modeling appropriate behavior; that I develop some behavior modification strategies and consistency in dealing with Jared's oppositional behavior at home; that I continue with my support groups; and that I obtain play therapy for Jared through a mental health professional.* I had always wanted somebody to instruct me in what to do for Jared, but this was too much — completely overwhelming. A referral was to be made to the public school system by the liaison educator so that a consultant could go into Jared's current and future learning environments to advise the educators how to do their parts.

I showed Jared's teacher the report. She too was overwhelmed. "We're not doing time concepts yet," she said. Jared was having considerable difficulties at school. And he and Jacob were having problems getting along. When in "a mood" Jared still took advantage of Jacob and undermined his sense of fairness. Eventually Jared stopped taking and grabbing from Jacob and became more skilled at negotiating. His debates were one sided of course and truth hid in the folds of tears, smiles and reasons without logic, which served well to confuse Jacob. "He makes me feel invisible," Jacob said one day. I knew what was going on and would intercept for him.

People often said, "Let them work it out themselves, brothers are suppose to fight." But I felt that if I allowed Jared to fulfill his needs without regard for Jacob, I would be encouraging him to stay hidden amongst his aggressions and self-imposed hate. Mean spirited people get away with hurting others all the time. Only those strong enough to see through the deceit can protect themselves. No, I had to be on constant watch to protect Jacob. Besides being blinded by his love for his brother, he lacked the ego strength to protect himself. The feedback I received from other people was correct though. Brothers are suppose to fight. It's normal. But it was getting harder and harder to get to normal from where we were all by ourselves. I called the mental health professionals that the psychologist had suggested but one wouldn't take the Medicaid insurance, and the other wouldn't have an opening for three months.

Jacob was getting stronger every day, despite everything. The emotional healing I saw take place in him after attending his new school for three months was profound. It wasn't my imagination with me seeing just what I wanted to see. Never did his eyes shine so bright or his cheeks look so rosy. He even carried himself differently. He was calmer and less "anxious." His nightmares subsided somewhat and he began sleeping later in the mornings on weekends. He was eating all of the lunch I sent to school with him. He drew everyday and played his piano with passion.

It's what Jared needs I decided; that special school with its healing powers. The younger children were especially catered to at the school. I envisioned it to be the place were Jared's tough exterior could be dismantled and his tender heart allowed to show itself openly. I thought it a place where he could go back to his toddlerhood if he needed to. He was seemingly like a toddler in so many ways: When he took something in his hands, it became his. If he wanted something he took it. And he still cried, whined, sucked his thumb and drooled. The children at the other school were ostracizing him by now and the teacher was clearly at a loss as to how to teach him. So I placed him in a Kindergarten class at Jacob's school.

The class size was fourteen with two teachers. The room a soft pink color with a play loft and a rocking chair. A child's waist height sand box and a water play trough stood in the corner. It was a doing place where the children helped with baking, gardening, building, and learned finger knitting. There were no academics to speak of, only songs, stories and poems. The emotions were key to learning, always being called upon through the senses: the sensation of dirt against the skin, the weight of the hammer being lifted against gravity and then falling, the tingle of wool wrapped around little fingers, the smell of the food or of the teacher's hair etching a memory; surely to be recalled again someday in another place, another time. It was a peaceful and quiet place. The children laid down for naps after lunch listening to the teachers read fairy tales or sing lullabies. Aftercare was provided in the same room so they didn't have to move around the building.

The classroom head teacher was most receptive to Jared joining her class. As always I provided a bit of his history. When she heard it I thought she was going to cry. "I'll rock him if he cries," she said. "And if he gets frustrated or angry, I'll have him bang nails." Her empathy for and interest in the spirit of my little boy lost warmed my heart. It left me feeling empty too, though, with pangs of jealousy; Jared would be with someone much more patient and gentle than I.

Just when I was feeling like there was no help, and that

nobody cared, I received a call from the County Mental Health Department. The Robert Wood Johnson Foundation cared. It's a foundation that makes grants to improve health and healthcare for all Americans and it was funding a pilot project called The Partners Project for children labeled severally emotionally disturbed. Evidently, of the 7.5 million children in need of mental health care nationwide, 40% are considered severely emotionally disturbed and yet they are the most underfunded and under served group of all.

Jacob's name had been submitted to participate in the Partners Project by Barbara, of all people, some two years prior. He was one of 150 children chosen. As soon as I heard Barbara's name, I shut-down. I didn't want a repeat of what had happened with Jared; I wanted to be involved in my child's care. Plus I hated the idea of Jacob being referred to as *severely emotionally disturbed*. However, when the woman on the other end of the phone explained what kind of services the project was offering, I changed my mind.

Evidently it was discovered some time ago that the traditional methods of care weren't working for children considered severely emotionally disturbed. In fact, most mental health services for children are thought to be "bundled" carry over practices from the adult mental health system. But like so many things, there is a lack of agreement between professionals as to what really works for children with emotional and behavioral problems. In addition to these problems, the existing systems of care are terribly fragmented. A child might be in the child welfare system, the public school system, the mental health system, and the juvenile justice system, all at the same time for various reasons related to the emotional problems, yet the systems don't communicate with each other in order to provide effective care. Duplication of the same services is very common.

Traditionally the older child with severe problems is removed from the home and placed in an institution of some sort for several weeks or months, even years. The family is typically discredited, blamed, and shut-out; never becoming full participants in their own child's care, or allowed to take some responsibility. But institutionalized care is very expensive and systems don't keep kids forever, they generally return to some type of family unit. So somebody came up with the idea of taking the money that would have been spent on institutionalized care, making the families equal partners in decision making, and with all the systems working together, devise a service plan that was individual to the child's unique needs and of value to the family in caring for the child.

Some families function better with some respite. Some children need self care training. An older child might need job training. A lot of children go to summer camps in order to build social skills, but they might need a mentor to go with them and help them therapeutically. Some children do better in a classroom with the help of an aide or a tutor. These types of services were proving to be of value not only to families and children, but to teachers, therapists, and counselors too. The name for this type of care is called "wraparound" because it is community based and individualized. When I heard the word "wraparound" I thought of Sherrie and how she had said: "You just keep Jacob wrapped up tight and he'll be okay." She was right, really. He always did better during the summer with structured activities. If left unstructured for any length of time, he would be harder to engage in daily living activities.

So the Partners Project was being used to promote communication between the various agency professionals, to cut down

on the duplication of services, to move away from expensive
institutional settings, to work effectively with families, to save
money by providing alternative methods of service that would
help children learn how to function in their own communities,
and build services in the communities at the same time. It
seemed like a win-win situation to me. The dollars allotted for
a particular family were being managed by managed care coor-
dinators. The managed care coordinator's job was to work with
the family in determining what services they needed in terms
of what was working and what wasn't. In essence, the Partners
Project was about redefining the mental health needs of children in a modern society, but it was about efficient use of the
public dollar, too.

When the managed care coordinator asked me what I
thought we needed I told her it wasn't Jacob I was worried about;
it was Jared's problems that were tearing me apart. It was ironic.
Jared should have been in the project, he was the one with the
most problems, serious problems.

"You could try family therapy," the care coordinator suggested. "Partners isn't designed to meet the needs of siblings
but clearly family dynamics effect everyone's mental health,"
she said with genuine concern in her voice. Then she provided
me with a list of government funded community mental health
agencies that offered family therapy. I chose one of them based
on a friend's recommendation. After three sessions of information gathering by the therapist, better known as an "intake assessment," the boys were taken into a room for play therapy.
"They need help with their grief issues," the therapist said. I
don't know what it was I expected from "family therapy," but
as I sat in the waiting room alone, I found myself thinking: *What
about me? I'm the one living with these children everyday and I need*

to find ways to cope. I need someone to help me sort out my feelings about Jared. I need someone to tell me how to change behaviors. It was up to me to teach the child right from wrong.

"You don't have to continue with the same intervention if you don't think it's helpful," the managed care coordinator responded, after I shared with her what was happening. "The purpose of the Partners Project is to save dollars as well as provide care. If we continue with a service that is of little or no value to you, then we are wasting money. Is there another type of treatment that you think might help? You don't have to depend on the list of government funded agencies that I gave you, either. Partners will pay for services through a private agency too." As soon as she said that, the agency that came to my mind was the clinic suggested by the child development specialist when Jacob was in Kindergarten.

So I contacted the private clinic and scheduled an appointment. Before the first session I was sent a questionnaire in which to fill out and send back. It asked about Jacob's history, his current behaviors and my concerns. Pictures of our family were also requested. It was time consuming on my part to fill out the form and gather the pictures, but very much worth the effort. We were assigned a fellow experienced with adoptive families as he had adopted himself, and there was no time lost doing an intake assessment — the first meeting was a working meeting.

The therapist talked with me first. I shared with him my concerns about the boys' relationship. I told him I was frustrated and confused trying to parent Jared. I admitted to spanking. I told him I didn't want to yell. I told him about our daily routine and the various things I did to avoid conflict. I asked him what he knew about attachment disorders. He was very easy to talk to. I especially liked his straight-forward style. "I don't approve of spanking," he said, but I didn't feel that he was judging me. Actually, he made me feel good about myself. He affirmed me by acknowledging my commitment as well as the sacrifices and the consistency well established in our home. After talking with the boys, he sent us home with a behavior modification program. The program was designed to modify my behaviors too. If I lost my temper, I lost a poker chip. If I lost too many chips, I was going to have to put money in someone's piggy bank.

Hope loomed in the air on the drive home. The boys and I chatted and laughed. I think they liked the fact that I was on a program too. It wasn't just about Jared and his problems or Jacob and his problems — it was about all of us — Mom was going to actively work on her problems too.

For a while I thought behavior modification was the best act in town. You would think I had never heard of it before. My enthusiasm toward it was primarily due to the fact that I needed desperately to feel that I was doing something; that the behaviors really were predictable and could be changed. The boys and I carried poker chips in our pockets. Pennies, stickers and suckers served as rewards. It was a time of concentrated effort with me a part of the equation now. I wanted to be a good parent. But behavior modification still wasn't effective with Jared. When he lost a chip he seldom knew why and he always thought I was just being mean to him.

The therapist said there was no such thing as an attachment disorder which I found confusing. If there was no such thing, where did the label come from? I wondered. The therapist seemed to know a lot about the subject matter. Jared was having difficulty with attachment issues, it was true, he said. But his primary problem was that of self-worth; he didn't think himself lovable. He recommended Joe and I catch him "off-guard" and tell him we loved him when he least expected it. Even when he did something bad I was to say, I love you. "Do you know how hard that will be for me?" I asked. "Yes, I do," he said, "but you have got to do it. If Jared doesn't feel some attachment to you by the time he is 10, he probably never will." Those words were enough to scare me into swallowing my foolish pride. I knew the therapist was right. The urgency in his voice echoed my own internal panic. It was clearly a now or never situation.

So I forced myself to say to Jared "I love you" when I was irritated with him although I'm sure my body language said "I can't stand you." Joe did much better at it than I. He was a patient man. This intervention strategy did help. Jared's verbal opposition decreased somewhat. But like always, he was so consistently inconsistent that sometimes the strategy seemed to have merit, other times it felt much like throwing pennies into a fountain. But it got placed into my now assorted bag of tricks and pulled out at random like everything else. Joe was good at reminding me to keep using it, which helped a lot.

I was feeling a little more in control of the situation by now, but I still couldn't believe Jared and Jacob weren't fetal alcohol effected. There had to be more to the picture than just the past. I asked the therapist what he knew about fetal alcohol but he, too, changed the subject. However, he thought Jacob was attention deficit and hyperactive and suggested I have him evaluated by the doctor on staff there at the clinic. Jared wasn't officially his client so he couldn't voice an opinion about him.

I read the book the therapist suggested on attention deficit and Jacob's behaviors definitely fit the diagnostic guidelines: he was physically over active, fidgety and squirmy, easily distracted, he had difficulty completing tasks, he often blurted out the answers to questions before they were completed, and jumping off of the dresser was an extreme example of his inclination to engage in physically dangerous activities without consideration of a possible consequence. He wanted what he wanted, too. But I didn't want to hear he was attention deficit. That meant he was impulsive and prisons are full of people with impulse control problems.

The therapist said that if Jacob was diagnosed attention deficit/hyperactive, a medication would be prescribed that would help him to settle down. I associated the word hyperactive with emotionally disturbed of course, and I didn't want that word to follow him either. So I decided against the medication. Also, I was accustomed to constantly having to redirect Jacob and he wasn't as over active as he used to be.

Joe didn't want to use medication, either. He and I weren't married yet, but he was so involved in Jacob's care and well being, that he made sure his opinions were heard. He didn't feel the way I did about the label of attention deficit, but he wouldn't even consider the idea of medication. He had his personal reasons. As a child he was administered a stimulant for his "reading problems." Evidently the medication kept him awake all night and then he was tired during the day when his brain needed to be alert for learning. After four years he refused to continue taking it. He was 11 by then and his parents didn't push it. That was over 30 years ago, but Joe wasn't about to change his mind.

We saw the therapist for about four months. In addition to working with us as a family, he worked individually with Jacob and with Jacob and Jared both on healthy competition and sibling rivalry issues. He even tried to help me with Jared's teacher.

Things were falling apart for him at his new school.

The school turned out to be a disastrous placement for Jared. Within two months I was being paged at least once a week to come and get him early. Dismissal was the consequence for kicking another child, being uncooperative or not attending with "listening ears." Within another month early dismissal increased to twice a week. On the days when field trips were planned, I was asked to keep Jared home. In time, even on 'good' days, people avoided eye contact with me when I went to pick him up. The psychologist at the Learning Clinic had said this particular type of a school setting wouldn't be structured enough for Jared but I didn't listen to her.

I had been talking with the head teacher over the phone since Jared joined her class. She had encouraged me to call her at home in the evenings. I wanted to build a working relationship with her, but something felt strained and I didn't know what it was. After a while, she started asking me things that made me feel like Jared's negative behaviors were the result of our life style or something. "Do you have an established bedtime routine?" she asked. "Are you at home with him in the evenings?" Then her questions started making me feel like the problem was with me. "Are you giving him enough attention?" "What have you been doing to help him grieve?" It was hard not to feel defensive. Then I started getting feedback that young children shouldn't have to attend aftercare and that their mother's shouldn't work outside of the home and had I considered home schooling. At that point in time, I couldn't have afforded to quit working even if I had wanted to. The adoption subsidies weren't nearly enough to finance my staying home and juggle the "special needs" of the boys at the same time.

I felt the teacher was trying to make things work. I wanted

desperately to make the school work for Jared, too, so I tried even harder to change his behaviors. The pressure was incredible. I put him to bed earlier; I scolded him for kicking others; I worked with him on active listening as best I could and I followed through on my threats to withhold treats if he wasn't cooperative with the teachers; I processed and processed with him; sometimes I spanked. I had a notebook going back and forth so I could monitor and talk with Jared about specific behaviors as soon as we got home. I wrote in it faithfully as did the assistant teachers. I asked if I could help out in the classroom but the head teacher said no. I asked if she would speak with our therapist. She said she would but that he would have to call her at one particular time during the day only.

In time the opening question was, "Do you know what Jared did today?," when I called the teacher. Then one day, to my surprise, she said, "All the children planted grass seed two weeks ago for our Easter baskets. The only one whose didn't grow was Jared's." She was implying something but I didn't know what. When she said "I believe in karma and the idea that we chose the mothers we are born to," I knew then, and that was enough. Jared didn't have a choice about any of the things that happened to him — babies and children never do. So I packed up his things, put his little hand in mine, and we walked out of the classroom together.

In the days that followed I kept thinking about what the woman said about karma and choices; I was constantly thinking about what other people said. I was so discouraged that I thought maybe I was kidding myself. Maybe Jared was just a "bad seed" and far too damaged to ever heal. There was definitely something about his person that seemed to attract the negative. Other children didn't like him. A fight always broke out when he joined a group. Animals didn't seem to like him either.

When he asked for a "bird in a cage" that he would name "Petey," I thought that a good idea, getting him a critter to look after and care for; something living that he might form an attachment to. So I bought him a cockatiel and he named him Petey. But Petey didn't like Jared. Anybody but Jared could pick Petey up. Every time Jared put his hand into Petey's cage, Petey bit him.

Then Jared wanted a rabbit. The rabbit wasn't gentle to begin with, but he especially liked hacking away at Jared. In time, he wouldn't let Jared touch him at all. I finally gave up on feathered and furry pets and bought Jared an ant farm; the plastic encasement would keep the insects contained I thought. I don't know how they did it, but those ants got out and attacked Jared. And size had nothing to do with might; Jared was traumatized by the experience.

Then one day I received a telephone call from an education consultant connected with the public school system. Based on the referral made by the education liaison at the Learning Clinic, Jared had to be evaluated again. I was all ready so confused at this point that I didn't want him evaluated any more. So I told her I was busy that week. She called again the next week and then again the week after that. She finally caught me one day. "Please let us help you," she said. Her voice was so kind that I gave in.

The evaluation took place in our home which I found most helpful. However, when Jared was found to be "high-functioning autistic" (in some circles this is called Asperger's Syndrome) because of his isolative play, one-sided interactions with people, and his preoccupation for tying things up, I didn't find that helpful at all: Jared suddenly had four heads instead of two. I knew enough about autism to think there was a mistake and I questioned the evaluator. "He has to have a label in order to receive special services at school," she said. It was true — no label, no luck. I don't know whatever happened to the mild pervasive development disorder diagnosis.

Labels, labels, labels. I didn't want any more labels. I just wanted our Jared back.

Chapter 4
Is This Child Really Lovable?

I didn't take Jared back to the school. I knew it was just a matter of time before I would be asked to take him out any way. Joe suggested I take a leave of absence from work in order to stay home with him. So I gave up my job and told my employer I would be back in September. There wasn't anything else to do really; it was late spring by now. Joe and I were getting married in August, but until then he would help me with our living expenses. There was so much to do before August that I thought it probably best that I didn't work. We had to sell my house, fix-up Joe's house, and plan a wedding. Joe wanted to stay in close proximity to his family, so it was decided we would keep his house and sell mine. After twenty years of housemates and bachelor brothers, the old place needed a face lift and a bit of a woman's touch.

My not working would give me more time to work with Jared. I knew I had to change his behaviors and his attitude if he was to be successful in any school setting. So I wrote up a schedule of learning type activities that we would work on in the mornings. I was determined to keep him structured-up. I was going to home school him. I bought learning work books, children's sing-a-long tapes, a chalk board, and some simple wooden puzzles. I was optimistic. I was going to insist he learn to dress himself too.

Mornings were still just as ugly between he and I as they had ever been and there was no sign of things letting up. I kept thinking that maybe I just wasn't giving him enough time to dress himself. So after I got Jacob off to school, I laid his clothes out on the bed, told him to get dressed, and then left the room. Two hours later I found him huddled in a corner in his underwear and the clothes still laid out on the bed. This went on day after day. He could take off his pajamas independently which lead me to believe we were making gains, but he refused to dress himself. "Leave me alone. I don't have to get dressed. You're being mean to me," were his typical comebacks to my pleas. I tried behavior modification. I tried yelling. I tried spanking. Then I gave up.

Sometimes when I looked at Jared I wondered, *Who is this child in my home?* After almost two years, I still didn't know him. He wasn't going to dress himself and his "odd" behaviors just kept getting worse. He hated having his hair cut now and would cry in the car both going and coming from the barber's office. He wouldn't brush his teeth because the toothpaste "burns me" he said. He was still fussy about what clothes he would wear and he was adamantly opposed to wearing anything new. He formed an attachment to a particular pair of jeans and would let me have it if they weren't available. Every other night I washed those jeans while he slept in order to keep the peace. And while he slept I thought about what a failure I was as a parent.

Jacob was doing well, though, and this made me feel better. He was developing into a "real boy." Mr. Miller's opinion of him was polished. Jacob's end-of-the-year first grade report read: "Jacob is a highly sensitive child who truly cares about his fellow humans. He is also himself deeply affected by kindness or unkindness. He has a unique gentleness and kindness in his being which I'm happy to see emerging so beautifully."

Joe was adamant that I never show favoritism toward Jacob. Not that I could — Jared with his relentless demands made sure of that. I really didn't want to show favoritism, though, because I felt that if I did it would encourage Jared in his need to compete in order to be first. His need to be first was insatiable, like a hunger that is never satisfied. He often cheated and bent the rules in order get the advantage. It wasn't healthy. So I discouraged competition of any kind when I saw it. Joe seemed to think Jacob was showing-up Jared all the time. I didn't think that was true. As his little brother's keeper, Jacob wouldn't intentionally keep Jared from succeeding, I felt. Nevertheless, I made a conscious effort to always be fair — whenever I bought something for Jacob I bought Jared the exact same thing.

Joe knew my feelings toward Jacob were different than my feelings toward Jared. I felt close to Jacob. He was mostly cooperative and he didn't lash out at me with hurtful words. It was rewarding to see him change and grow, finally surrendering his fears.

It was Jared's constant resistance that took the pleasure out of parenting him. Every little thing was resisted, even things he would have liked. I wasn't getting away from spanking him like I had wanted to when he argued. Instead of one or two swats, it was three or four now. I would put up with his resistance and defiance for as long as I could by calmly redirecting, repeating myself patiently, counting to three, giving positive feedback, taking things away, even ignoring him. I took time-outs and went on walks only to return to the scene and have the negative feelings swell up again, unresolved. I didn't like spank-

First Grade Report ~ 1992

Jacob has made such remarkable progress
this year. There are not enough superla-
tives to describe how far he has come. He
has calmed down in his outer actions as
well as his inner being. He appears to be
much more at peace with himself. He
rarely loses patience with himself or
others anymore. His tendency to be disruptive in class has almost completely
vanished. No more noises, calling out
etc. It's wonderful.

Although slow, he is conscientious about
his school work and works hard to do the
best he can. Usually he becomes quite
absorbed in whatever task is at hand -
but if he does not, he is easily distracted by anything going on around him,
and then he falls behind. This lack of
attention is not from lack of good
will, but appears to be a tendency to dream and float away.
At such times it can be
difficult to pull him
back.

Jacob is a highly
sensitive child who
truly cares about
his fellow humans.

He is also himself deeply affected by
kindness or unkindness. He has a unique
gentleness and kindness in his being
which I'm happy to see emerging so beautifully.

Jacob's tendency towards forgetfulness is
a concern which is all that prevents him
being totally reliable. No matter how
hard he tries, sometimes he just cannot
seem to remember things.

Academically Jacob has done well. He
tries hard and has been able to do everything which we do albeit slowly at times.
But his own pace is fine.

Jacob has grown beautifully into the
class and has really made himself a place
in it despite having joined us later in
the year. It's been a good year for him.

Mr. Miller

ing anymore than I ever did except by now it had taken on a life of its own. After a spanking Jared was incredibly compliant and would remain so for a couple of days. Then the opposition would start again. I'd brace myself and maintain for most of the time up to two weeks. But it seemed the longer I went, the more oppositional he became. Then I'd lose it and the cycle would start all over again.

I always felt bad after spanking Jared. He would stand there looking forlorn and all to himself, innocent, as if he really didn't know what he had done to deserve a spanking. I would tell him over and over again why he got the spanking, but it didn't seem to convince him, which would only make me feel worse. Never before in my life had I felt so torn and conflicted toward another human being. A little voice kept telling me he was deceiving me: *Jared is full of hate and distrust; damaged. He is bad.* Certainly the things he did were bad, but I didn't want to believe he was bad. So I would apologize after a spanking once I had time to think. Somebody told me apologizing was not good parenting — that it would put Jared in charge.

"That's okay," he would say "I forgive you." He had a super human capacity for forgiveness it seemed. Sometimes he would say "I'm sorry too," which would make me think: *Oh, so you did know what you were doing,* but I would push those thoughts aside. Then he would let me initiate a kiss and hug. Sometimes we even cuddled; me welcoming the moment of "closeness" like the starving welcome food. It was all so sick. We were putting a new twist on the meaning of "child abuse" — I couldn't make the much needed physical contact with Jared until I hurt him first.

I don't know how it was that I actually thought I could home school him. He still hated any kind of academics and I hated working with him. He'd scream and cry and I'd yell. I couldn't think of clever and creative ways to motivate him enough to keep him engaged. I had always admired people who had that kind of creativity and patience with a child. I couldn't keep him structured up with household activities, either, without first fighting the resistance. It was exhausting. I gave up eventually and let him wander, stay under the table or in his little house, or go around and tie things up, while I worked to get the house ready for sale.

I always felt guilty when I left Jared to himself to wander. Not that he would wander far. He knew how to be just close enough to get my attention and irritate me too. If I was in the kitchen, he was hungry even if he had just had lunch. If I was in the basement doing laundry, he was in my dad's room playing with things or carting tape players off. If I was working in the yard, he wanted to ride his bike. I would let him with the stipulation that he ride on the sidewalk only. "Okay Mom, I will," he'd say with a big smile. As soon as I would turn my back, he would be in the street. When he was asked not to do something, he would eventually do it anyway. "Okay Mom," he'd say, "I wouldn't play with the garage keys anymore," or "Okay Mom, I won't play with the garden hose nozzle." A few days later the items would come up missing. I'd go searching and find them under his bed along with other "missing" items from around the house. When he was asked three times not to throw the ball at the house, he kept doing it anyway and broke the window. The day he tried to fill the oil tank with water from the hose, I wanted to kill him.

When I tried helping Joe with his house, Jared would be right in my face. Anything I was working on he was in the was the yelling Jared hated, I knew that. I yelled at him a lot, it was either that or spank. In time, even on 'good days' when I didn't yell or spank, I barked out orders and reprimands in a scornful and shaming tone. I never thought I could be that kind of a parent. I was a good parent when it was just Jacob and I. I resented Jared now. Things would have been a lot different without him.

The house was finished in spite of it all and Joe went back to work. He would return seven weeks later, just in time for the wedding. Jacob went on to his summer programs while I worked on selling my house and getting things packed for the move. Jared stayed home with me. I didn't want him to. I wanted him to go away.

I did send him away one weekend. He and Jacob stayed with a friend for a day and night. Jacob did fine. Jared on the other hand became extremely anxious and insisted on walking my friend's dog around the block — about 10 times, as I recall. When he wasn't walking the dog, he was pacing the floor or hiding under the kitchen table. At night he fussed and cried. When he came home, he was more difficult than usual. I felt terrible for leaving him and had to wonder if he interpreted the visit as the prelude to "another home."

I was trapped: I couldn't send him away but I couldn't stand him either. I hated my life. Home wasn't safe anymore nor the haven it used to be. It was a dark place of discord and discomfort. Pretty soon I was slapping Jared's hands to keep him from touching everything. When he cried I closed my ears and my heart. "SHUT UP!" I screamed at him. Then one day, to get him out of my personal space, I pushed him — not hard enough to hurt him but just enough to reject him. When I reflected upon my actions, I was truly ashamed.

Something awful was happening inside of me; I was not a

mean person by nature. All of my adult life I had tried to live by the Golden Rule: Do unto others as you would have them do unto you. Now the very core of who I had believed myself to be was being shattered and destroyed. I loved Jared, yet I was losing my compassion for him. This was, in and of itself, frightening. I had always believed it to be compassion that makes human beings so great; distinguishing the civilized from the uncivilized, perhaps. I was ashamed of what I had become. And when I looked at Jared, I was ashamed of him too.

In my heart I was harboring feelings of distrust, shame, and disgust toward him. I couldn't trust him around food. If I sat out a basket of berries or a bowl of chips and didn't watch him, he'd eat the whole basket or package all by himself. It didn't matter that I put meals on the table consistently and always made sure there was more than enough food, his greed was forever present. I was distrustful of the way he seemed to make it a point to leave peanut butter and jelly on the bathroom door frame on his way to the sink to wash up. I was distrustful that he wasn't deliberately urinating on the floor in his room and on the walls in the bathroom. I was ashamed of him when, wide awake, he had a bowel movement in his sleeping bag during a camp-out. I was disgusted with the way he hauled around bags of the bits and pieces of things he'd taken apart as if they meant everything to him; more so perhaps than love itself. It reminded me of a bag lady hauling around her worldly possessions in a shopping chart covered with plastic. One day when I caught Jared wandering down the street I wanted to let him keep going.

Discouraged and despairing, I felt certain I was missing something. There had to be more to the situation and I just hadn't put it together yet. But I couldn't figure out what it was.

Just before Jared's file was to be closed following the adoption, the worker asked me if I would like to have copies of anything from it. In addition to the nursing notes documenting his life with Julie, I asked for copies of every evaluation completed on him. Eventually I received a stack of paper ten inches tall. I didn't go through it at the time however. I put everything in a file. So I retrieved it at this time and in a state of sheer panic, I went through all of it.

Counting the two that I initiated, there were 19 evaluations. Each focused primarily on the early abuse and neglect during Jared's first two years of life. Each said the same thing but with a different slant. Some were done to satisfy the legal system in order to terminate Julie's parental rights; others were done to determine what kind of help Jared needed. Fetal Alcohol Syndrome was noted very early on, but never carried over. *Jared might be mildly retarded,* the day treatment center's evaluation read, to my surprise, but fetal alcohol was not listed as part of the equation. Each evaluation rang of little hope but faithfully acknowledged "a referral will be made to."

I was devastated. The evaluations confirmed my feelings of hopelessness and despair. There was something terribly wrong with Jared and love wasn't enough to fix it. Fear of an evil lurking in the shadows, waiting to leap out just to remind me nothing was sacred, began to swell up inside of me. My dad said I was putting too much faith in psychologists and not enough in God — "You need to pray!" I was praying, but my Creator wasn't answering me.

A copy of the personality profile evaluation that was completed on me was in there too. My responses to the profile indicated no "significant personality disorder" — although I felt I had one now. Then I saw my present life in bold letters: "Ms.

Shilts feels that she can 'save these boys' from the terrible early neglect and abuse they suffered."

I had actually believed that back then. What a joke I was. It was all a joke. I had thought young children were resilient; their little hearts capable of healing. I didn't know it at the time, but when I met Jacob and Jared I was looking for something to believe in. I became a therapist in order to help others; to be a part of the solution instead of the problem. But as I began to age, the days grew long and I was empty inside wanting for something to believe in; something that transcends time and justifies human suffering. If I wasn't rummaging through the past to see if I had missed it, I was longing for tomorrow in the hopes that I might find it there. It was magical meeting Jacob and Jared and being thrust into the world of children. Childhood is the age of innocence. I wanted so much to believe that such an age could still exist among man. I had been a sentimental fool.

Everything looked different. I should have paid attention to that bad omen I sensed seemingly so long ago now. There were no answers; theories; or preparedness. There was no help nor light to lead the way. Nobody was coming and my Creator had forsaken me. I was all alone. Alone with the unknown. I was in a weakened state, too, and I didn't have the strength anymore to fight the darkness on Jared's behalf.

It was too late anyway. He was sick — sick in his soul. The darkness was devouring him; signs of the invasion were becoming more and more obvious. He was detaching the heads, arms and legs from his action figures and playing with the trunks with seemingly little awareness that the limbs were missing. I feared that the dullness of his eyes, the flatness of skin color and the ever present grease in his hair were signs of a spirit either dead or dying. He always looked dirty and unkept, no

matter how often I cleaned him up. I feared his fixation for tying things up was now practice sessions and part of a master
plan for suicide in the event of adolescent depression. With an-
guish, I feared the true meaning of why he was picking at himself now; scratching his mosquito bites until they bled and tearing the scabs off his sores so they wouldn't heal. I feared the
way he crawled around on the floor on all fours and howled
like a lone wolf. One day when he was under his favorite chair,
I heard him say in a thin voice "I don't belong in this world,"
and I feared it was true.

I kept thinking about the fact that there is no distinction
between childhood mental disorders and adult mental disorders. Now I had to wonder if Jared's maladaptive behaviors
were the sneak preview to an adult life plagued by demons:
schizophrenia. His loss of contact with the environment and
the adjustment difficulties made me think so. He wasn't in touch.
Love meant nothing to him. Perhaps it was the uninvited voices
of schizophrenia that made him howl like a wolf; trying to convince him he didn't belong in this world. I was suddenly overcome with a fear so profound it paralyzed me.

Jared could be anything — schizophrenic, oppositional defiant, conduct disordered — the behaviors fit each. At best, he
had the makings of an anti-social personality disorder. He was
the "getter," everyone else the "giver." He was needy yet so
deceitful, antagonistic, calculating, and manipulative. He was
impulsive, self-absorbed and couldn't understand the social
consequences of his actions; a child without a conscience. An
unattached, damaged, deranged, severely emotionally disturbed
child.

Oh, what had I done? I had sole responsibility for the mental health of a fragile youngster. I wasn't angry with Barbara anymore. I felt I should have left Jared in the child welfare system — "the unadoptable child" — never to be named or viewed in the light, America's shame always to be hidden, and me, free from blame.

Chapter 5
Family Support

I was going to send Jared back to Child Welfare. I had to. I wasn't prepared to deal with a mental illness and if he had an already well established anti-social personality disorder, wrapped in childhood disguise just waiting to fully test its wings in the teen years, I feared I wouldn't meet it with compassion. I didn't want to be a child abuser and tyrant, living in the shadows of shame and unpredictability. But then something happened: "somebody" came.

Some weeks prior to the autism label, I received a three-by-five card in the mail from the Developmental Disabilities Department of Multnomah County, a department of the government that helps children who have physical rather mental handicaps, with Jared's name on it. There was evidently an open enrollment process underway and I was requested to sign the card and return it on Jared's behalf. I had no idea what was being offered, but I signed the card and put it in the mail anyway. It was at about this time that I received a telephone call from a woman from the Developmental Disabilities Department Family Support Program identifying herself as a "Case Manager." Jared's name was chosen out of hundreds to receive services. "There isn't enough money to go around for all of the children who need help," the Case Manager said, so enrollment in the program was for one year only.

The services the program offered were as the name implied, family support. It was a fairly new program, evidently. Like the Partners Project it was family centered and paying for services out in the community. "Whatever services are needed to support your family and help Jared succeed in the community will be paid for," the case manager said. She was very easy to talk to. When I shared with her our situation she suggested I have Jared evaluated for a sensory integration problem. "Sensory integration therapy has been known to help autism," she said. I didn't even bother to tell her I didn't think Jared was autistic. I didn't want to have another evaluation completed, either. But since all the things I had tried weren't working I decided to do it. It would be the last one, I decided.

When Jared was found to have moderate to severe sensory integration dysfunction, I felt terribly foolish; this information was within my own profession. I had never practiced sensory integration therapy because it takes specialized training, but I knew of its history and the theory behind it.

About thirty years ago an occupational therapist with a Ph.D. in psychology, named A. Jean Ayres, felt there was something going on inside the brain of children who couldn't put puzzles together, had trouble learning to dress themselves, had problems learning in school, and couldn't pay attention to any task for longer than a few minutes. So she set out to determine what wasn't working well in the brain and to search for a solution to the problem. She went about it differently than others, however, because she believed some of the answers would be found in a better understanding of how the brain processes sensations. This idea lead her into the field of neuroscience, which is the science of the brain and the nervous system, and eventually to the discovery of sensory integration dysfunction.

The central nervous system is a very complex system made up of the brain, the brain stem, the spinal cord, and billions of nerve cells, called neurons. We may not be conscious of it, but the neurons are constantly picking up sensations about the condition of our body and the environment around us. The eyes pick up light, the ears pick up sound, the inner ear picks up the forces of gravity, muscles and joints pick up the sensation of sitting or standing, the nose picks up smell, and the skin tells us if something is hot, cold, rough or smooth. The sensory information from these sensory systems is then sent to the brain where it is integrated and used to plan, organize, and direct our actions and thought. The process of integrating sensory information is a powerful organizing principal of the nervous system and key to a normal human developmental process. Dr. Ayres didn't get the credit for it, but this concept won the Nobel Prize in Physiology/Medicine in 1981.

It's elementary really — the genes dictate where one starts in his ability to integrate sensory information — but the integration itself begins in the womb every time mother moves. After that, it's a developmental process that takes place during childhood when the child moves, talks, and plays. Dr. Ayres believed the sensory integration that occurs when a child moves, talks, and plays is the groundwork for reading, writing, and good behavior, as well as the learning of mental and social skills. Although not exactly the same, Ayres' ideas were much like Piaget's. He had said the first seven years of a child's life are for moving and play in order to give the child a sensory-motor intelligence that serves as the foundation for intellectual, social, and personal development. Intelligence, Piaget believed, was is one's ability to adapt to, and cope with, his or her environments.

Dr. Ayres found that if the brain is doing a poor job of integrating sensory information, the result can be mass confusion for the child. In anybody, child or adult, such confusion will influence the person's ability to adapt which in turn influences his or her ability to learn. Few people can integrate sensory information perfectly, but for some children the problem is serious enough that the confusion shows itself in unwanted behaviors and emotional problems.

Jared had never been adaptable; his inability to dress himself was but one example. Children who have lead deprived lives typically have sensory integration problems. The children who have come to the United States from Russia and Romania to be adopted, after spending their early years in orphanages with little or no sensory stimulation, are being found to have severe sensory integration problems. Obviously, the deprivation Jared suffered in the early years of his life had influenced his brain's ability to organize sensory information. He wasn't allowed to move and explore the environment like kids are supposed to do. He wasn't touched enough either, which influenced his sensory development. But I would have never connected his inability to adapt to sensory integration problems — I thought it was just emotional problems. So did the Learning Clinic. Sensory integration dysfunction was not tested for there although Jared's inability to adapt certainly showed up. When I read the following description that Dr. Ayres wrote on the behavior problems associated with sensory integration dysfunction, I felt she was describing Jared:

The child with sensory integration dysfunction is apt to give his parents more trouble than other children. He is less happy - things are just not right within him. He is fussy and cannot enjoy being with his family or playing with other children. Losing a game is very threatening to his incomplete self-concept, and so he ruins the game. Sharing his toys or his food may be difficult. He is forever trying to make himself feel successful and important, and so he cannot think about the needs of other people. Because his brain responds differently, he reacts differently to circumstances. He is overly sensitive and his feelings are often hurt. He cannot cope with everyday stress, or new and unfamiliar situations. Because others do not like his behavior, they dislike him and make trouble for him.

Evidently, it was not new knowledge that some children couldn't integrate sensory information like they are supposed to, but most people believed nothing could be done about it. Dr. Ayres disagreed. She thought that if a child was put into a situation which would require an adaptive response, sensory integration would occur. So she used swings, among other types of equipment, and the child's intrinsic motivation to move and play, in a therapeutic way; always controlling the movement in order to help the child obtain an adaptive response. Once there is an adaptive response and the sensory information is integrated, the brain is more organized and ready for another level of organization, and then another, and then another.

While the results of the therapy might be immediate, although subtle, and typically noticeable only to the parents because they are the ones who live with the child, the true goal of sensory integration therapy is to increase the child's adaptability and thus enhance his development in all areas, which emerges over time. This is where Dr. Ayres lost a lot of people: sensory integration therapy is a process, not a quick fix, and it takes time to see the big changes. Those who have never observed sensory integration therapy first hand, or don't live with the child, think it doesn't work which has kept it from becoming common knowledge. Consequently, most parents and professionals don't even know what sensory integration dysfunction looks like. Even if they do know but don't understand the process, they won't recognize that something can be done about it.

The initial results of sensory integration therapy for Jared were astounding. Within eight treatment sessions he was dressing himself! At six-and-a-half, he could finally put on a shirt. He couldn't dress himself before because his brain couldn't conceive of, organize, and carry out the motor action: place the shirt over the head, arms into the sleeves, then pull it down with both hands. Dr. Ayres called this process praxis, which is a fancy word for the term "motor planning," which means the ability of the brain to conceive of, organize, and carry out a sequence of unfamiliar actions. At the clinic obstacle courses were used to facilitate this process in Jared's brain. All of his motor skills were affected by this problem. The tumbling and gym classes required motor planning. He knew what the movements should look like but he could not sense what they should feel like. His dislike of the swings and slide, movement in combination with his feet leaving the ground, were early signs of sensory integration dysfunction. Children who don't crawl before they walk, or walk before they run, typically have sensory integration problems.

Learning about Jared's sensory integration problems had a profound effect on my perceptions and my parenting. I had always felt there was a reason as to why he wouldn't dress himself — that it was a couldn't do as opposed to a wouldn't do — and I should have trusted my intuition. My trying to teach Jared to dress himself before he could motor plan was like trying to put a house up without a frame. A frame is on the inside of a house and not visible to the naked eye, but without it the house won't be as strong. And the problems Jared was having with food, sharing his toys, playing games, adapting, and perhaps even the mood swings, where not necessarily "character disturbances" at all.

The information I had on "unattached emotionally disturbed" children did not mention sensory integration dysfunction. So I threw it out. All of it. I didn't need anymore confusion. Until I helped Jared with a frame for his house, I wasn't going to speculate anymore. I wasn't going to live in fear either if I could help it.

I felt that if Jared's brain was still changeable that meant his spirit was too. But I had to shift my focus to the central nervous system and work to rehabilitate his brain. He was almost seven but I didn't let that cloud my vision. I had a lot of faith in neurorehabilitation and the human brain's ability to "heal itself" because of my work with stroke patients. With rehabilitation therapy, a person can regain the use of an arm or hand after a stroke simply because the brain is able to build new pathways around the damaged area.

I didn't fully understand the theory of sensory integration dysfunction or its treatment, but I didn't let that get in my way, either. I know what I saw with the motor planning and if Jared could have accomplished it without therapy, he would have done it a lot sooner because there was plenty of opportunity. But I had to hurry! His teachers and peers were putting more and more demands on him all the time — I had to help him get a frame for his house built.

So I took him to therapy throughout the summer. His gross motor skills blossomed. Our Family Support Case Manager told us about a baseball club for handicapped children so I enrolled him in that. It wasn't appropriate for him because the other children were either in wheelchairs or wore helmets for severe seizures, but he enjoyed it for a while. I took he and Jacob to the park often. Jared was no longer resistive to playground equipment.

I concentrated on the various ways Jared could get sensory input from the environment and let him examine and explore things all he wanted with his hands. I even bought him old typewriters and telephones at a second hand store so he could take them apart and haul around the pieces if he wanted to. I bought him a back pack for carrying his things which he would wear sometimes for hours. I stopped sending him to his room and allowed him to ride his bike whenever he wanted to.

I understood now why Jared had been adamant about learning to ride his bike. Bike riding is a pure sensory integration activity because it requires balance as well as coordination. A bike is also lower to the ground than a swing or slide and a way in which he could integrate all by himself. I knew now of course he had to go further than just up and down the block on his bike, so that meant I had to ride with him for safety and I wasn't real comfortable on a bike.

By the end of the summer Joe and Jacob were joining Jared and I on our riding expeditions. It was not easy riding bikes with Jared. He had to be ahead of Jacob. If he lagged behind which he tended to do, he would cry. Sometimes he'd put the brakes on unexpectedly causing Joe or I to either run into him or crash and burn trying to avoid impact. We weren't very patient, but determined. If we ran into him, he'd cry, we'd yell and he'd cry some more, and then we'd get rolling again.

I enrolled the boys in swimming lessons which was more stress than I wanted. I had to supervise the lessons in order to assist the instructor in getting Jared to pay attention and stay with the group. Fortunately, because the boys were young I could take them into the ladies dressing room to help them keep on task. Every activity was work with Jacob and Jared. It was work to get their attention, work to get them to understand what I was saying, work to get them to engage, work to keep them on task, and then work to get Jacob to stop so we could move on. It was as if they weren't aware of or connected to anything going on around them or in the environment. I used a lot of enticements to get and hold their attention, which worked well: "Let's start getting ready for bed so we can have a story," or "Let's get done eating so we can have ice cream," or "Hey guys take a look at this."

At six-and-a-half and nearly eight now, the boys were incessant chatter-boxes even away from the table, so much so that it interfered with their listening. They wandered, too, when chatting. I had to hold their hands when we walked across a parking lot, for example, because they would wander and step out in front of moving vehicles. And yet they were fearful of crossing a street, often thinking an oncoming car was closer than it really was. They were still moving too, constantly; it never stopped.

Things were still changing all the time, too. One day Jared would act like he heard me and would respond very appropriately, the next day, he would act like he didn't have a clue as to what I had said. One day he would seem to have a skill, the next day it would be gone. One day Jacob seemed able to problem solve, the next day he could become extremely frustrated over the simplest of problems.

We made another break-through that summer when I enrolled Jared in a summer program, for four weeks, four hours a day; which was just enough structure to hold some of the opposition at bay. It was a learning program that had the children draw pictures in order to learn words and concepts. Jacob had attended it the summer before and really liked it. Jared was able to last the duration without complaints. He was difficult for the teachers to manage though; I could see the strain in their faces. At the end of the session it was suggested we have him tested for a learning disability. This is when we discovered he was *severely learning disabled*.

I looked up learning disabilities in my college text book on neurological rehabilitation and this problem too is very complex. No two children with a learning disability will present with the same set of symptoms or the same degree of severity. Some children have problems learning things verbally, some in the learning of math, reading, and in the acquisition of spoken and written language. Some have problems with nonverbal learning too, like understanding right and left and up and down, for example. Some have difficulty understanding the meanings of facial expressions and the behaviors of others — the social nuances. There are also maladaptive behaviors associated with learning disabilities: hyperactivity, short attention span, impulsivity, perseveration, distractibility, overly emotional and temperamental, gross and fine motor coordination problems, memory deficits, concept formation and problem solving difficulties, and speech and language problems. And while some theorists believe learning disabilities are a result of psychological and/or social problems, the majority believe they are the result of some type of brain dysfunction.

The way the evaluator explained Jared's learning disability to me was that he was having difficulty integrating information he sees and hears. His eyes and ears were sending information to the brain separately, which is normal, but then his brain couldn't integrate it. The information was being treated as two unrelated pieces when in fact each piece needs the other to be complete. In short, he was a "visual learner" and he had an expressive language disorder which meant he couldn't express verbally the thoughts that were in his head. It didn't surprise me he had learning disabilities; sensory integration dysfunction and learning disabilities typically go hand-in-hand.

Once I had time to think about it, the folks at the Learning Clinic had said Jared needed multi-sensory and visual cues for learning. According to the evaluator at this time, he needed special one-on-one assistance utilizing visual cues in order to learn. Tutorial services consisting of an aide going into the school to work with him, or me taking him into the clinic was available at $65 an hour. I was considering this option but when I drew a picture of a boy brushing his teeth in order to accommodate Jared's "visual" learning style and it didn't work to get him to brush, I decided to wait on tutorial services. Plus I wanted to see what the public school would offer first.

It was a fruitful summer. Joe and I had a nice outdoor wedding. No longer afraid, I was able to prepare for the wedding with a new found freedom and much more energy. I was grateful to have Joe by my side; he wasn't a quitter. He worried too because he loved the boys as if they were his own children. Within three weeks after the wedding he contacted an attorney and started adoption proceedings. The boys seemed to love him, too, and I know they liked the idea of he and I getting married. "Mom's getting ready for: The Marriage," they would say in a very serious tone and then giggle. It was the funniest thing: Jacob and Jared didn't seem to know what was going on around them, or when someone was sad, but they sure knew when people were happy. They must have known when people were stressed, too, because they always moved more when there was tension in the air.

Although our managed care coordinator, her clinical supervisor, and the psychiatrist overseeing our case through the Partners Project had never heard of sensory integration dysfunction before, I was granted permission to have Jacob evaluated for sensory integration problems and the Partners Project paid for it. Interestingly enough, he was found to have sensory problems too but they weren't serious enough to warrant individual therapy. His problems were the opposite of Jared's. He craved movement and needed intense "thrill seeking" type of sensory input.

In anticipation of rain and winter weather, Joe and I set up a playroom for the boys on the main floor of the house. I found some old mattresses, made slipcovers for them, and laid them out on the floor. Joe made a swing out of a piece of wood and wrapped it in soft carpeting then hung it from a beam in the ceiling. Jared didn't like the swing and once on it he wouldn't make it move, so we had to tell him to pretend it was a pony. We also started rough-housing with him. He didn't like it at first, which I expected, but we stayed with it. He had never acted out sexually so my fears subsided in that area. However, I decided he had to have human contact. We didn't tickle him because that brought on tears, but we wrestled and rolled on the mattresses with him. He was so little and scrawny that wrestling with him took little energy on my part and my being able to make contact with Jared in a positive way was most encouraging. Pretty soon he did like it. Soon we were all having a lot of fun. I noticed that after a rough-house session both Jared and Jacob were able to pay attention better. Jared was more inclined to engage in a task, less oppositional, and actually rather pleasant to be around.

By the time school started Jared was home in body and soul. His eyes shined bright, the grease was gone from his hair and his skin took on that rosy happy kid color. Everybody noticed it. "Jared's presence has changed somehow, he seems more aware of what's going on around him," someone said.

So we started the school year out on a hopeful note. I went back to work part-time and started feeling better about myself as a person. Jacob stayed with Mr. Miller while Jared started first grade at the elementary school in our new neighborhood.

I took with me to the school the evaluation that stated Jared was learning disabled with a language disorder; I thought it would save time and money. I also shared the evaluation completed by the Learning Clinic that specified how the teacher should work with Jared using multi-sensory tactile and visual cues. To my surprise, the evaluations didn't seem to matter because Jared was not found eligible for a special classroom or special help. The only extra help he could receive was one hour a week of speech and language therapy. And even though he was labeled autistic, occupational therapy couldn't be obtained on site. "That therapy doesn't come to this school," I was told. And even though sensory integration therapy was being used in a school district across the river from us, it was not allowed in our district.

At this time I didn't understand the public school system very well at all. I was getting the picture it was like everything else, though — up to me to figure it out. Later I would discover that in America every school, every school district, every State, and every County does things differently. The emphasis of any given school is determined primarily by the school board and parental influence. Some people want the school to emphasize the arts; some the sciences; some the languages; some sports; some want scholars; some are big on self-esteem. Jared's little inner city school emphasized self-esteem building.

The first grade teacher was quick to say she didn't think Jared was autistic. I shared with her that I didn't think he was either. The speech and language therapist didn't say anything except, "I'll work with him on social skills and have him play games with another student I'm working with." She was most kind. Jared definitely needed social skill building. At home he interrupted constantly when others were talking and cried when asked to wait his turn. Then when his turn came he'd say defensively "Forget it, I can't remember now," even if it was just within seconds. I couldn't imagine how he was going to manage in the classroom being one of 27 children. When I asked the teacher about using multi-sensory tactile and visual cues she said, "Oh yes, we have blocks here that he can use to count with."

I continued taking Jared out to the private clinic once a week for sensory integration therapy. It was over sixty miles round trip from our home but I could use the Medicaid card so I was grateful. We were lucky, too, only a few children with Medicaid insurance were taken at a time because of the time consuming paper work and low reimbursement rates — any other children were placed on waiting lists. We just happened to get in before the waiting list doors closed again for another six months.

I wish I could say I sat in on the therapy sessions in order to learn all I could about Jared's particular sensory integration problems, but most of the time I didn't. Most of the time I sat out in the waiting room dazed and exhausted, trying to process all of the information coming at me, the whole time not wanting to hear any of it, and thinking about what a mess I had on my hands. The sensory integration problem was just one piece to a very complex puzzle. I had a child who couldn't communicate, some of his learned helplessness behaviors were so well established that I couldn't foresee them ever being uprooted, he had emotional problems, then there was the learning problems, and I still believed he was somehow effected by exposure to alcohol in utero. And then of course, there was the problem with my poor parenting.

To combat my feelings of being completely overwhelmed, I tried not to look at the whole picture if I could help it. Instead, I looked at things in pieces. I broke each piece out from the others and then broke each of those down into even more "manageable" pieces, which I then looked at one at a time, and in relation to the brain as best that I could. I was going to have to learn how to communicate with Jared. Since I didn't know how to draw, I thought about he and I taking sign language classes together. As far as the learned helplessness was concerned, I decided I was just going to have to keep pushing him. My faith in sensory integration and its promise of adaptability was blind to a degree but it was faith nevertheless, and faith is powerful. I had no idea what might be fetal alcohol related behaviors now with everything in such a mess, so there was no point in dwelling on that, I decided. And as far as the learning problems were concerned, the school was going to have to teach him. I was finished with that aspect of Jared's development. I didn't know how to teach a severely learning disabled child and my trying was harmful to our forming a relationship.

Besides, I already had my hands full. Jared was still a most difficult child to care for. He still fussed when I combed his hair, he wouldn't try different clothes, and he wouldn't brush his teeth. Although he wasn't as lethargic as he had been, he was still very hard to wake in the mornings. He still sucked his thumb, drooled, cried, whined, and put dirty things in his mouth to chew on. He was always biting the sides of his mouth and tongue and now he wouldn't eat foods with nuts in them — "This has lumps in it!" — he'd say. He could still get lost in the house going from room to room but the aimless wandering had decreased considerably and he wasn't hiding under the chair anymore — just the table from time to time. He wasn't quite as resistant with simple tasks although he still wasn't about to apply himself if something required effort. And he still argued like a defiant teenager.

He stopped taking the action figures apart. He stopped tying up Jacob, the cat, himself, and focused strictly on inanimate objects now. His moods weren't as extreme and he wasn't as fearful about going into a room alone. These were all little gains but each a triumph in their own right.

I also had to work on Jared's moral development, his attitude, and his ability to get along with others — no small order when I didn't even have a relationship with the child. He had no desire to please me and why should he? Especially now. Damage had been done. I had wanted him to go away. I had felt disgust for him. He knew that. To realize that I had wanted to break his spirit was a horrifying thought in retrospect. His spirit was ugly, the opposition keeping love out, but at least he was alive inside. It was really all he had to call his own too — something that life, biology, nor genetics could steal from him — and he would need it when he went out on his own into the world someday.

Feelings of guilt hung over me like a dark cloud but I refused to let them drag on me and keep me motionless. There wasn't time. If Jared and I didn't form a relationship soon and if he didn't start feeling better about himself in a big way, we were going to lose him. It was a race against time, with the darkness nipping at my heels. But my Creator was with me again strengthening my resolve to keep moving.

Jared's moral development was of course at the heart of all my worries. When he began drawing pictures of guns and gravitating toward horror oriented toys at the store, I knew I had to take action. And fast. Without a sense of self a person can't discern right from wrong. If Jared had a sense of self it was seemingly nonexistent. His self-concept was incomplete; his self worth poor — he saw himself as bad. It wasn't as simple as him having a need for self-esteem anymore, that was something I only read about in a magazine while waiting in a doctors office. And like reading an article on the pleasures of touring Europe, Greece, or Ireland, complete with photographs, I could wish, but I knew we wouldn't be going there.

Jared wasn't bound with rage nor did he show violent tendencies but clearly he was at risk of learning all the wrong things. He wasn't connecting consequences with actions. How was he to know fires can kill people or that knives can make them bleed? I was going to have to watch everything he played with and everything he saw until he was stronger on the inside, I decided. So I threw out all the toy weapons and the action figures. Then I hauled the Nintendo and the television up to the attic.

I had never let Jacob or Jared see a violent movie, but I did let them watch cartoons on Saturday mornings. I grew up believing cartoons and kids go together. Cartoons are very violent. Then Nintendo came along and everybody was getting their kids one. I didn't want my child to be left out so I bought

Jacob one when he was five. I didn't like it when he played it though because he cried or got angry when he lost or couldn't get to the next level and he always fussed when it was time to turn it off. Jared didn't know how to play Nintendo but he liked to watch Jacob.

It wasn't difficult for me to make the decision to do away with Nintendo and television. I had been thinking about their influence on children for a long time. The private school Jacob attended discouraged them. They were considered "bandits" — believed to have the ability to rob from the child the opportunity to be "in-touch" with himself and his own innate drive for creative expression. All parents who enrolled their children in the school were encouraged to adopt this value and remove television and Nintendo from the home. It all sounded a little far-fetched to me and I was reluctant to buy in until now. But I was thinking in terms of brain development too — anytime the brain is used actively as opposed to passively, the dendrites that connect brain cells are made stronger — and watching television is a passive activity.

Jacob was upset when I put his Nintendo in the box but once out of sight, out of mind. The only time he mentioned it was when we went to someone else's house and they had one. To my surprise he and Jared didn't miss the television. I did though. "There is a need for balance, Donna," Joe said. So we rented videos to watch on weekends. Joe was right. Popcorn and a movie on a Saturday night became something to look forward to and a special treat for all.

Even more surprising to me was the pleasure I found in not having to listen to all that television and Nintendo noise. Jacob and Jared made constant noise as it was. Little noises: toe tapping, finger thumping. Subtle noises: throat clearing, tongue clicking, thumb sucking. Big noises: running, jumping, climb-ing. And from Jared, the — *Mom make me happy* — noises: cry-ing and whining.

I had to be able to problem solve around Jared's learning style. He was a "visual learner." This concept was so foreign to me. So I asked Jacob's teacher Mr. Miller, if he had any advise as to how I might influence Jared's moral development via pic-tures. I respected Mr. Miller's opinion. "Read him fairy tales," he said. "Fairy tales bring the elements of right and wrong to-gether in an imaginative picture form, which is how all young children see things, learning disabled or not." So I delved into the rich tales by The Brothers Grimm. I read the classics — *Snow White, Rapunzel, Hansel and Gretel*, and the not so well known — *The Raven, The Two Brothers, The Water of Life*, and *The Blue Light*. "The evolution of humanity is mirrored in the tales," Mr. Miller said. With Jared's fears and gloom and doom attitude, he al-most couldn't bear the dark passages. But in time, with story after story and their inevitable happy endings, his spirit started responding and optimism began to slowly find its way into his heart. Eventually I went on to reading more modern day sto-ries; those declared by the experts to build moral character in children.

And then "real" make-believe play between Jacob and Jared unfolded, ever so naturally. In time the cartoon super hero themes were replaced with fairy tale themes. Listening in, I'd hear of spectacular events in which someone obtained power because he used a magic stone or a magic wand. The boys would journey through the house dressed in garb appropriate to the role each had chosen — old hats, backpacks filled with 'trea-sures' holding secret powers, curtain rods were staffs, my old bathrobe the king's gown. They'd talk each role, action and plan out, with Jacob providing the special sound effects.

After a while, the boys were playing for hours together, harmoniously. Jared was much more giving to Jacob and more willing to compromise without resistance. Jared being able to engage his imagination was of great comfort to me. I've always thought imagination a wonderful thing; perhaps one of the gatekeepers to the soul. To see Jared really play was to see his spirit being socialized; his play purposeful. He was using his brain creatively and focusing on thought and content.

When I commented one day to my dad about how well the boys were playing together, he said "I think it's because of all those stories you read to them."

Sometimes if I could relax and let myself forget about what I should be doing with Jared to enhance his development, I would join the boys in their play. I wasn't comfortable with imaginative play anymore and had lost my knack, but they defined my role and lead me, so I didn't really have to do anything but let go. For a few minutes I could see the world through their eyes; an experience which is in and of itself, magical. Jared beamed when I played with them like this. Sometimes he would say something endearing like, "If your kids want to come with us too, tell them to just hop up on your lap and hold on tight." It was during moments like this when I found our Jared again. There was no crying or whining, fears, or anxieties. He wasn't shattered and broken, he was happy.

Jacob was eight by now and Jared nearly seven. Christmas was right around the corner and hope was alive at our house.

Chapter 6
Care Of The Soul

I t was a busy place, our house. Joe and I worked hard and intensely with the boys. It made all the difference having a partner who worked just as hard as I did. Never letting up, always watching for results, we stayed focused. Hardly a day went by when we didn't hug or rough-house play with Jacob and Jared; I lived each day as if it was to be the last. We took them and a friend of Jacob's to Mt. Hood to play in the snow on inner-tubes. We went on hikes in the woods, walks in the neighborhood. We kept them moving. We told them what good boys they were, too — constantly — following up with a kiss or a hug.

I kept thinking in terms of sensory input and sensory stimulation. I kept children's tapes playing in the car. I set out clay, play-dough, crayons, water paints, paper, felt pens, tape, glue, and safety scissors on the dining room table and left them there. This was a big move for me — that table was always a mess. Jacob loved it. He could go to the table and make things, draw, and paint whenever it suited him to do so. Jared liked to cut with the scissors and use the scotch tape — lots of it.

We got Jared glasses, too, and I had his head size measured accordingly. It wasn't growing and neither was he.

Joe never opposed my ideas regarding what might be something we could try with the boys and he always followed my lead. He believed in me. Plus he saw for himself the changes. And they were coming along, slow but sure. "The boys are doing better all the time, Donna, and that's because of you," he was always saying. I don't know if I could have kept going if Joe didn't believe in me the way he did.

Joe was at a disadvantage when he came back from sea. During the weeks he was gone, I would implement another new parenting technique or make a new discovery about Jacob and Jared and forget to tell him. He'd come in and attempt to resume where we had left off with a given technique only to find out, "We're not doing it that way anymore." He had to adjust his social life, too. Friends or family were accustomed to stopping in to see Joe regularly — he was so social and very much liked. But we simply couldn't have people over on school nights. Any change in routine and the boys would be more difficult to manage. Joe recognized this and made the necessary sacrifice; it was perhaps his biggest adjustment.

Joe and I supervised Jacob's and Jared's self-care activities every day. We worked diligently with them on going into the bathroom to wash and brush without playing, stopping, looking, and touching something in route. We worked with them constantly to pay attention to whatever the task at hand. We had them draw pictures of teeth brushing, hand washing, and hair combing to act as reminders to stay on task. Jared still chewed on his toothbrush, he wouldn't use toothpaste, he wouldn't rub soap into his hands, and he would forget to comb his hair altogether. We worked with the boys constantly on not chatting at the table so that we could finish meals in a timely manner. We started them on learning to make their beds, empty the dish washer, and set the table. Jared was assigned the top rack of the dishwasher where there was only two types of items — cups and cereal bowls. He had to have a picture of a place setting in order to set the table. We used enticements always. I thought that if we did these daily activities over and over again, especially for Jared, they would eventually become second nature, and then Joe and I could "semi-retire." This thought — work now, rest later — kept me going; I wanted capable and independent children who could be self sustaining someday.

In spite of the work, things were better for us at this time than they had every been. And then like always, just when I was starting to breathe easier, things flipped upside down again.

Although Jacob was doing fine in school and had never temper tantrumed or raged while there, he was becoming more and more difficult at home. He was sneaking cookies and candy; I was very rigid regarding when he could have such treats. And if he wasn't storming around the house kicking things that just happened to be in his way, he was looking to argue with me over ridiculous things. In the past when he argued with me I would structure him up real tight — take total control. But that technique wasn't working anymore. It seemed the stricter I was, the more oppositional he became. The tension in his body was obvious, reminding me of a time bomb just waiting to explode. I couldn't understand it, either; he had not raged in months. Then one day there was an explosion. I said he couldn't have a cookie and he kicked in the back screen door. When another rage surfaced just a few days later I knew we were in trouble.

I had to do something to help Jacob conquer the rage inside of him but I didn't know what. My thinking naturally fell back unto my "professional" and now consumer knowledge base. At the psychiatric hospital raging teenagers were placed in padded cells. At an inner city "alternative" school for children considered emotionally disturbed here in Portland, cells are used, but they're not so padded. Well, I wasn't going to build a padded room in our house. It was a home, not a hospital or prison, and I was a parent with love in my heart.

Ironically, the administrator at Jacob's school had suggested I read the book *Holding Time*. It was a book he had read when his son was young even though there was nothing "wrong" with his son. He thought it might help me with Jared. "It tells you how to help your child to be happier, more cooperative, more self-confident and less demanding," he said. I did buy the book but I didn't read it — I was too busy and too confused at the time. So I finally sat down and read it. To my surprise, the technique advocated in the book utilized the brain to reach the child emotionally.

Holding Time is a book written by a psychiatrist named Martha Welch who drew from the research on primate and infant bonding as well as her own clinical work with Autistic children. She found that by holding a child a particular way, at a particular time, two biochemical systems in the child's brain will reach a balance and thus create an optimal level for learning and emotional development. So she wrote the book to show parents how to hold and when. It was written for any parent who wants to rear an emotionally well-balanced child; single parents, adoptive parents, working parents. As a working single parent herself without a lot of time and energy to devote to her son after a long day, she would hold him. After holding time her son was most content to do his studies or play by himself (he was an only child), for the remainder of the evening.

As I read the book, it reminded me of how I had held Jacob very early on and fed him from a bottle. I had been doubtful, yet something had worked and brought change. And I was doubtful now but being pulled to try the holding technique. So I put it to use for the first time when Jacob was very angry but not yet in a full blown state of rage. Unfortunately, by the time I got him on my lap and my arms around him, he was out of control. I was terribly nervous to be in such close proximity under the circumstances, and I fumbled which gave him the opportunity to free up one of his hands. Before I knew it he had a fistful of my hair and was pulling hard, calling me names at the same time. The rage that poured out of him was terrifying. But I couldn't let him go otherwise the opportunity for resolution and thus biochemical balance would be lost, which is critical if the child is to benefit. When he pulled my hair completely out of my scalp the pain was excruciating. Then when he bit my upper arm I screamed out in pain and started crying, but I couldn't let him go. It would harm him I felt to see what he had done without bringing resolution. Instead I said, "I love you Jacob. No matter how much you've hurt me, I still love you. I'll always love you." I said this over and over again and though he struggled, he didn't continue to attack. Finally he stopped struggling and melded into my arms much like he had done as a little fella when he allowed me to feed him. When his eyes met mine, I knew something had taken place deep inside of him.

This entire process took one hour and twenty minutes. It was physically exhausting and emotionally draining. But I know what I saw afterwards and I know without a doubt that I did the right thing to use it. Jacob seemed happier and more at peace with himself than I had ever seen him before. That evening when Jared started talking about his recent acquisition of birthday presents, Jacob said, "I'd rather have holding time now instead of presents. Holding time lasts."

Thereafter, every time Jacob became agitated I did holding time. The sessions were never as long nor as intense as the first and I didn't get hurt again. Within approximately two months, the rage was completely gone. His frustration and anger remained but he never raged again or destroyed property. Holding time was the most beneficial and effective intervention I ever found for Jacob. I was so grateful I found it when I did, too. He was only eight and still small in size. I didn't stop holding with him even after the rages were gone, either. Every week for nearly a year we had a 20 to 30 minute holding time session. It was easy actually compared to the work that went into the behavior modification and structure techniques. I would do one thing differently however, if I were to do it all over again. For that first holding session, I would try to find a caring therapist to help guide me, but I would definitely do it again.

I did holding time with Jared too, of course, hoping to foster a bond between us, but like everything else, it was hit and miss and didn't seem to hold. Jared didn't have the rage inside of him that Jacob did; other than yelling and opposing, he didn't get angry. So when I held, there was no resolution to speak of. Holding was good for me, though, as a way of coping with the opposition. When frustrated with him, I could hold. He hated it of course, that I would take him in my arms and hold him when he was being a stinker. While holding I would say things like "You're a good boy and I love you." He didn't like that either of course and would close his eyes. Or he would say, "My ears can't hear you!"

Joe and I were also working with Jared on learning how to get along with other children. Some people said, "Let the other kids socialize him," but I knew that wasn't going to work. Other children didn't like him and mean begets mean. But Jacob had friends and there were neighborhood children around so I invited someone to our house to play almost every Saturday. I had to watch Jared constantly. If he even looked like he was going to hit or take something from another child, I redirected and modeled for him how to ask for things. This seemed to have little impact because when he wanted something, he wanted it, and there was no way to reason with him in order to insure him I wasn't trying to make him unhappy. "You're being mean to me," he'd say. But then eventually he'd settle down and go back to play. I operated this way with the other children too. No one was allowed to take from Jared or hit him. This could make for strained relations between myself and the other child's parent at times, especially when Jared was obviously the antagonist.

Jared really was getting better. He was having more good days than bad now. My being able to distinguish a good day from a bad day was an accomplishment within itself. On bad days his eyes would glaze over, his skin color would be gray, he was more oppositional than usual, and his thinking seemed even more scattered. On bad days he went into his own little world.

The bad days always made me anxious and the opposition wore me down. Once in a weakened state, negativity would set in, and I would want to give up again; it was hopeless. When negative, my heart was hard: Jared was bad — calculating and manipulating constantly to get his needs met. I was forever at war with myself to think positively instead of negatively, my old ways of thinking fought with the new, my desires to nurture fought with those wanting to disregard, while my intellect wanting to acknowledge brain function fought with my emotions in their wanting to blame the spirit. The strength of my opponents always emerged when I least expected, catching me off guard. As was the case the day Jared announced to me that he was so happy to be going to a new school, that he had hated the other one. "They were always trying to trick me there," he said.

I was so irritated when I heard this. He had calculated to get out of that school. Despairing, I was reminded of the deep seated issue he had with trust. He clearly didn't trust anybody and it stood in the way of everything. When he struggled Joe and I would try to guide him but he resisted our help. "You don't know!" or "You're lying," he would say. Even with Jacob he kept his guard up. It was pathetic and heart breaking to see a little boy trapped within the confinement of his own bitter reflection: people were deceitful and not worthy of credibility — genuine caring perceived as nothing more than trickery.

Upset now, I shouted at him, "If you think you're so smart, then you figure it all out! I'm not going to help you any more."

He started crying then, real tears, and said, "Don't you know I can't live without you?!" This only made me feel worse. Of course he couldn't live without me. I was his lifeline to humanity; the relationship a necessary pretense and a shield with which to combat his aloneness. Hopelessness filled my heart again, leaving me cold and unresponsive. And then I realized something. If Jared felt he could not live without me, that meant he was attached to me.

This is when I started talking to Jared a lot. Inside, surrounded by layers and layers of mental and physical difficulties, was a little boy who felt he couldn't live without a particular human being: me. And I had done nothing but let him down over and over again. It wasn't all his fault. There was suffering in my own soul, too. I told him I was sorry for the mess things were in; the mistakes I had made. I told him I couldn't remember what it was like to be a child. I told him he was lovable. I told him I believed in him. I asked for his cooperation and suggested that if we worked together as a team, we might be able to put the pieces together. I asked him to talk to me and tell me when I hurt his feelings. I asked him if he would be patient with me.

So it seemed Jared was attached to me, but unfortunately, I wasn't attached to him. There was little joy in being his parent. All that crying and whining were constant reminders that I couldn't give him what he needed. At times I thought he should have been an only child. He would often ask me, "You like me more than Jacob, don't you Mom?" At other times I thought I was the wrong parent for him. I just didn't have the patience, he was so much bother.

Jared still hated new clothes and I couldn't figure out why. I washed everything first, assuming it was the 'store smell' that bothered him. Finally, he agreed to try a different pair of jeans but they had to be "made soft first" he said. Thinking he didn't understand that his new shirts were "made soft" too, I insisted he wear them to see for himself. The next thing I knew, there were holes in those shirts where the tags had been. This irritated me. Then when he came down with the chicken pox, he used the commercial carpeting on the stairs to scratch them! He cried as if in pain when he scratched, but I couldn't keep him from scratching. I followed doctor's orders regarding over the counter medicine and the usual home remedies of oatmeal baths and calamine lotion. He hated having lotion applied to his skin, especially over his joints - "Don't put it where it bends," he said. As if possessed, he kept scratching and scratching until the skin on his back was nothing but one big welt from the shoulders down. I couldn't comfort him.

The incident made me feel anxious and fearful; alone with

the darkness. My fears were always just below the surface anyway, waiting to pull me down, paralyze me, and fill my heart with doubt. They taunted in a tone so ugly and demeaning: *Self-injurious behaviors-severely emotionally disturbed-damaged-deranged.* It was a haunting chorus. Then the school problems began again.

After about five months, Jared didn't want to go to school anymore. He cried to stay home and kicked and screamed when I put him in the car. I couldn't get a sense of what was going on for him from the teacher. Every time I checked with her it was: "Oh he's doing just fine; he's not Autistic you know." I kept telling her I knew that but it didn't seem to matter.

I wasn't satisfied with these reports. I had to know in concrete terms exactly what Jared was doing in school. I also had to know how he was getting along with peers. I didn't have the desire to volunteer as I had with Jacob; I didn't want to see what I might see. So the Family Support Case Manager offered to go and observe one day for me. It was ideal really because Jared had never met her, so he wouldn't be self conscious and try to perform. She agreed to log for me his every move, emotional response, and the things he said. She observed from 10:00 in the morning until 1:00 in the afternoon. Her note taking was excellent. The behaviors she documented were typical of Jared and, unfortunately, most discouraging:

<u>10:00</u> 'All kids sitting, Jared standing. Kids counting, Jared chewing on coat sleeve, watching. Leaves group, goes to desk and takes out paper and yellow crayon. Looks at book for a few minutes while sucking thumb. Starts coloring. Teacher takes away coloring book and asks him to join the group. He whines, stays at desk and continues to write with crayon. He does not return to group, head down on desk, thumb in mouth, then

makes marks on paper for a while. All children getting out journal paper. Teacher approaches Jared and asks if they can have a good day like yesterday. Jared is writing on paper. Teacher stops to talk to him, he is writing on desk. She encourages him to finish like yesterday. Jared got frustrated and crumpled paper. Upset because it had a rip in it, teacher tapes it. Jared working quietly and has been for about three minutes. He is now beginning to talk to himself a little bit. Jared is under desk. His head is on floor. Teacher says he can take nap after lunch. She gently helps him get off floor and into desk.'

10:15 Speech therapy - 'Very pleasant relaxed atmosphere. Game playing. Jared says other child is so good at it and wins the most. "Didn't you win last time Jared?" therapist asks. "No," states Jared. He and other child have been playing Go Fish and conversing for five minutes - Jared is totally in tune. Switch to discussion of seasons, Jared is arranging cards on a tray, but is focused on conversation. Therapist puts points up. "Did I do a good job today?" asks Jared. "Of course, you always do," says therapist. "I do?" asks Jared.'

11:00 Return to classroom - 'Jared has thumb in mouth, head down. Math problem presented. Jared is attending head up - I can see him pointing and counting books. Jared continues to sit quietly sucking thumb.'

11:10 Library - 'Jared sucking thumb and listening quietly. Boy beside him crowds him. Jared gets into a shoving match with girl next to him but it stops.'

11:30 Lunchtime - 'Jared chose seat by wall and ate while watching kids. At end of lunch he did some wheeling and dealing for cookies with boy across from him, large dark haired boy. Quickly shut lunch and ran outside when lunch was gone. Worked hard to shut it!'

Recess - 'Boys up steps and down slide. One interaction with same boy that he traded with at lunch was stopped by PE teacher - because boy pulled Jared's shirt. One other sort of chasing game with small red-headed boy. Climbed and jumped through monkey bars. Promptly ran to line up when he heard bell.'

12:00 Return to classroom - 'Quiet time. Jared is reading book - thumb in mouth. Starts trying to tell kids that he knows how to spell BOING. No one listens. He gets loud and teacher notices and listens to him spell it. He gets a little wiggly. Begins to jump.'

Math workbook time - 'A sub is helping - Jared goes to get some blocks to work with. I hear him say "3 + 6 is 9." He is chatting pleasantly with desk partner from time to time. Teacher redirects him from talking. Doing something with crayon at his desk, he is singing — room pretty active. Teacher works individually with him for a moment. Jared is on floor but then gets himself back to work. As group corrects math problem together, teacher brings him up to her desk to get help. Group working well together. Project finished and group getting restless. Jared is still beside teacher. He returns to desk. He is sucking his thumb and rocking. Group is suppose to return books and return to group. Jared stays at desk. He is dropping blocks on floor and crawling. After two invitations he does come to group. Group lines up for music.'

I couldn't fault the teacher for Jared's problems. She was really very nice and she cared. She made Jared student of the month two times. After the Family Support worker's visit, she shared with me that she was getting a divorce and fighting for the custody of her only child. "I wish I could help Jared more," she said, "but my cup is empty."

By spring Jared was going to the principal's office on a regular basis for being disruptive. Evidently he wasn't working alone either; three other boys were faithfully involved as well. I could just see Jared following along, not knowing if any of it was right or wrong; possibly thinking it was the way to make friends. I talked to the principal and tried to explain Jared's problems. He was tolerant and he listened but it clearly wasn't his problem. Besides, Jared looked normal. At home I would lecture and lecture Jared about what not to do at school. "Jared, it's not appropriate to be disruptive in school."

"It's not?" he responded in a tone of genuine confusion. He wanted to do what was right I could tell, he just didn't know how. "Is there a book that will teach me what to do Mom?" he said, with sincerity, those big brown eyes opened wide. This is what made parenting him so difficult. I never knew what he could comprehend and what he couldn't. And I had never heard of therapeutic interventions that focused on teaching a child school skills or right from wrong.

Mornings were even more difficult now with Jared not wanting to go to school. It was so much stress having to get myself to work on time and having to deal with him, too. So I quit my job — again. I never got used to having to give up things for myself, but that is how it always was. I couldn't manage well when Joe was gone; it was just too physically and mentally exhausting. By simplifying and giving up in order to reduce the stress, I was better able to cope. I was resentful about giving up my job. It meant further social isolation and less money in the household budget which meant no extras. I felt parenting was the most insignificant work I could do, too, after talking with a career oriented woman one day while at a fundraiser. "And what do you do?" she asked me. When I told her I was a busy mother, she said, "Oh, I see. You're just a mom."

My dad and I were drifting apart. I couldn't talk to him about anything anymore. He thought God had sent Jared to me to improve my character and that bothered me a lot. Parenting my "special needs" child had done nothing but bring out the worst in me. My dad also thought I was putting too much faith in brain rehabilitation and not enough in God. He was right to a degree. It was hard to keep the faith in anything sometimes when there was no help or a place in which to turn. We had access to the various government funded mental health agencies for play therapy and psycho-therapy, but that's not what Jared needed; talk wasn't working. This is when I realized that the children's mental health system needed serious revamping. It wasn't going to happen in our time though.

And by now I knew that even though it was supposed to happen there, in reality the school system wasn't prepared to help either. I had the documentation to prove Jared was learning disabled, and it was obvious he needed extra help, but he had yet to qualify for more help. Evidently, a child has to reach a level of maturity and be considerably behind academically before a concentrated effort is made to address his needs adequately. This meant Jared would have to continue to fail until something changed.

When and if Jared qualified he would be entitled to a team of professionals: a special education teacher, clinical psychologist, counseling psychologist, speech and language pathologist, occupational therapist, and physical therapist are typically the basic team while other specialists may be called in for consultation or supervision. Each professional would evaluate and work with him according to their individual professional responsibilities and goals at various times throughout the day. Their responsibilities and goals would over lap, but at times the evaluation results would differ, which would be to Jared's disadvantage. Professionals take pride in their work, and while they may wish to work together, many feel a need to prove their professional expertise when they are arriving at differing evaluation results. This might then lead to problems in professional territoriality. And once there are territorial issues people have a tendency to stop talking to each other. The result is fragmented and pieced together services for the child. This is most unfortunate, because in reality, none of the treatments by themselves is complete given the complexities of learning disabilities and no one profession has been proven to be superior over another.

The occupational therapists in the school system are typically suppose to address the motor planning and motor control problems associated with learning disabilities. What techniques are used to do this is up to the individual therapists. Dr. Ayres showed that sensory integration therapy could help children with learning disabilities to achieve more in school and feel better about themselves. According to my college neurorehabilitation text, sensory integration therapy is a framework in which all professionals could work from for a more holistic approach. But Dr. Ayres' work was discredited in this area too, because someone misinterpreted her writings and thought she said sensory integration therapy would correct learning disabilities. She didn't say that — learning disabilities cannot be corrected. She said sensory integration therapy will organize the sensations for use and thus influence the brain's capacity to perceive, remember, or plan motor movements, which are required for all learning. In other words, once the sensations are more organized the higher level learning can take place and that which is learned can become integrated so that it stays with the child. It's a framework within which to work and Dr. Ayres was always clear about it being followed by academics, self-care training if that is a goal, social-skill building, etc. But since so many people have difficulty understanding the theory of sensory integration dysfunction and its treatment, few occupational therapists are free to use it in a collective way within the public school system.

In addition to these problems, there is a more fundamental problem plaguing our public school system that the general public does not know about. The school therapists, teachers, and special educators are terribly over burdened. Every therapist I talked to, including Joe's sister who had worked in the public school system for five years, said children in need of special help are not being identified simply because there is too much need. And those who are being identified, don't receive enough help. By the time the paper work is taken care of, a therapist may get only a half-an-hour a week with a child. There is also a problem with our education laws for 'special needs' children. They dictate that all handicapped children be mainstreamed to regular classrooms throughout the day, often times without an aide or extra support, burdening the teachers, and resulting in even more fragmented and pieced-together help. The child with the learning disabilities — the invisible handicap — is at a terrible disadvantage under such circumstances.

No, it was up to Joe and I. I knew now why people will often say of a "special needs child" — "Well at least so-and-so has his family" — it may be the only real support the child will ever get. Poor Jared. He had his family all right, so he was a part of something, but we didn't understand him, we couldn't give him the support he really needed; I couldn't even defend him and mean it with all my heart. It was a hopeless situation by all accounts.

Joe was always encouraging me to go out with friends when he was out at sea, but when I did I couldn't relax enough to enjoy myself. I would pretend to be listening to conversation or interested in a movie when in reality, my mind agonized over all that could go wrong at home. Joe's little sister and my father babysat for short periods but the older the boys got, the more difficult it became for them to maintain the needed structure. Plus they argued with Jared — he could make anybody argue with him.

About the only thing I had for myself was my hobby of sewing. I had taken the sewing machine out of the attic that winter and proceeded to make Jared a quilt for his bed. I had never attempted a project of such magnitude before but it somehow seemed appropriate to the situation. A quilt has to be made in several stages, each stage so detailed and complex, requiring its own time, its own attention. I had no patience for the details at first. They were tedious and time consuming, keeping me from the next stage to the end product, which is all I really cared about. But eventually I came to find satisfaction in each stitch, each star, each block. The feel of the fabric at my fingertips was calming and reassuring. I was making something that would last, something permanent; something for Jared.

The familiar hum of the sewing machine was like finding an old friend, one who knew my history from way-back-when so there was no explaining to do. I lamented silently and alone. Things were not the way I had thought they were going to be when I decided to adopt Jacob and Jared. I thought that within a couple of years I would have them emotionally stable and then we could enjoy life. I had no idea I was going to have to rehabilitate them, live such a rigid existence, or give up so much. I was given new life when I discovered what it felt like to make a little four year old boy named Jacob happy. Now it was all I could do to maintain some dignity. I always thought Jacob would go to college. Now I had to wonder if he was even going to make it through high school with his frustration and anger problems, and low self-esteem, or if he was going to run away, get on drugs, and drop out of life entirely. Jared didn't even have a future. I had thought we would be nothing less than a healthy and happy family but we were a dysfunctional mess. And I was "just a mom" but I had never worked so hard in my entire life.

Joe's sister and I were consoling and helping each other over the phone nearly every day. Her son was in the third grade and having considerable difficulty too. He was overly emotional and socially immature; he couldn't "keep his hands to himself" according to the teachers and principal of the school. At home he was raging a lot and nearly unmanageable, keeping the entire family in chaos. Then one day the school psychologist suggested they have him evaluated for attention deficit and hyperactivity. He was attention deficit all right and needed medication in order to be able to concentrate and keep his hands to himself.

Joe's sister was a problem solver, never letting something go by without at least attempting a change. She too struggled constantly with seeing good in her child, trusting him, understanding the behaviors, and leading a normal life. We kept each other going by sounding out our latest problem solving idea, our expectations, our frustrations, and our disappointments. We discouraged each other from thinking too much about the future. Her husband felt that their son's biggest problem was her; that she just wanted control. But that wasn't true. She wanted her son to be able to get along with others and she wanted his school work to reflect his IQ of 140. She was a good mom. She kept telling me I was too.

After learning a lot about attention deficit, Joe's sister convinced me we should have Jared evaluated. She felt certain he was attention deficit and hyperactive. "I just know he is!" she said. It didn't make sense to me. Jared wasn't physically over active and his attention span seemed fine when he was doing something he wanted to do. Nevertheless, some of his behaviors did fit. So I enrolled him in a social skills group for boys his age with attention deficit, and I made an appointment with a doctor to have him evaluated for medication. If medication was another piece to the brain puzzle, I wanted it.

But the psychiatrist said Jared wasn't attention deficit so he couldn't prescribe medication. "He's just emotionally disturbed," he said, as if that was the extent of who Jared was. Then he politely excused me from his office. We were there for a half-of-an-hour, if that. I was angry. Jared needed help. If he had attention problems that was all the more reason why he needed help. If he couldn't concentrate in school how was he going to succeed or learn to comply? Without success or acceptance by others, how could he ever be anything but "disturbed" living in a world where others don't go? I wanted to tell the psychiatrist how hard Joe and I were working but I never got the chance.

Our work wasn't in vain either. Little gains were being made. Although Jared's social skills were inept, he was not hitting other children anymore. He would retaliate when provoked but he didn't initiate now. For some reason I felt this was as much a credit to his true nature as it was to our parental guidance. I liked this about Jared, very much. He and I were reaching some kind of an understanding too — he wasn't saying "You're being mean to me" anymore. He was starting to express his feelings too.

I had to give him the room to express his feelings which wasn't easy for me when I was upset. One night I was lecturing him about a given behavior, going on and on; asking him questions but never pausing long enough to let him talk. He opened his mouth a few times and tried to speak, but I was determined to have my say for as long as it took. Eventually he gave up trying. When I realized he wasn't going to say anything, I didn't like that either. "And what do you have to say for yourself young man?" I asked.

"Well I don't know, now. You wouldn't even let me damn talk!" he said. Our whole family laughed at this exchange. There were moments like this, when things were just right, and Jared's true inside self would appear and put the proper perspective on everything. That was the Jared I loved. He wasn't arguing just for the sake of arguing. He was accepting and tolerant, yet able to be honest with himself and others. He was connected. Those were the moments that kept me going.

I took Jared to the social skills group anyway for six weeks. It was designed to teach impulse control primarily, so I enrolled Jacob as well. Joe's sister took her son too. It was a real family affair. When I watched Jared maneuver among the other children, it was obvious to me then that he was not tracking. Whatever was happening, he wouldn't get it figured out until the group was well into the first step and already anticipating the next. I felt sorry for him. I don't know if he got anything out of the group or not. He always looked a little bewildered upon leaving and would sometimes take Jacob's hand as they walked down the hallway together. Jared was lucky to have a brother like Jacob; he was his lifeline to unconditional love.

I don't know why I worried so about Jacob's schooling, probably because the security was false; teacher specific. Mr. Miller was wonderful with Jacob, seeming to understand him so well. His end of the year second grade report read: "Jacob is such a fine, moral and kind child; unusually so for one so young. I want now to draw out a bit of strong fiber, to help him maintain these unique gifts of his. He will need some strength in his inner being in order to preserve these qualities when he moves out into the world as an adolescent/adult." Mr. Miller was a rare and gifted teacher.

It was amazing Jacob did as well as he did. Other than me expecting him to do his best, he got little support. I was always so busy with Jared. This is why I resented Joe or anybody else thinking I showed favoritism. I didn't. I couldn't. Jacob was always second. And Jared was always miserable, no matter what I did. There was no way to please him and be equitable at the same time. His perceptions weren't even reality based. One day when he saw two equal piles of clothing stacked up on the couch he asked which one was his. When I pointed to it, he wailed "Jacob gets more than me." Pretty soon it was "Jacob gets everything!" which wasn't true but I was going to hear that for a long time.

Then one day, two weeks before school let out for the summer, Jared was attacked at school by a deskmate who wanted his cookies. I became quite upset. The principal thought I was over reacting. Maybe I was, but nobody knew Jared as I did. Every act of deceit, selfishness, greed, and aggression validated for him that no one is to be trusted. This incident served to remind me of Barbara's words "Jared will always be a victim" and with it another bite of humble pie. How was I to protect

Jacob has developed so beautifully this year. The difference in his sense of self, as well as self-confidence is markedly improved over last year. He still carries within him a sense of wistfulness which I cannot quite pinpoint its origin or cause. It's almost as though he is not quite certain who he is or what he is about in this world.

Jacob takes a real interest in whatever lessons we are about and he gets deeply engrossed in his own work, so much so that he can lose complete track of time. He may concentrate of some small details and not complete the total project in the time allotted. He is extremely conscientious about wanting to complete whatever tasks he has to complete although he is sometimes forgetful that he has something to complete and needs to be reminded to do so. He is always willing to do whatever is asked of him. I no longer encounter the resistance which he displayed in first grade.

Jacob still needs to be assured that he has done well, or knows something, as outward praise is most important to him. He will sometimes repeat his old habit of interrupting to point out that he already "knows" that, or "I was going to say that."

Jacob is doing very well with his reading. Indeed, he is one of the best readers in the class. His writing is also coming nicely, although he writes slowly.

Mathematical concepts he can understand usually, but he is slow to do the calculations. Artistically he is doing beautifully, with his painting, drawing, recorder and singing.

Academically and artistically Jacob is in good shape.

My real concern with him is strengthening his inner being, that part of him which gives him his self-assurance and the ability to focus clearly, remember what he has done and why he has done it. The artistic work, music, literature and recitation we do will all help strengthen this.

Jacob is such a fine, moral and kind child, unusually so for one so young. I want to draw out a bit of strong fiber, to help him maintain these unique gifts of his. He will need some strength in his inner being to preserve his unique qualities when he moves out into the world as an adolescent/adult.

It's been a wonderful year for Jacob.

Mr. Miller

him from predators? How was I to cultivate in him a capacity for genuine caring if living meant degradation at the whim of those more powerful?

After this incident I felt as if we were going to drown in a sea of human despair and it wasn't just our own — predators and victims, families in crisis, doctors without faith in the power of the human spirit to overcome — it was all around us. There was nobody to look after our Jared. And I knew we would lose him for sure if I couldn't teach him how to take care of himself.

So I did something that was cruel and aversive therapy, which I detest — I put tabasco sauce on his thumb. I didn't know what else to do. At seven-and-a-half he still cried, whined, drooled, and sucked his thumb. I had put him on a behavior modification program several times to stop the thumb sucking but it never worked. Personally, I really didn't mind if he sucked it at home or at bedtime; he seemed to need it. But to Americas toughest children, crying, whining, and thumb sucking might mean, "Pick on me," "I'm weak," "I'm different." And given Jared's ability to antagonize, whether it be intentional or unintentional, he didn't conjure up feelings of sympathy or support in others for him. He just couldn't continue sucking his thumb in front of peers and that was all there was to it.

I continued trying to find someone who would medicate him and went to our pediatrican's new partner. She was familiar with attention deficit, but she didn't know us and Jared's case was too complex. She thought he ought to have a thorough evaluation and offered to make a referral to a psychologist. I turned her offer down. Time was too precious. Psychologists can't prescribe medication so another referral would have to be made to see a psychiatrist. Jared's mind would be probed yet again and subject to the past, detouring us from the future and detaining us from getting help for his brain.

And then it dawned on me — if Jared was fetal alcohol effected, the attention deficit would show itself there! So I called the doctor's office who had said Jared was Fetal Alcohol Syndrome to make an appointment to see her again. But there was a waiting list and it would be three to four months before I could get him in.

I knew there was a Behavioral M.D. specialized in diagnosing fetal alcohol effects practicing in Portland, so I called her and Jared was seen right away. When she said "Jared is so severely fetal alcohol effected that I am amazed he functions as well as he does," I was completely stunned. I wasn't surprised that he was diagnosed with fetal alcohol effects, but I didn't expect him to be so severely effected. I asked the doctor why he cried so easily but she didn't know. When she said she thought he would benefit from medication I was overcome with feelings of gratitude. I was also incredibly relieved. It was evaluation number 23. We could stop now.

Then as quickly as my hopes rose, they fell. The doctor wouldn't prescribe medication until after Jared went back to school when she could consult with his teacher; my account of his difficulties wasn't enough. We were half way into the month of July.

I was doomed. With two more months of unstructured time, Jared's behaviors would worsen. He was already so difficult and there were no programs for kids "like him." I would be alone, too. Joe wouldn't be back home until late August. I would be alone, cooped up in the house with Jared. Had I been thinking ahead, I might have been able to get the Family Support program to help me find a therapist to go places with him like the Partners Project was doing with their kids, but it was too late now. Our year was up. The evaluation done by the Behavioral M.D. was the last thing the program paid for. Not that I wasn't grateful for it, that doctor didn't take Medicaid insurance either.

Once again, and in the face of needing help, I felt powerless. Despite my feelings of desperation, I couldn't bring myself to have a dialogue with the doctor and state my needs. It wouldn't have mattered, though, even if I did. Doctors don't like to make such decisions all by themselves and, unfortunately, it's not standard practice to consider the parents equal partners in care. I felt terribly insignificant, even to blame, as if I had done something wrong to warrant being in her office.

My faith in everything was waning but I had to keep believing Jared was going to make it and that things would work out. If they didn't, I feared I would lose what little hope I had left for humanity. So it was for the care of my own soul as well as Jared's that I found the strength to carry on.

Chapter 7
"I Need You With Me"

I t was another long summer. I did some yelling and a little
spanking, but I made it through with my integrity intact. I
wasn't much of a drinker, but on really bad days, I did that
too — double shots of vodka with o. j.

The boys and I got out of the house almost everyday and
kept moving. Besides the fact that I wasn't about to stay inside,
I did it for the sensory integration piece too. Jared had had sensory integration therapy for six months but I never stopped
thinking about it in terms of the process and its promise of adaptability. I thought about it unconsciously more than consciously,
though, and I didn't think in terms of adaptive responses as
much as I did just movement in general.

We did swimming lessons, hiking, bicycling, neighborhood
walks, garage sales, the library to watch a puppet show or check
out books. Joe's sister had to get out of the house, too, so we
would pile all the kids into her van for hiking, swimming, playing at the park, going to Discovery Zone (a gross motor play
facility for children), and roller skating. Between the two of us
we had five children and a lot of hyper-motor activity. We must
have been quite the sight herding them around, fussing with
them to "Stay together," "Get back here," "Don't touch that,"
and the ever faithful, "No, no, sweetie, he didn't mean to hit

you." Jared always had to be towed of course, crying, whining, and accusing me of hurting his arm. People often stared at us. We did camp outs with the rest of Joe's family, and went fishing and crabbing when Joe was home. Jared loved being on the water. He said it "gets me relaxed" and that it reminded him of sensory integration therapy for some reason.

Sometimes Joe's sister and I would simply lounge beside her swimming pool, sipping on iced tea, dazed and frazzled, watching our children play. They loved fantasy play and they didn't need toys or weapons to help them along. They made up their own wild, creative adventures, with each child contributing, and traveled the universe on the wings of their imaginations. The imaginary struggles encountered seemed very real to them, calling on acts of courage. "Can you get out of that cave?," I heard one say to the others one day. "I'll try," was the earnest response. They were unique children. Most of the children who came around our house, or who Jacob and Jared played with when we went places, couldn't engage in creative and imaginative play; they had to have toys, television, Nintendo, or a fight to keep them entertained.

Jared had his problems at times; so sure others wanted nothing more than to cheat him. If he wasn't doing well at all, he would go off and play in a dark corner someplace by himself.

One thing that helped a lot was to keep the boys on a certain sleep-wake cycle. Then they functioned better during the day and life was a little easier. In bed by 10:00 and up at 8:30 whether they were ready to get up or not was the best. They would wake in excellent moods if I let them sleep until they were ready to get up, but sometimes that would be at noon and then they wouldn't go to sleep at a reasonable hour at night. I tried doing things their way - letting them go to bed and get up when they pleased - but after a couple of days, and no matter how much sleep they had, they would be incredibly crabby, fussy, and resistive to having to do even the simplest of tasks.

We started talking about the effects of alcohol on the developing baby's brain at our house that summer. Jared was severely fetal alcohol effected. It was real. To ignore it, lie, or deny, would surely be crazy making. Jacob was effected too; I'd known it all along. So one day I had he and Jared sit down beside me on the couch and I told them nicely that Julie drank too much when she was pregnant with them because she didn't know she shouldn't. I explained that their memory problems, attention problems, and sensory integration problems probably had a lot to do with the fetal alcohol.

Jacob took it hard and voiced his indignation. "Well Julie should have gone to the library and gotten a book about it!" he shouted. I agreed with him. I had never put Julie down in front of Jacob and Jared but I wasn't about to defend her either. I felt bad about telling Jacob, he wasn't ready for it. And then when the opening lines of a movie were, Hey man, what's with you? *Did your mama drink beer when she was pregnant?*, I felt really bad.

My telling Jared on the other hand felt absolutely right. He let out a big sigh of obvious relief and said, "So that's why I can't think straight!" much to my surprise. This was the wonderful thing about Jared, he kept expressing himself, providing insight into who he was and how he viewed the world. He was a cutie really and the way he saw things was quite unique.

Jacob didn't want Jared and I to talk about "IT" — the fetal alcohol — he said. Whenever we did, he would leave the room. I refused to stop talking about it though, his brother needed support even if he didn't. People didn't like Jared and it wasn't entirely his fault.

One day, Jacob stood as if frozen when I explained to a friend of his that Jared was fetal alcohol effected. His friend had been over all afternoon to play. The three of them, he, Jacob, and Jared had gotten along quite well all things considered. Then something happened and Jacob's friend became agitated with Jared, calling him names and hitting him. Jared was crying. From the information I gathered from their individual reports, it sounded like Jared got confused and the other child misinterpreted his intentions. So I explained to him that Jared had difficulty understanding things sometimes because he was fetal alcohol effected; that he wasn't intentionally being mean. Then I explained what fetal alcohol meant in very simple terms. When I was finished, the child took Jared's hand to shake it and then he apologized for calling him names. The exchange was warm and caring, innocent and non-judgmental, free of malice or blame.

Then in a jovial tone, the child said something to Jared that I would have never anticipated. "So that's why it seems like you're drunk all the time!" Jared smiled big, as if somebody had told him he was a genius or something. Jacob hung his head in shame and fixed his eyes on the floor. I just stood there, not able to say anything for a moment. It was all so painful. The child's words were incredibly descriptive. Jared's poor lip closure, the drooling, the spitting when he talked when excited, the biting of the sides of his mouth when he ate, the weak hand grasp, the way he seemed to touch things surfacely without force or intent, and of course the scattered thinking, did in fact seem like someone in a haze or a fog; someone drunk. Poor Jacob, I didn't know what to say to console him. Neither he or I wanted to hear the truth put to us that way.

Other than stirring up emotions, the fetal alcohol label really didn't change my perceptions nor my decided upon course of action for Jared's mental health care. I was learning to reframe, tolerate, and accept, and my efforts at brain rehabilitation were effective too — Jared did better when he was kept engaged and moving. A proper school was our greatest need now and the real cornerstone, I felt, to what life had in store for Jared. It was essential he have some sort of success academically otherwise he would never go to school willingly. And he had to go to school. It was his developmental work or occupation, just as a job is the developmental work of a man. There are alternative schools operated by the mental health system for children with emotional problems, but I didn't want Jared in one of them because of what he might see in terms of inappropriate behaviors. Plus, I knew education in such a setting is not the focus.

It's unfortunate, but the mental health system for children, in general, doesn't see education for troubled kids as important as the psycho-therapy and socialization process. In most psychiatric hospitals and residential treatment centers only a couple of hours a day are allotted for school and classroom time. The remaining hours are spent talking, processing conflict, or working in social skills groups, for example. And interestingly enough, there have been reports that as high as 50% to 70% of the children who engage in juvenile delinquency and criminal activity have learning disabilities.

I didn't know if Jared was considered behind academically in school already or not. He was writing but it wasn't completely legible and I knew for certain he couldn't recognize his name in print; he couldn't remember his birthdate either. The paperwork for continued special services from the public school system had already been finalized. Jared was to be evaluated at some point during the upcoming school year to determine what else he might need. If the Autism label wouldn't work to meet his needs, the label severely emotionally disturbed would be considered.

A label like that could destroy Jared. I had recently learned what is said about the children labeled severely emotionally disturbed in the public school system — "The SED kids: they're sad, mad, bad, and can't add" — "They can't learn." I knew Jared well enough by now to know that if he was perceived as bad, he could be very bad. I wasn't going to allow that label to be placed on him. I would not accept that he couldn't learn either. But he had to be someplace where he wouldn't be left to stay under a desk, where the effort was concentrated, the services less fragmented, and the social stigma not allowed to follow him.

I had no idea where to go to get help for Jared, or even what he needed, really, in terms of how to teach him. All I had to go on was what the folks at the Learning Clinic had said — that he needed a multi-sensory approach to learning with visual cues. Obviously, just the counting with blocks wasn't enough. When the boys attended the social skills group for children with attention deficit, I met a parent whose adoptive children attended a private school for learning disabled children, something I didn't even know existed until I talked with her. She said the public school couldn't teach her children how to read but that the private school did in one year. The pre-adoption class trainers were always saying the agency looked for people who are resourceful to be adoptive parents and now I knew why. So I called the private school and scheduled a visit.

It was a small school in the suburbs that used the Orton-Slingerland method for dyslexic children — a true multi-sensory approach that is used in Sweden and quite a lot in elite boarding schools in our country. Reading and writing were being taught using the eyes, the ears, the voice, the hands, and the whole body by having the child stand at the chalkboard to write and sound each letter out. The school was only one of two in the entire Portland Metropolitan area teaching learning disabled children with this approach. The average classroom size was seven, each child grouped according to ability. The main courses of reading and writing were offered in the mornings with the child moving throughout the afternoon to other classrooms for math, science, art and music. Time concepts, telephone use, handling money, and using a calendar were at the core of the curriculum. Tickets and stickers were provided for completed assignments, earnest efforts, and appropriate behaviors. Everything was highly structured and the day's activity schedule provided in picture form.

After evaluation and a lengthy discussion with the school administrator, Jared was accepted. I did not tell her Jared was labeled emotionally disturbed. With 80 miles in transportation daily and tuition, the costs would exceed the adoption subsidy. Evidently, the public school system here in Portland, will fund an alternative school for a child, sometimes as much as $60,000 a year which includes the cost of transportation, as long as it is not religious. But this school had a bible study class every third week so it didn't qualify. It was a good thing we had the adoption subsidy. Also, for a parent to get the public school system to fund an alternative school a lot of effort is required to find out who to talk to, documentation — proof that the public school is not able to teach the child — which typically equates to years of failure, and then a lawyer sometimes. Jared couldn't afford anymore failure and I didn't have the energy to fight the system and him, too.

I was extremely anxious while Jared was being tested. Given

his resistance in general, low tolerance to frustration, and negative attitude toward school, I didn't know how he would do. I talked with him before hand and lectured and lectured about how important it was that he try real hard to do his very best on the evaluation and not whine or complain.

He whined and shut down a few times during testing when frustrated and he was a little resistive the administrator reported to me afterwards but he made it. The administrator felt confident he could learn. Her only concern was the behaviors. "I hope we can turn these behaviors around in a reasonable amount of time otherwise I won't be able to keep him." I appreciated her straight forward communication style. Then she laid out the rules. "I need you with me! Whatever behavior it is we are working on here at school, you must work on it at home as well. I need your word that you will follow through on this. Also, there will be homework. This will not be easy on you but we'll start out slow and increase as we go. The assignments will be clearly outlined. Go by the outline, not by what Jared tells you. He'll try to rally your sympathy and probably tell you we are not nice to him here." *Now how did she know Jared so well already? I thought to myself.* I gave her my word that I would follow through. Then I took in a deep breath and wondered to myself if Jared and I were actually going to be able to pull this one off.

I met who was to be Jared's homeroom teacher, Mrs. Pettit. She was a tall woman with the most beautiful eyes I had ever seen and a presence that was stately and refined. Like Mr. Miller, she was confident and sure of herself; she said working with learning disabled children was her calling. Jared would be with her in the mornings for reading and writing. She also had responsibility for teaching him the school skills: getting his notebook out, putting his bag away, hanging up his coat, standing in line without touching others, raising his hand when needing help, saying please and thank-you. "They're the little things that help to make life harmonious for everybody," she said.

The first weeks of school were agonizing for all of us. Jared hated the demands being put on him. Several times he yelled at me for sending him to a "school like that." Mrs. Pettit used her "teacher apple notes" to give him verbal feedback on his behaviors. Her words were positive, and the notes were always signed, Love, Mrs. Pettit, but I could tell she was having a difficult time. Then she called me one day. As soon as I heard her voice my heart sank; it would be bad news. "Jared yells at school", she reported first, "and he said a bad word today." Then the conversation circled around to "Jared seems very impressionable to what he sees and hears. It must be hard for you when your husband is at work."

There it was — our dirty laundry — with me as the culprit. Of course Jared learned the yelling from me and the word shit too. I became extremely anxious and thought I was going to start crying. I didn't know where to go next to try to get help for him. Then suddenly, something happened inside of me. That bad mom tape always playing inside my head clicked off and a good mom message came on: *You're a good mom. You work hard, you're doing the best you can, and you love that child.* I was doing the best I could. I shared this thought with Mrs. Pettit. I came off as defensive, even angry perhaps, but I wasn't angry. I was just so frustrated and desperate. I had already shared with Mrs. Pettit the fact that Jared had been exposed to alcohol while in utero. I didn't share with her his early history for fear it would become the infamous black cloak that it was, but I thought I better do it now. Jared probably wasn't going to make it at that school anyway, I had concluded.

Student: Jared
Subject: Writing Class
Date: Sept. 7, 1993

Thank you for looking and listening carefully as I gave instructions this morning. It is important to pay attention so you

Teacher: will know how to do your work correctly.
Love, Mrs. Pettit

Student: Jared
Subject: Writing
Date: Sept. 9, 1993

You really kept your pencil moving today. It really helps the whole class to be able to cover all that I have planned when you listen and obey the 1st time. Jared, you must feel so ☺ when you do such

Teacher: good work. I love your neat letters. ♡ Mrs. Pettit

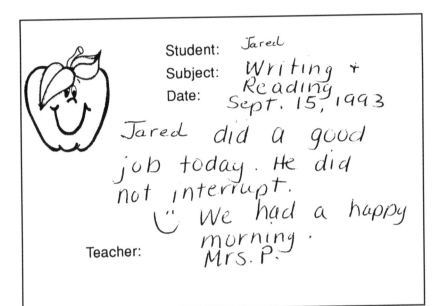

Student: Jared
Subject: Writing + Reading
Date: Sept. 15, 1993

Jared did a good job today. He did not interrupt. We had a happy morning.
Mrs. P.

Teacher:

We talked for a long time. Mrs. Pettit interrupted me for clarification now and then, occasionally she interjected a thought or an idea, but mostly she just listened. She was concerned for Jared. I could hear the compassion in her voice. I also told her that when stressed I had a habit of yelling. Then she said something that words alone could never express what it meant to me. "I think you are a good mom, too. Now, I want you to get yourself a cup of tea, put your feet up, and relax. I have your child during the day and we're just getting started."

Mrs. Pettit put Jared on a tally system right away. Evidently he was difficult from the moment he walked into her classroom in the mornings starting with putting his things away and making ready for the day. He wouldn't put his book bag where it belonged, instead, he would throw it at her feet. He wouldn't get his notebook, hang his coat, or take off his hat. These were just a few of the unwanted behaviors needing to be changed —

9-14-93
Whew! Mrs. Pettit had a hard day and she is tired. She had to give Jared many reminders to form letters in the r, to write on

his papers, to stop making noises, to put his pencil away, and to not talk loud during reading groups. Mrs. Pettit was not able to teach all of the juicy information she had planned,

Jared, I want Wednesday to be wonderful!
♡

Student: Jared
Subject: **Writing**
Date: Oct. 14, 1993
Thank you for getting
started right away on
your letters today. The
lesson goes well when you
do your part and work
hard the whole time.
Teacher: Mrs. Pettit
OOOXXX

the entire list was long. So Mrs. Pettit and I picked just six to work on first. She was a pragmatic woman. Each time Jared followed a rule and responded appropriately he earned a tally. He could receive up to six tallies in a day, each tally worth ten cents, payable as soon as he got home. I was also getting him to school a half-an-hour earlier, as per Mrs. Pettit's request, in order to help with the transition. She asked that I pursue follow-up with the doctor and get Jared on medication right away, too.

I was already trying to reach the doctor for the medication but she wouldn't return my call. I had gone back to work again three days a week. I needed to do this for myself. It took my mind off of all the problems and acted as a thread to humanity. Because I was out in the field all day, I wasn't able to call the doctor during her office hours. Instead, I left messages on her answering machine. After four messages, I asked our Family Support worker if she would call the doctor for me even though we weren't on her caseload anymore. I was able to call her because she was a friend of mine. Her son had a learning disability, too; he still didn't know how to read going into the fifth grade. She and her husband couldn't afford private schooling or even private tutoring for him though because they had three other children too. And the school system wouldn't pay for it because her son was thought to have "emotional and behavior" problems rather than a learning problem. "He's not learning because of his attitude," the professionals had said.

Finally, the doctor called. Then Mrs. Pettit talked with her and it was decided for certain Jared couldn't pay attention well enough to learn without medication. But the doctor was still slow to act — we were going into the month of November. It was Mrs. Petit who told me what to do at this point. "You call that doctor's office and you say loud and clearly into the message machine: *You promised you would help us and now we need your HELP!* "

I did just that and Jared was placed on the stimulant Dexedrine right away. His resistive behaviors and much of the arguing ceased immediately, profoundly, astonishingly! It was amazing. I didn't even stop to think about the long term effects or the negative side effects such a drug would have on him — there wasn't time. With the help of medication he was being given a chance finally. A chance to work at something; to use his brain; to at least try. I was being given a chance too, now that the burden of resistance was lifted from my shoulders. A chance to pretend I had a child who wanted to please me; a chance at a loving relationship with him; a chance to build something decent perhaps. The calmness that settled over the house, filling the air with harmony, brought comfort to my soul and with it the promise of peace waiting for me just around the

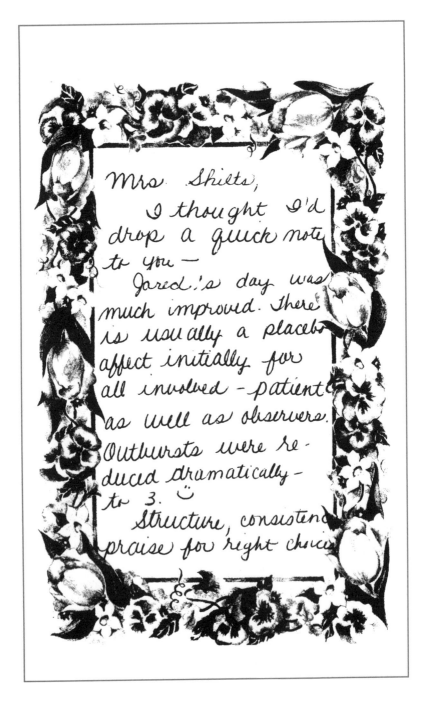

Mrs. Shilts,

I thought I'd drop a quick note to you —

Jared's day was much improved. There is usually a placebo affect initially for all involved - patient as well as observers. Outbursts were reduced dramatically - to 3. ☺

Structure, consistent praise for right choice

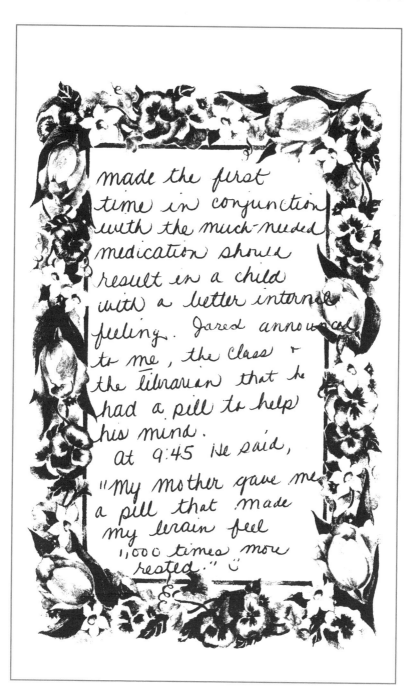

made the first
time in conjunction
with the much-needed
medication should
result in a child
with a better internal
feeling. Jared announced
to me, the class &
the librarian that he
had a pill to help
his mind.
At 9:45 He said,
"My mother gave me
a pill that made
my brain feel
1,000 times more
rested." ☺

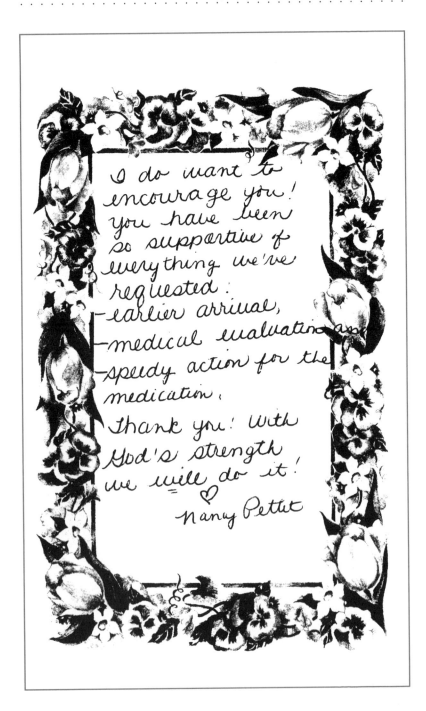

I do want to
encourage you!
you have been
so supportive of
everything we've
requested:
—earlier arrival,
—medical evaluation an
—speedy action for the
medication.
Thank you! With
God's strength
we will do it!
Nancy Pettit

corner.

With medication Jared's school performance improved. His teacher apple notes were saying such things as, "For a little boy, you do BIG work!" — "You worked so hard today" — "I love you." Jared was so proud of himself. He loved the word BIG, too. Mrs. Pettit was grateful for the medication. She and I talked weekly over the phone; we had an excellent working relationship going. I wrote her notes regularly inquiring about Jared's behaviors and what I could do to help. I let her know in every way I could that she was valued and greatly appreciated.

Jared was writing and reading the Bob Books by December. The dark cloud that had hovered over him those first months of the school year finally lifted. He loved going to school now. Then something amazing happened. Our Jared showed a passion

Student: Jared
Subject: Writing
Date: Nov. 18, 1993

For a little boy, you do BIG work! Your word blending and writing is good. You are capable. You have been teachable, too when you allow me to show you how to do things. I ♡ you. Mrs. P.

Teacher:

Student: Jared
Subject: Cooperation
Date: Nov. 19, 1993

BIG DEAL Alert!!

Make a big deal of Jared's cooperation: he stopped listening to the earphones and moved on to the next group (ON TIME) today! He is capable.
teacher:
Yay! "wow!!"
Love,
Mrs. P.

for learning. By his own initiative, he would sit down to write; always so serious in his demeanor. The amount of interest he was taking in learning and applying himself was incredible. When he drew beautiful animal pictures free hand from a book, I was astounded. It was as if something inside of him had magically been unlocked. He even expressed this himself in his own unique way — "You know Mom, every time I learn something it is like the wall in my brain gets torn down one brick at a time."

Then the "love" notes to me started coming in — "Mom you are the vairee Best MOM in the werld" — and I cried. Our Jared was capable, he loved learning, and he was developing more than I ever thought possible.

When at the Christmas play, seeing Jared on stage with his classmates, I sat tall. My heart swelled with pride and new understanding. Jared didn't look any different than anybody else. He had dignity standing there with his peers — those with learning difficulties too. When he spontaneously started playing an imaginary flute and I looked around and saw the pleasure this innocent act brought to the adults in the audience, I was filled with thanksgiving. There was something special in the air and Jared's light was shining through finally.

Jared adored Mrs. Pettit. It wasn't just the teacher apple notes that won her way into his heart — she had a very special way with him — he didn't want to displease Mrs. Pettit. I think it was the first time in his life Jared ever wanted to please anybody. I was not envious of Mrs. Pettit, what she did for him I could have never done. Then Jared started buying her little presents with his allowance, refrigerator magnets saying such things as: *#1 Teacher, Teachers make all the difference*, earrings, and stuffed animals. His note cards would say *To Mrs. P, Love, Jared*.

Student: Mrs. Shilts-
Subject: Kindness
Date: Nov. 18, 1993

Thank you for your encouragement and notes of affirmation. Be of good cheer — Jared is a sweet, loving and kind boy — like
Teacher: his mom. ☺

Mrs P.
о оо xxx

Jared 12/93

When Mrs. Pettit said to me one day "He's soooo tender hearted," I let my breath out completely. To myself I thought: I *hope so.*

He was just as oppositional with me as ever in the mornings until the medication took effect — which wasn't until he arrived at school. Waking him was still one of my biggest problem. I couldn't say, Jared it's time to get up, and expect him to come to standing on his own. I had to physically bring him to his feet and if I turned my back, he'd lay back down and go to sleep. Once I had him standing I then had to tell him what to do. He wouldn't move or he'd stumble around if he did, and I would get irritated with him. I would keep at him to hurry up and he would argue. Too many times I would end up yelling at him. It was a terrible thing yelling at the start of a day. It couldn't have been fun for Jared either.

Even more depressing was the fact that after three years, a very tight schedule, pictures of what to do posted around the house, and things always the same, Jared still couldn't do his self-care type activities unless I reminded him and then supervised accordingly. He was still fussy about his clothes, having his hair combed, and getting his face washed. His teeth were yellow now because he wouldn't brush them. Now when I said it was time again for a hair cut he'd say things like, "No, I think I'd rather have long hair," as if he suddenly felt the need to make a fashion statement. He still whined all the time at home and often at school. He had taken on some funny little ideas by now too. He wouldn't sit on the upstairs toilet seat because "I'll fall in," he said. He liked to cinch his belt real tight. In fact, so tight that he went through two imitation leather ones in a period of six months. And he wouldn't wear anything but his hiking boots — "They make my feet feel heavy, Mom."

I began taking Jacob in for therapy just after Christmas. As soon as Jared started having academic success, Jacob became

MoM one of my presents to you is Love!!!

MoM you are the vairee Best MoM in the werld

extremely argumentative and suddenly stopped being so dang neat and tidy. We couldn't ask Jared any questions now to see what he knew without Jacob jumping in and providing the answer, even simple questions like those he was answering when in Kindergarten. The little stinker. Joe was right — he did like showing-up Jared. Though surprised, I was glad for Jacob that he too was facing change. He didn't have to be the "perfect child." It was sad too in a very human way, this unveiling of Jacob's real work at hand. He was Jared's "victim" so it seemed, enslaved to the caretaker role and helpless to reject him, but Jared was also his unbeatable rival, so-to-speak, he couldn't defeat him without defeating himself too. This is when I realized just how essential Jared was to Jacob's well being. Finally for the first time, I knew I did the right thing to keep them together. It was hard to know if I was ever doing anything right, so this discovery gave my hopes a big boost. Jacob evidently thought I was doing pretty good because one day he said, "You know, I think it takes a special parent to parent a kid like me."

Against Joe's wishes, I put Jacob on medication too. This caused hard feelings between Joe and I but I had to do what I had to do. He was home for five months out of a year, I was home for twelve. Twelve months, 365 days, twenty-four hour days, day in, day out. I was tired of having to redirect constantly. Plus Jacob was struggling to keep up in school — his learning problems were finally showing themselves.

In February, we transferred Jacob to Jared's school. We had to. Mr. Miller moved on and the new teacher couldn't control the children. The class was noisy and chaotic, wrecking havoc with Jacob's hypersensitivity to sound. It was a sad day for us when we learned of Mr. Miller's departure. He had been the caretaker of Jacob's soul, his "inner being," for two years. Jacob came to him angry — and rightfully so — he had a lot to be angry about, but Mr. Miller, through patience, "firm but gentle guidance," nurturance, and tolerance, willingly reached out and helped to redirect the anger and in turn, shape Jacob's broader social consciousness. Jacob came to admire him. I think he instilled in him a silent respect for authority figures, too.

It was another intense winter. Jacob was nine and Jared had just turned eight. The homework and the fostering of real study habits in Jared was grueling work. Each child had to read to Joe or I four nights a week for twenty minutes. Jared was progressing in his reading, but each new level was demanding and required a lot of concentration on his part. Nobody could talk when he read and the house had to be made quiet of all extraneous noise.

The boys had to give speeches, too, which was the most difficult of all. Over a course of two weeks, they had to write two minute speeches, memorize them, and present them in front of their peers. I didn't think such a task was possible with Jared. And I don't know which step was more stressful — the writing or the memorization. My job was to find the information in the encyclopedia for him. His job was to copy it. It was agonizing for him. He wanted his writing to be perfect according to the way the words looked in print or he'd cry and have to erase. When he memorized, he couldn't make a mistake, the dog couldn't bark, and Jacob couldn't ask me a question without him having to start the speech all over again. But he was successful. Repetition was the key — over and over again — that and taking only little pieces of the project one at a time. I utilized the long drive to school to work on the memorization too which helped a lot. In March Jared wrote his first "story" — Mi dog and I will go to the moon! — all by himself.

Mi dog and I will go to the moon!
won day
we will take pichrs uf the moon
we will go
in a sadlitel
we will go on the!
moon won day
We will see hoa far
a way the moon
is the end

Jared 3/94

It was all I could do to manage and keep the school happy as well as the boys. In addition to the school work, Jacob's individual therapy, piano lessons, and Weeblos, there were singing lessons for Jared to advance to piano lessons eventually, and Tiger Cubs. Whenever I could, I scheduled all afternoon activities for directly after school. With exception to award nights for Weeblos and Tiger Cubs, we never went out in the evenings. I kept our schedule very tight. Up at 6:15, I took care of myself first then took care of Jared. Fortunately Jacob could take care of himself as long as I reminded him to stay on task. Breakfast was at 7:20. It had to be supervised always otherwise the boys would chatter. Then it was an allotted five minutes in the bathroom for grooming. Supervision was mandatory there too because if in the bathroom alone or together, they always found something else to do. We were out the door at 7:40 in order to arrive at the school by 8:10. At 2:30 it was round-up time. School dismissal was at 3:10. After therapy or activities we were home by 5:00. While I fixed dinner I would have Jared do his school work and read. It had to be this way. If I waited until after dinner there would be a lot of crying, whining, and arguing because he was just too tired to apply himself. What was really interesting, though, was the way Jacob and Jared both would come alive at 11:00 at night on a weekend. They could read, write, do math, focus on mundane tasks, and follow directions without missing a beat at midnight.

I stopped fighting the time it took for the boys to eat dinner. Their own time frame was at least an hour. They would eat a little bit and then chatter, eat a little bit and then chatter; never finishing everything on the plate. Jared was a terribly messy eater. Food would end up on his nose or drip down his chin annoying the heck out of me and making my chin itch, but it

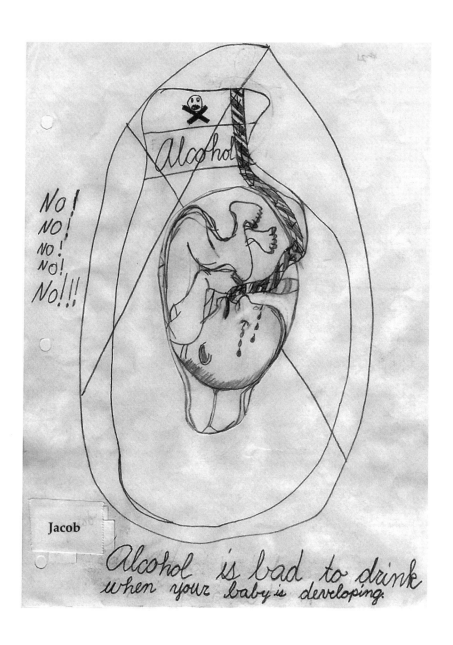

didn't bother him - he was totally oblivious. Jacob had his own style of eating too. He would take a bite, chew on it for a while, then pocket it in his cheeks. Then he'd take another bite and chew and pocket. There was no swallowing. He'd bite, chew, and pocket until his cheeks were so full he'd look like a chipmunk. Then he would take a swig of juice and wash it all down in one big gulp. I had no idea what the advantage was to this style of consumption. They had these little fixations about what they would eat too. For over a year it was peanut butter and honey sandwiches and cut up apples in their lunches. They didn't like surprises. If I put something different in their lunches, or did something differently, they could become quite bewildered. One day I forgot to cut up their apples and they ran to Mrs. Pettit for help. "Mrs. Pettit, Mrs. Pettit," they said, looking forlorn, she told me later, "our mom didn't cut up our apples today." Sameness meant sanity at our house; and I was their rock.

While the boys chattered and ate, I would make lunches for the next day; clean up the kitchen; talk on the telephone. It was a way of life really: the need to pay attention to the boys' likes and dislikes; the constant problem solving and strategizing in order to avoid conflict; the never ending search for positive ways in which to get them to do things; the constant pursuit of trying to keep them connected and be patient too. After dinner I would help Jacob with his piano lesson and homework while Jared played. It was a juggling act trying to take care of each child adequately. Sometimes the only way I could make it feel even was when I rough-housed played with both at the same time. Then it was bedtime and story. It was becoming harder and harder for Jacob to go to sleep at a reasonable hour, so following stories, I would let him read in his bed for a while in order to relax.

In order to balance out the rigid weekday schedule, I made sure the boys had a lot of free play time — down time I called it — on the weekends. They liked this very much. And since I couldn't go any place, I worked on this book. But first I would have the boys pick up their rooms and help me around the house for a little while on both Saturday and Sunday mornings. The reason for this type of activity was two fold: Firstly, if Jared moved his body and engaged his brain first thing in the morning for a few hours, he was better able to get along with others throughout the day. Secondly, Mrs. Pettit had advised: "Don't ever let Jared's room get too messy or he'll be overwhelmed and you'll have a fight on your hands trying to get him to straighten it." She was right.

In the quiet of the night, working on a quilt for Jacob by now, I thought about our Jared. He was on his way finally and hope was no longer an elusive quest — here today, gone tomorrow. My Creator sent us Mrs. Pettit because without her we would have never made it. The future was filled with promise now. But we weren't out of the woods yet. Jared needed time for the seeds of a purposeful life to take root and we were on soft ground; anything could happen. I worried about the school calling; about getting to the drugstore on time so we would never run out of medication; about how I was going to go to a mandatory school meeting and get the homework done and Jared to bed on time, too, when Joe was gone; about how I was going to keep Jared from crawling into his little shell; or about how I was going to get people to be nice to him.

Then I was informed Congress wanted to cut adoption subsidies to adoptive families. Evidently, a small group of parents and professionals worked for five years to get Congress to fund adoption subsidies in the first place; they were very much needed given the needs of the children and no resources available. Since then, the fight has been to keep those funds from being cut because whenever money for children is put on the chopping block, the adoption subsidies are questioned. Joe and I couldn't afford to keep Jared or Jacob in the school, or the various activities, if we didn't have their subsidy money. All of it had always gone to their care. I struggled to keep feelings of bitterness out of my heart. I wrote a letter to my government regarding the adoption subsidy, in the hopes someone would see Joe and I weren't stealing or squandering the tax payer's dollar. I sent the letter but I was left with the worry; Jacob and Jared's subsidies were at the mercy of their fellow men. Then the school did call.

Shortly after his stream of successes, Jared received his first Classroom Warning from Mrs. Pettit for being "stubborn." He was gloomy and tearful for having upset her. He didn't like having a mark on his school record, either. I guess I should have been pleased that he was remorseful over this; remorse is indication of a conscience. Except there was one thing missing. A conscience is the distinction between right and wrong coupled with a sense that one should act accordingly. Jared didn't get it. After the warning he kept at it. "Grumpy," "Jared needs reminders to stop on time," "He keeps the rest of the class from being ready," the apple notes were reading, and almost two weeks had passed since the warning. That was Jared. Once "in a mood," he could dig himself a hole. To combat those moods at home, I worked him. With me by his side, he had to do little jobs: carrying things, sorting clothes, picking up the yard, stacking wood, etc. Joe was so irritated with him one day that he taught him

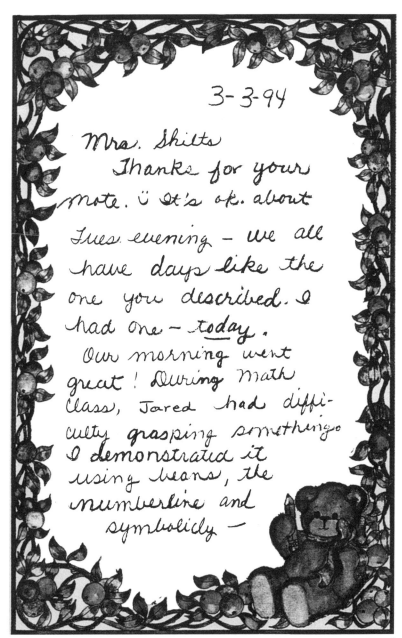

3-3-94

Mrs. Shilts
    Thanks for your
note. ü It's ok. about
Tues. evening — we all
have days like the
one you described. I
had one — <u>today</u>.
Our morning went
great! During math
class, Jared had diffi-
culty grasping somethings
I demonstrated it
using beans, the
numberline and
    symbolicly —

continued

Then, Jared, became Stubborn (note the bold capital S!) He was not cooperative at all. His peers and I were not pleased (and we voiced our displeasure). Therefore, NO math ticket and thus, THE WARNING! Reason — Jared would not say "5" (the answer) audibly — when he did actually voice "5" it was so muffled that human (perhaps Divine) ears could not possibly discern the answer.

Please sign The Warning + return tomorrow. — Sorry. Great Morning! Yucky Math, Great afternoon.   ♡ mrs. P.

how to clean the bathroom from top to bottom. With enough activity, Jared would eventually come out of those moods. That is how it happened at school, too. He eventually crawled out of his "hole" and he and Mrs. Pettit were back on working ground. She was a special lady, "Mrs. P;" she never held any of it against him.

I continued to process with Jared all the time, too. I couldn't tell you how many times we were late going places because I would drop everything and process a behavior or conflict. Most of the time I didn't know why I bothered, it was like talking to a wall. But every once in a while Jared would surprise me and

say things that made me feel the talks were actually getting through; that he was seeing himself in the equation. One day when I asked him how his school day went he said — "Remember how grumpy I was this morning?" — Yes, I responded — "Well, I didn't get any tickets or coupons today."

That spring I got out the puzzles, cards, and games. The boys and I did a little learning activity frequently. I didn't have the patience to work with Jared daily but I was good at making suggestions, putting things in his path, or utilizing the drive to school to work on counting, categorizing, and memorizing. Teaching him the rules to games was not easy. Jacob and I had to wait for him to make his decisions and we couldn't talk when he was thinking. Sometimes he'd change the rules of the game to benefit himself and of course there was no way to reason with him. "You guys are cheating!" he'd wail or "You just want Jacob to win!" But being able to have a family game of UNO or Rummy finally even amidst Jared's crying and whining, made me feel like we were starting to resemble "normal" people finally. Jared was building Lego constructions. They weren't elaborate but they were sturdy and complete. On holidays and teacher conference days, I kept him moving. We went to the children's museum, the library, the museum of science and industry and arts and crafts festivals.

Then we started soccer. Jacob was on one team, Jared on another. Jared was actually very athletic by now and he loved sports. I had to be right there with him though. His emotional outbursts, whining and pouting often got him into trouble with the coaches and time out on the sidelines. Because he was aggressive, he was often ostracized by team mates. For a long time I thought he understood the rules and just wanted his way. Then one day he was sent to the sidelines when I wasn't watching so

I didn't know what happened. I asked him about it when we got home but he wouldn't tell me and became tearful. "You'll just think I'm bad if I tell you," he said. This made me feel terrible. I said I wouldn't think him bad, but he still wouldn't tell me. It was most frustrating. Finally he said, "I don't know what happened!" So I drew a picture of the playing field and asked him to show me where to put stick figures to represent himself and the other players. To my surprise his visual memory was excellent.

Once we had the figures placed accordingly, I then asked him to point and show me what happened. "Well you see, I was over here and I got the ball. Coach wanted me to pass it to this kid. I didn't want to. I had it and I could have scored." This is when I knew: Jared didn't know it was a practice, he thought it was a game! I explained to him then that it was a practice and not a game and that the coach wanted the kids to learn how to pass to each other. Jared was genuinely surprised. "It was?" he asked. "Well I didn't know that!"

This little tiny piece of information was incredibly valuable to me and a reminder of Jared's learning style. I talked to all four coaches at the next practice and explained to them that Jared was learning disabled and attention deficit. It was amazing how things turned around and I didn't even have to tell anybody what to do. One of the coaches said, "So that's why he's impulsive" and to his fellow coaches, "He's going to need drawings you know guys!" The next thing I knew, the game strategies were being drawn out on the grass in the simplest form just for Jared. His eyes locked unto the index finger that was being used as a pencil and he listened intently to the instructions. Afterwards he looked up and said "Okay Coach!" Heroes were in our own community I discovered that day, and

Jared became a part of the team. Again, this is where therapeutic support from a Partners Project type model would have helped us immensely.

That summer it was basketball camp, swimming lessons, and nature study classes where Jared was allowed to touch things in addition to watching and listening in order to learn; it was the closest I could come to a multi-sensory approach. I stopped hovering so much and forced myself to let go. It wasn't easy; I constantly worried. Whenever I could enroll Jacob and Jared in activities together I did so that Jared would have emotional support.

I sent Jared to the basketball camp alone however, which was a mistake. It was the wrong kind of a camp too. There was too much noise, too many children, and not enough adults. When the instructor voiced his complaints regarding Jared's behaviors at the end of the first day, I explained the situation and offered some pointers. When he was still unhappy at the end of the second day, I gave up trying to offer working solutions, and begged him to let Jared stay the last three days. "If you feel the situation is intolerable I won't bring him tomorrow, but I sure would appreciate it if you would let him finish out the week." The instructor was a nice enough man — he let Jared finish out the week — but he didn't like him. It was a negative experience for Jared and I should have taken him out. The neck ribbing of his shirts were torn and soaked with saliva from him sucking and chewing on them throughout the day. Again, an aide at his side would have made this a more positive experience.

We hiked and we bicycled, went to the park, or played in our backyard that summer too. The neurorehabilitation of Jared's brain was working, slow but sure, and I was thinking more in the way of sensations for the brain than I ever had before. I let the boys dig holes, make mud pies, and build forts on the patio. Joe built a platform in our walnut tree and hung a swing, a trapeze bar and a rope to climb. Every kid who lived on the block came to our house to play in the backyard or in the playroom; some of them had sensory integration problems too. It was good socialization experience for Jared. Jacob became quite popular. "Gee Mom, if I'm popular in my neighborhood, maybe I'll be popular in life too," he said to me one day. On some days, the neighborhood kids went to the park or swimming with us. I still liked kids and it seemed like they liked minding my rules.

The communication between Jared and I was getting better. "Don't put your swimming trunks on now Jared. You can do that at the pool," I said one day in brisk and unbendable fashion.

"But I can't keep track of all my stuff when I do that Mom," he said. It made all the difference when Jared talked to me. When he didn't, I had no way of knowing if he just didn't hear me, if he was ignoring me, if he was being "stubborn," or if he just didn't care.

Jared was climbing all the time that summer. At the park he climbed trees while his brother and the other kids played in the sand. At first I'd panic when he got out of my sight and go looking to see if he was on the other side of buildings. Pretty soon I knew to look in the foliage of trees. Sure enough, there he would be, crawling around having to keep himself balanced, or hanging from branches like a little monkey. When he started hanging from door frames and ceiling beams in the basement at home, I let him. He was building a frame for his house; getting to know his body. With exception to Joe, most people thought I was silly to believe in sensory integration, its process and the promise of adaptation for new learning. But Joe and I lived with Jared, we knew what we saw; there was a noticeable difference in his moods following whole body balancing type activities and a willingness to at least try to do things.

At the close of summer I was looking back on the year in wonderment. It had been a time of incredible emotional growth and learning for all of us. As a family, we had never functioned so well. We even went on a real vacation during spring break. That winter I found a respite provider which I think helped a lot. For one weekend a month, Friday afternoons through Sunday evenings, Jacob and Jared stayed away from home. It cost us a $100.00 but it was well worth it. On the weekends they were gone I got to sleep in and do whatever I wanted. I was much more patient with them when they came home and just knowing that in three weeks I was going to get some relief again, I was better able to cope with the pressures. It was amazing what money could buy.

The woman I found to provide the respite had been a foster mother at one time so I thought I would be getting experienced and knowledgeable help. She was very enthusiastic at first and promised to put Jared on a tally system if he needed it, keep other children from picking on him, and keep the television off. But it didn't work out that way — all the money in the world won't buy cooperation — and I was always having to hear about how bad Jared was when I picked him up. It was terrible listening to the negatives. I brought some of this on myself. In an attempt to get her to take Jared's needs seriously, I shared with her his past, but also some of my day to day frustrations. "It's all going to come back at you when he reaches adolescence," she said once when Jared was especially difficult, "You know that, don't you?" By summer she was burnt out and so was I, so we moved on.

I quit working altogether that summer in order to take care of Jared. I wouldn't be going back, either. It was all too much. I couldn't keep up with everything: a job, the house, the yard, the activities, the driving, the school work, and be patient with the boys too. While they were in school, I would get respite. I didn't mind giving up my job so much this time. It would be for only a short time, I thought, and Jacob and Jared weren't going to need me forever.

Chapter 8
The Connection

J ust when I was beginning to feel I had a handle on things — that sameness, understanding, firm but gentle guidance, purposeful activity, medication, behavior modification, the correct learning environment, whole body movement activities, and effective communication were the formula for Jared's care — the bottom fell out again.

It all began in the fall, when school started again. Joe and I always hated it when school started because it was so much work getting the boys going. Then there would be nine months of the tight schedule, the morning chaos with Jared, the resistance, the homework, the activities, and the constant pressure to stay on top of things because it was the only way to avoid conflict and still keep the boys engaged.

This year I wanted us to get off to a good start so I decided I wouldn't fuss with Jared about getting himself ready independently in the mornings. By now I was getting him up, asking him to make his bed and having him get dressed without supervision. He was almost nine, it seemed that having him make his bed was a reasonable expectation. The whole time I would call from the kitchen or check on him every few minutes. I always found him playing. Sometimes I would yell at him to get going. Once I started yelling he would slow down and I would yell some more. Then he would yell back. On really bad days it was verbal warfare. I didn't want us to live this way; I wanted to be supportive. So I decided I would make his bed for him in the mornings and then sit in the rocker and direct until he was completely dressed. This new approach worked very well for a while and served to alleviate that part of the morning stress.

Then one morning the alarm didn't go off and I got up late. I couldn't stay in Jared's room so I asked him to get himself ready while I went down to start breakfast. He came unglued and yelled at me "If you don't help me, I'll go back to being mean to you like I was before!" I was completely devastated, hurt, and discouraged. I had been manipulated. *Jared is a child without a conscience*, a little voice called out. *An unattached child. His heart is hard. He cannot feel empathy. Selfishness, deceit, greed, and his insatiable need for control are deeply embedded; there will be other victims someday.* Hopelessness overcame me again. After Jared left for school, I crawled back into bed to sleep my anxiety away.

Again, I wanted to give up. I had gone from one method to the next, thinking each would be the magic piece to the puzzle, but there wasn't one. Jared obviously couldn't be helped. He needed to be housed in an institution perhaps, away from society. But then I thought about the love he had for Mrs. Pettit. It was his idea to buy those refrigerator magnets for her, not mine. And when I looked back over the previous four years and where we had started from, I couldn't deny tremendous gains had been made. I couldn't give up yet, I had to keep trying. I just hadn't found the right parenting approach that's all, I decided. I had been too nice to him. I let him push me around.

All he had to do was cry and I'd come running. He still cried a lot and whined all of the time; that had never changed. I was going to have to be tougher. I wouldn't rough-house play with him anymore; it was too friendly. I was the adult, he was the child. He needed to be held accountable for his actions as it is done in the treatment centers. I was going to have to keep taking things from him.

So I went back at it headstrong and determined. When Jared was argumentative and bossy, I worked him. He washed wood-work, cleaned the bathroom, emptied the dishwasher, and sorted dirty laundry. I had to stay on him of course, directing and redirecting constantly. He wouldn't use both hands so I had to make him by placing them accordingly on given objects. He'd yell at me in resistance but I refused to give in. I got out the chips, the behavior charts, and the money jar. When he misbehaved I took his chips, his money, his bike, or his play time. After dinner it was homework and directly to bed. I still read to him but I refused to rock him in the rocker or cuddle with him. "Why do you think I'm so bad?" he wailed one day, but I let it roll off. He was deceiving me — trying to rally my sympathy for his own gains — the willful and malicious child.

I refused to help him in the mornings. He had to make his bed, get dressed, and report to the table at a certain time. I used a timer for this. If he didn't make it, he had to forgo breakfast — it was a natural and logical consequence. When he yelled about this, I put him out on the front porch to wait by himself until we were ready to go. If he didn't get his shoes on in time, he had to carry them and put them on in the car. He never made any of the time lines of course and mornings became nothing but shouting and yelling matches. He was pretty mean to me with his words, but I wasn't going to give in. I could be just as stubborn as he was. Then my friend who had moved to Mt. Shasta came to see us and stayed over night, I had not seen her or confided in her in over four years, and she was appalled with me. She never came to see me again either.

Weekends became especially difficult. I couldn't find enough things to keep Jared busy, so on really bad days I made him stay in his room so he wouldn't argue with me or cause problems for Jacob and his friends. He was always bugging Jacob. One morning when Jacob was sleeping Jared wanted him to get up. I asked him to leave Jacob alone, explaining that he needed to sleep a little longer. Jared said, "Maybe he does, maybe he doesn't. How do you know?" When I asked him how he would feel if Jacob woke him when he was tired he said, "I wouldn't mind," which I knew wasn't true. I always processed with him this mean and selfish attitude but it was like talking to a wall.

I processed every little conflict, but Jared simply couldn't see himself in the equation, everything was always somebody else's fault. He and I were always arguing. Stupid arguments, too. For example, one night he wet the bed. I didn't get upset about it but when I asked him to take the sheets off of the bed and take them to the laundry room, he refused to acknowledge that he had even wet it. We went back and forth about it for a while. At times like this I couldn't keep myself from yelling at him. It was so frustrating. Finally, he said "Okay, I wet it. But not all of it." It was crazy making. He couldn't be reasoned with either. One time he wanted to wear Jacob's coat. I told him that was fine but that if Jacob wanted to wear it, he would have first choice because Jared had four coats while Jacob had only two. "You're being a jerk!" he shouted at me, in between tears. When I tried to reason with him, he put his hands over his ears and walked off. We taped him arguing and blaming on a cassette tape but that didn't work. I had him do self-talk but that didn't work either.

It was all crazy making. One night Jared was afraid to go up to his room for a book because the hall light was burnt out. I suggested he run up and turn the bathroom light on as quickly as he could. His response was, "But there are only magazines in the bathroom." Another time he was pretending he was a dog and licked my legs. I went along with it for a while but then he wouldn't stop. The emotional outbursts were still with us, as was the moodiness. On really bad days, he crawled into his own world; staying under tables or hiding in his "cubby holes" around the house. He was still destroying his toys, tying things up, and resistive to wearing new or different clothes. Wherever he had been in the house he left a trail of something: food crumbs, peanut butter and jelly on the walls, snack wrappers, clothing, broken bits and pieces of toys, tree twigs, bark he had peeled from the twigs.

My new hard-line approach wasn't working though. I wasn't living in fear as I had before but I was frustrated all the time. The constant battle for control is what parenting an attachment disordered child is all about. What a hassle; it was too much work. And the more control I exerted, the more obstinate Jared became. I felt like anything but a nice person. When I looked in the mirror, I was ugly. When I looked around me, the world was ugly — a gray, broken, and fragmented body of nothingness.

I was yelling at Jacob. I was yelling at my dad. Then Joe and I started having problems. He didn't like what was going on between Jared and I. He thought I needed to "lighten up," "relax," "calm down." I couldn't relax. It was ridiculous, working so hard and not being able to succeed. No, there had to be something that worked, and I wasn't going to relax until I found it.

I started calling around looking for professionals who treated attachment disorders. I had to face it, I decided, Jared was an unattached child and character disturbed as well as severely fetal alcohol effected. He couldn't feel empathy toward others and apparently he wasn't going to. I couldn't teach him. I couldn't rehabilitate his brain.

I couldn't find a professional who treated attachment disorders, either, so I started reading information on emotionally disturbed children again. It was always so readily available. The parent group newsletters I got in the mail often focused on attachment disorders and emotional disturbances. In fact, since I had adopted Jacob and Jared, attachment disorder and emotionally disturbed was no longer reserved for children who had suffered as severely as they had — those labels were the norm now. If a child was adopted even at two months old, and he or she had problems, it was thought to be because of an attachment disorder.

So I started Jared in play therapy that fall in order to address the issue of grieving which is thought to be at the core of the problems and conflicts for the unattached child. It was the first time I had taken him in for individual therapy since his discharge from the day treatment program. Unfortunately, the therapist was young and knew nothing about fetal alcohol. I tried to educate him. I also spent forty-five minutes with his supervisor finally convincing her to read one of Jared's 23 evaluations rather than have him endure another psychological test. The psychological was for the records, a mandatory requirement after twelve weeks of therapy. The therapy backfired, though, as was evident when Jared started shouting at me, "That's not fair!" every time I asked him to do something. I don't think he knew I wasn't the one who had deprived him in his early years. To know that I wasn't, he would have to differentiate one situation from another and he didn't seem able to do that. He was very literal. Once I said, "Keep you eyes peeled," when we were looking for something, and he said, "I can't do that. It'll hurt!"

After that I hauled the boys and myself around for six more months for more of the traditional therapies. Jacob had individual psycho-therapy which he benefited from a lot, it seemed. He loved the individual attention he received from the therapist. But then one day he declared "If I keep having behaviors, I'll get to keep seeing my therapist," and I wanted to cry. *How long was all of this going to go on?* I asked myself. It was like swimming up stream and I was getting very, very tired working against the resistance.

We had family group therapy, which was frustrating because Jared couldn't understand what was being said; he was always one step behind and everybody in the group noticed it. Then I went to two parenting classes which utilized the natural and logical consequences approach. With exception to Jared's play therapy and Jacob's psycho-therapy, Joe and I paid for everything ourselves. When those techniques didn't work for Jared, I started seeing a psychologist on an individual basis because I thought there was something wrong with me. Some psychologists say people can't make us unhappy unless we let them. Mine kept asking me what I did to take care of myself. *What was I to do to take care of myself?* I wondered. There were no professional respite providers; no place to go; no escape. During one of our sessions, I asked my psychologist not to ask me anything, just tell me I had dignity.

Fortunately, Jared's school placement was stable. It was like the glue that held us together. It wasn't without problems though. Jared didn't have Mrs. Pettit that second year and the new teacher had different expectations. She wanted Jared to move faster and keep up with the group. She didn't like the way he fussed to bring his work to completion even though it was time to move on. She wanted to use some sort of a timer to get him to move on but I knew that wasn't going to work. When I used the timer with him at home, he'd wail, "No, no, not the timer!" through his tears. Then he would approach the task frantically yet blindly, as if the timer was some kind of man-eating shark, sure to attack as soon as it dinged. He would likely really fuss if forced to use a timer in front of his peers. The teacher wanted to find something that worked, though, and when I explained to her that Jared was severely fetal alcohol effected she wanted information about it. She was to be commended — she was the only person who had ever asked for specifics regarding fetal alcohol. It was because of her request that I discovered some very disconcerting and upsetting news.

I went to the university library to see what I could find on fetal alcohol. Hundreds of studies were listed documenting the damage alcohol does to the developing fetus and the behaviors associated with it, as well as the prognosis throughout the life span. I didn't want to learn what I learned. Jared was Fetal Alcohol Syndrome and not simply Fetal Alcohol Effected. His getting lost in the house, the "Well how do I do that?" question, the "there are only magazines in the bathroom" statement, where indicators of an information processing problem. The information went to his brain but then got lost someplace in route when it came to knowing what to do with it. This problem and the play without purpose, the wandering, the impulsivity, and the self-care problems where the group of signs and symptoms that together indicate Fetal Alcohol Syndrome.

People had tried to tell me Jared was Fetal Alcohol Syndrome but I wouldn't accept it. I didn't want to accept it now, either. How could I? Between it and fetal alcohol effects is a massive difference in disability and prognosis: The adolescent years for Fetal Alcohol Syndrome children are pretty bad: lying, stealing, criminal activity, lack of empathy, low motivation, depression, fourth grade level reading and third grade level math is about all they can do. The *maladaptive* behaviors present the greatest challenge for professionals to treat. Adulthood is even worse: depression, suicidal ideas, chronic mental illness. They need special training in order to obtain a job and someone to provide economic support and protection because they are socially and sexually exploited by others. Many become homeless.

I also discovered that at least 100,000 children in America have been born with Fetal Alcohol Syndrome in the last decade. And although there is not an exact number, it is believed that 500,000 children have been born with fetal alcohol effects in the same amount of time. While the children with Fetal Alcohol Syndrome may be identified, the children with fetal alcohol effects are typically not identified. Doctors are the only ones who can identify them but they are not doing it for several reasons: Confirmation of the mother drinking while pregnant is necessary to make a diagnosis but a lot of women don't want to say they drank for the obvious reasons. And even though the effects of exposure to alcohol in utero present with certain facial features, no two children will present the same. The features change as the child ages, too. There are other contradictions as well. For example, children with Fetal Alcohol Syndrome typically have a smaller than average head size, but Jared's head size was large. It's hard to be certain of identification. The key is in the behaviors — there are certain types of behaviors specific to organic brain damage. But evidently, even if the doctors are familiar with the behaviors associated with fetal alcohol and certain of a diagnoses, they are hesitant to label the child because they think nothing can be done to help him. Consequently, parents and caregivers are working without the proper tools, attempting to parent children they don't even understand, while the schools are expected to educate without the proper modalities, resources, funding, or support.

In a numb and almost catatonic state I went to the mall and did some shopping, then I went on home. I didn't get a chance to tell Joe what I had discovered because he became upset with me over the items I had purchased. For the first time ever, I bought Jacob and Jared completely different things. I bought Jacob some hiking boots and not Jared. It wasn't that I didn't want to buy Jared some boots, he needed them the most, it was just that there weren't any in his size on sale. I bought him something else instead. Joe thought I was showing favoritism. "That's not fair to Jared." But I didn't care anymore about being fair. And I didn't care about Jared's feelings. "You just have a bad attitude," Joe said and I suddenly felt incredibly lonely. He didn't understand. Nobody understood.

Then I did something that was totally out of character for me. I packed myself a bag of clothes and ran away from home. But before I left, I wrote out the boys' activities already scheduled to keep them structured up for spring break week and handed it to Joe. "Here, you maintain the structure for a while and then we'll see how your attitude is," I said.

I went to a friend's trailer in the country. There was no phone, no kids, no dog, no structure to maintain, no laundry, no meals to cook, no arguing, no resistance, no therapy sessions, and nobody telling me I had a "bad attitude." I slept through the first two days. In between sleep and awake, I did my grieving. Jared was Fetal Alcohol Syndrome. I just couldn't face it before. I kept telling myself that what ever had happened to his brain would be okay but it really wasn't. None of it was okay. He would never be whole and I couldn't fix him. His would be a wasted life. And if he were to leave home someday, it was up to Joe and I to find him some kind of a job that would work for him.

It was all so devastating. When I thought about another ten years with Jared and the work it would entail, I almost couldn't bear it. But, at the heart of all my despair was the empathy piece. It had been, and still was, above all else, the most important thing to me. There had been one disappointment after the other: Jared couldn't be an airplane pilot; he wouldn't go to college; he likely wouldn't obtain competitive job skills; it was all I could do to get him to wash his face and hands and brush his teeth; he had to go to a special school just to learn to read and write; he was born an alcoholic; he would sleep all day or lay on the couch and sleep if I let him. One dream after the other had slipped away. Begrudgingly, I had conceded. But to know I would raise a child who couldn't get along with other people, feel empathy, or likely ever know right from wrong, was too much for me. Jared suffered from organic brain damage — it couldn't be reversed — the missing piece would always be missing. I didn't know which was worse — a child without a conscience or a child without a heart, although it didn't seem like there was much difference between the two.

I slept through my despair for two more days. When I awoke, I felt a little better. Given Jared's early history, the Fetal Alcohol Syndrome and what I knew about it now, as well as the multiple homes he lived in, he wasn't supposed to be as functional as he was. He was reading and writing, and strong in math. Sometimes he felt pretty good about himself, it seemed. He wrote *My Life as a Boy* that winter. In reality, he was an anecdotal miracle and I had "saved" him. I guess it was a good thing I didn't know for certain he was Fetal Alcohol Syndrome, I might have lowered my expectations.

> My Life as a Boy
>
> I am a Inteagint Boy, I am in cunsiv, I am creativ, I am in times, I am special, I Love to ♥♥♥ drawing Birds and animals my brother Good at the peanoa and Good at ages. I am nine MY Brother is ten
>
> **Jared**

By the fifth day, I was ready to go on home. My thinking had cleared and my spirit was free from the negativity. I knew what I had to do. I would not send Jared away; that simply wasn't an option. I had made a commitment to him and I was going to see it through. When I took stock of things in a more positive light, I could see he was more stable than he had ever been. The school situation made a huge difference. Jared wasn't bad at school; he wasn't getting warnings; he was a hard worker. I wasn't the best parent for him, I knew that. One day when I was especially irritated with him, I said to Jacob that I thought I was the wrong parent for Jared. "I don't think he could be with anybody else, Mom," Jacob said so matter-of-factly. It was true. Not too many people would have put up with him. I couldn't separate Jacob and Jared, they loved each other dearly. And Joe loved Jared, they were buddies. In fact, Joe seemed able to understand and tolerate him better than I ever could.

Besides, there was no place where I could send Jared and have a clear conscience about it. The child welfare system was still the same except now there was a lot more kids and a lot more problems. Little children are being moved constantly. I heard about a little girl with Fetal Alcohol Syndrome being moved seven times in six months; Jared would never be able to handle change like that. Little toddlers born drug affected are being moved four to five times before age three; they are being separated from siblings, too. "Kiddy" prisons are now taking the place of residential treatment centers here in Oregon. No, for better or worse, Jared belonged with us. I would just have to parent him differently than people do with other children, I decided.

I wasn't going to live with the yelling and arguing, it had to stop. So I decided to parent him the way it is advocated for "unattached and character disturbed" children. It is believed that unattached children intentionally try to cause problems between a husband and wife. This is called "splitting" and it is a manipulation for control. It is advocated that a couple never show the child that they are in disagreement regarding discipline. It is also advocated that the "healthy" child in the home be empowered and the neurosis of the "disturbed" child acknowledged. So I made a plan and then called Joe.

Joe was happy to hear from me. "I'm sorry, Donna," he said, as soon as he heard my voice. "I've realized this last five days just how much work it is keeping the boys structured up. Jared has been so oppositional." I didn't tell him what I was thinking

over the phone. I needed to talk to him in person. So we agreed
to meet that evening at a motel half-way between home and the
country.

It was about 11:30 when Joe arrived at the motel while my
dad stayed home with the boys. He couldn't get away earlier
because Jacob had a Scout meeting to attend. We talked until
3:00 in the morning. I shared with him what I had learned, but
he refused to take a negative outlook on Jared's future. "We'll
look into a tree farm or a nursery business, something hands
on; don't worry about it for now." Joe was the best. And then
we made a pact. He would trust me on this new "parenting"
approach I was going to take, and he would stand by me no
matter what. The next morning we had a wonderful breakfast
at a cozy cafe and took a long walk holding hands before we
got into our separate cars to drive home. It was only the third
time since our honeymoon that we had been alone together.

When we got home I pulled out the hiking boots and presented them to Jacob. Jared started yelling at me, of course:
"Jacob gets everything because he's your favorite." Very calmly
I responded with, "Yes. He is. You've been telling me that for a
long time so it must be true." It felt terribly wrong to talk to him
like this. Then I told him I would buy him some hiking boots,
too, but that he had to earn them first by not yelling at me or his
father, by not blaming others, and by not interrupting people
when they talked. Tears swelled up in his eyes and he looked
over at Joe. Joe said quietly but supportively, "That is the way it
is Jared and your Mom and I think you can do it."

So we put up a behavior modification chart on the refrigerator and outlined the goals. I was so thankful Jared could read
by now. Within 30 days he had his new hiking boots. He never
accused me of favoritism again. The arguing and resistance

ceased. I wasn't comfortable with this approach but the emotional freedom I felt using it was incredible. For the first time ever, I didn't feel emotionally exhausted anymore. Jacob noticed the change in me. "I don't know what it is, but something is going on around here," he said one day.

When I shared this incident with my psychologist he said that type of a parenting technique was about setting boundaries, not parenting an "unattached child." He also said there is no such diagnosis as attachment disorder. So I looked it up in the psychiatric "bible" of mental disorders and he was right — there is no such diagnosis of attachment disorder. There is a diagnosis of reactive attachment disorder, which is thought to be the result of severe and pathological care, and considered uncommon.

I had always had my boundaries in order — saying no was one of my strong suits. In fact, some people called me a "no nonsense mom," as if that was terrible. I just didn't like the way I was always blamed by Jared. So just saying no wasn't the answer either. But I didn't really care anymore. Joe had hope but I had lost mine. I became very apathetic. There would never be joy in parenting Jared — only hard work, disappointment, shame, and sorrow. One day, I actually found myself thinking that if he was ran over by a car and killed, the world would be the better for it. Now when he whined and cried, I walked away, feeling nothing. When I found peanut butter and jelly marks on the walls, I said, "Oh, I see Jared has left me a present." He didn't do it again so I knew for certain he did it in the first place just to irritate me.

When Jared wouldn't go upstairs to his room one night because he feared "aliens" where there waiting for him, I insisted he go anyway, suspecting it was a manipulation. Jacob came to his rescue. "Mom, we watched a scary show on television at the slumber party last night," he informed me. The slumber party was Jared's first. I let him go to it in order to get him out of the house. I explained to the mother that I didn't want him to watch scary or violent movies. She said they were going to be playing games so I just assumed that meant the television would stay off, too. I let Jacob go upstairs with Jared that night, but it took a while to convince him our house was safe and that there were no aliens waiting to get him. One night he crawled around on all fours again, saying he was a gray wolf, and I experienced a pang of fear.

The piano lessons fell through. It was just too much work helping Jared practice and keeping up with the homework, too. He didn't enjoy practicing and if he missed a note it was my fault. The music teacher thought I was terrible for stopping the lessons. "Oh, he loves music!," she said. "Are you sure it isn't his mother who's not interested?" She was right and I felt guilty but I didn't care what she thought. I didn't care what anybody else thought either anymore. So while I monitored Jared in the waiting room, the teacher continued to instruct Jacob. I needed to be in the room with him because sometimes he had difficulty understanding her broken English — she was Japanese. Then one day when Jacob became frustrated and wouldn't accept her help, I explained to her that he was attention deficit with short term memory problems. "Oh, you Americans are always making excuses for yourselves," she said.

Scouts for Jared fell through, too. The arts and crafts frustrated him. The leader was wonderful with him but then he broke his leg and the group fell apart. I found another group but the leadership wasn't good and the children were often out of control. Jared was actually one of the more well behaved kids but he couldn't pull himself together as quickly as everybody else could when they were asked to settle down, so he was singled out all the time. I tried to keep him from "running with the pack," but he was a little boy and he wanted to have fun too. I tried to get the leader to let me help and keep the group structured up for him but he was young and very enthusiastic; he didn't need help and things were going to be done his way.

That spring I had thought I would be going back to work, so I started taking continuing education classes on sensory integration dysfunction. It interested me for several reasons: It had helped Jared in a profound way; it made sense-the idea of organizing the brain from the inside out-even if I didn't fully understand it; it was non-evasive, there were no surgical instruments or something to digest; play is something a kid does naturally or at least he should; and it seemed there was a huge need for it. I went to San Diego and Seattle. It was a great way to get out of the house and away from Jared. I didn't want to be around him. It was as if something inside of me had died.

It was Jacob who kept Jared company and my dad who provided the entertainment while Joe was gone: McDonald's and the Goodwill to look for "treasures" were the favorites. I always attended their soccer games, but for most of the practices, I dropped them off and went back home. Joe always went around with them when he was home: Scouts, soccer, fishing and boating; even a little rough-house play. He let Jared help him with woodworking projects. Joe was a patient man.

We sent Jared to a horse camp for a week that summer. It was the first time he had ever been away from home like that. He went with Jacob and a friend. Although I spoke with the camp directors first, I was phoned twice. We also sent him to a day camp for handicapped children as well as non-handicapped children. He liked that camp a lot and I was never phoned. With exception to these two camps, he was home throughout the remainder of the summer because I didn't want the hassle of trying to keep him and the camp personnel happy too.

I didn't want the work of keeping him structured up, either. So I ignored him a lot and let him wander and run in the neighborhood. He couldn't keep up with the other kids so he started biting them. He was biting his brother, too. I made him pay $5 to each person each time he bit; there were four times total. When that didn't work, I bit him back and that worked. He was looking more and more "disabled," too, as time went on. He was still little and scrawny, drooling slightly, irritable and unhappy. And he still liked it best in his own little world.

Fall approached again and a new school year began. Jacob was soon to be eleven, Jared was almost ten. The new year brought new teachers and new expectations although the same theme: Jared needed to work faster in order to keep up with the group. I tried to educate again as to the behaviors specific to fetal alcohol effects: Jared couldn't work faster and he couldn't keep up; if stressed he would perseverate and then not be able to move on; tears and emotional outbursts would result. I said I didn't mind as long as he was learning. But nobody heard me and I began losing my desire for teamwork. Eventually, I stopped talking to the teachers altogether.

I went back to school that fall, too. With each class I attended on sensory integration dysfunction, the more I learned about its significance on the child's social, emotional, and intellectual development. For example, I learned that the mouth is critical to higher level organization of the nervous system, and thus the higher level integration required for adaptation and skill building. Jared had always had oral-motor problems. So I bought some sensory integration equipment and I started working with him. Within five days, after just fifteen minutes of therapy each day, he stopped drooling completely and he stopped biting the sides of his mouth. He was also able to blow up a balloon for the first time. Inspired, I kept practicing and he kept changing — little changes, that only I could detect because I lived with him every day.

I kept reading and I kept studying. Then one day I found it: children who are hypersensitive to sound, hide under tables and chairs, who fuss with their clothing, cut the tags out of the clothing, cry when getting haircuts and their hair washed, hug on their own terms, have huge emotional reactions to minor scrapes and bruises, or have no reactions at all, and complain of food being too hot or having "lumps" in it, are suffering from a condition called *Sensory Defensiveness.*

Sensory Defensiveness is a type of sensory integrative dysfunction that refers to a self-regulation or sensory modulation disorder of the central nervous system which causes an over activation of a person's protective responses to incoming sensory stimulation, resulting in the person responding to certain harmless sensations as if they are dangerous or painful. It's a serious disorder and thought to be due to impaired processing in the limbic system, which is a complex set of structures in the brain, sometimes referred to as the "emotion centers" of the brain where we register feelings of fear, among other feelings, and is significant to our survival or self-preservation. When we are in a potentially dangerous situation, like walking to our car alone in a dark parking lot, for example, it's the limbic system which signals us to stay alert to sound and be prepared to fight or flee should something happen.

For children with impaired processing in the limbic system, various environments and key transition times can result in behavior disruptions. It is those behavior disruptions that everyone — parent, caretakers, and teachers — want to avoid, not just because we may not know how to handle them positively, but also because when sensory defensiveness dominates an individual's behavior, the habits and learned fears can cause other social and emotional problems which can then be very difficult to treat.

Both Jacob and Jared suffered from Sensory Defensiveness except Jared's nervous system was the more damaged of the two resulting in his defensiveness being severe at one time. According to his perceptions, his hair follicles, the insides of his mouth, his skin, and his bone joints hurt. "Don't put it where it bends," he had said when I applied lotion to his skin, referring to his joints. When I tried to hug him and he said "don't that hurts," he meant it. When his skin itched from the chicken pox, his brain perserverated, rendering him helpless to stop even though it must have hurt terribly. He liked to hide under tables and chairs and hang out in dark corners because it was his way of shutting out sensory stimuli when over stimulated. He didn't do well in the school that used the emotions for learning because it was too much sensory input at one time; he needed controlled sensory input. Even the swimming pool with its bright lights, strong smells, and the echoing of sound, was too much for him.

Jacob had had a need for control, too, in order to survive. According to his perceptions the world was dangerous and he had to be prepared to fight. He could shut down under such stress and then intense sensory input was required to bring balance to his nervous system. The head banging he did when so little, the rocking, the running in circles, the need for a quiet environment, the difficulty he had riding in the car, his need to touch everything, his preference for soft foods — scrambled eggs, white bread, and jello, his extreme behaviors in noisy, brightly lit and congested environments, and some of his difficulty sleeping were the sensory seeking/sensory avoiding behavior disruptions associated with Sensory Defensiveness. He was certainly angry due to the neglect he suffered, but mostly he was frightened. The world was a chaotic and confusing place from the start, at birth, when he was born in fetal distress.

All along it was the nervous system — always changing, always influenced by environment — that had baffled and eluded me. All of those electrical impulses pulsating through the sensory and motor neurons, searching to connect and orient, instilling fearfulness and wrecking havoc on the emotions when the mission was not accomplished, were the real enemies. That is one of the reasons why it seemed the boys were constantly changing. At any given time, in any given environment, they were either under stimulated and resistive, withdrawn, and isolative, or over stimulated and hyper-vigilant, defensive, and reactive.

To pay attention to sound and process information at will requires the ability to self-regulate. Jacob nor Jared, especially Jared, could understand what was being said to them when under or over stimulated. That is why I felt they weren't hearing me. It is also why Jared couldn't read out loud unless the room was absolutely quiet; he couldn't filter out extraneous sounds and orient only to the reading. Some people call this an auditory processing problem. When under stimulated, Jacob could not articulate his speech. In a just right state — neither under of over stimulated, fearful, or stressed — they did fine, no matter the environment, which only added to the confusion.

I went on to discover that recent studies are showing children exposed to alcohol in utero while their brains are developing are having considerable problems with self-regulation and the processing of sensory information; alcohol is *extremely* damaging to the brain of the unborn fetus. The Fetal Alcohol Effected and Fetal Alcohol Syndrome babies can be fussy, whiny, inconsolable at times, and have difficulty establishing sleep-wake cycles. Many have a weak suck or difficulty coordinating a suck-swallow-breathe pattern. The toddlers are in constant movement. The preschooler can be out of control. Educating and parenting the child can be extremely difficult.

I felt sorry for Julie when I learned this. Given her own problems and the lack of information surrounding how to care for her babies with their damaged nervous systems, I don't know that it was humanly possible for her to be a successful parent.

For me, making this connection — the mind-body-behavior connection — and understanding the "odd" behaviors finally, was extremely comforting, albeit bitter sweet. I was provided a handout on Sensory Defensiveness which listed the behaviors, including the behavior of hiding under tables and chairs, by the occupational therapist at the clinic when I was taking Jared for sensory integration therapy. "This may be of interest to you," she had said, but I didn't read it. I was too busy feeling overwhelmed, isolated, and disillusioned.

It wasn't too late, though, because children with Sensory Defensiveness were being helped with something called a "Sensory Diet," which, much like food nourishes the body, utilizes sensation throughout the day to "nourish" the brain in order to promote that just right state for new learning and decrease the behavior disruptions. It was designed several years ago by two occupational therapists named Patricia and Julie Wilbarger, a mother-daughter team, and it goes beyond the clinic walls by giving parents a framework in which to work from utilizing children's activities and the home environment.

So I went back at it filled with new hope and very much ready for what I was being advised to do — there was nothing left to try.

Two Years Later:
Home Is Where One Starts From

A t the time of this writing, Jacob is thirteen and Jared nearly twelve. The year is 1997, Christmas is right around the corner, and Joe and I have it easier now than ever before.

Jared has made tremendous gains in the last two years — more so than I ever thought possible. He has a second level purple belt in Taekwon-Do. When he performs for promotion, he outshines most of the other children. This is because Taekwon-Do is a whole body, right brain/left brain activity, which provides for him sensory integration, so he likes it. He is also an excellent horseman. The riding, the grooming, the handling — he does it all. Taekwon-Do and horseback riding are a part of his Sensory Diet, something he will need in some capacity for the remainder of his life.

The Taekwon-Do has improved Jared's self-image tremendously, I think. And while I enrolled him in Taekwon-Do for therapeutic reasons, he is so good at it now that I think it might also serve as a tool in which to protect himself in the future. At first, I thought he would use the martial art to hurt others or show off in order to fulfill his, at that time, insatiable ego needs, but that has never been the case. The instructors were very good about making sure the kids knew it was for self-defense and not to be used to show off or hurt somebody for the fun of it. Jared came to idolize the instructors and often repeated the things they said. "They're teaching us kids about things besides just Taekwon-Do, Mom," he informed me one day. "They talk to us about not stealing and cheating on tests at school, too." Heroes again — in my own community — unknowingly helping me to teach Jared right from wrong.

Jared is much more confident in general. He plays defense and midfield for his soccer team and is considered one of their most vital players. Jacob's coach picked him up two years ago when his own team folded, even though he was much smaller than the other children. "He has a heck of a kick," the coach said, "And I like his work ethic." By the end of the season the coach was calling him "Timex" because he "just kept on ticking." With incredible endurance for long distance running, he has won the medal for the most laps in his age group four years in a row at the annual school Jog-a-Thon. He's a "natural athlete" people keep saying. He is also a serious student and a fine artist, drawing regularly and producing beautiful works.

All that whining and fussing are gone. There are no gray wolves walking around on all fours at our house, there are no dark corners in which to hide; our world is his world. He does not lie on the important things, steal, or horde food. Willingly, he shares. He is fun loving and social. Much younger children adore him, he has an exceptionally gentle way with them. He emulates Joe. And interestingly enough, he is one of the most moral people I have ever known. Not only does he know the difference between right and wrong but he doesn't question it either, his feet are square on the ground. Last but not least — he feels empathy. When my dad died suddenly last year, rendering me helpless with grief, Jared was an empathic sponge offering heart felt and tender words of comfort, holding my hand, patting my back, not wanting to leave my side — nearly smothering me in compassion. So I got what I wanted after all.

Jared is also fairly adaptable — he rode the subway and maneuvered fearlessly and independently through the crowds of New York City two summers ago — although he still doesn't care for change.

No longer an extension of his brother, or in need of emotional support, he attended summer camps all by himself this last summer. As I watched from the sidelines I saw a thoughtful and helpful boy who anticipated and opened the van door for the camp leaders when they had their hands full; another time I saw him volunteer to carry something. The camp leaders were always glad to see him coming — he was their favorite — and I was proud. Finally the world was no longer closed to him and camps for the "handicapped" were a thing of the past. He was fitting in and it made him feel very good about himself, I could tell.

The camps weren't technological in nature, but fun: a little basketball before going to a bakery to mix and knead the dough as well as sample the fresh baked bread, for example. Last year he went to an overnight camp for five days. He came off of the bus dirty and scruffy looking, wearing shoes without socks and his coat without a shirt, but he made it and I was never called. He said the camp counselors became his friends. As his development continues to unfold, I am confident he will be more successful with overnight camps in the future.

It was his touch system that was blocking his development. Theory has it that if a child is tactile (touch) defensive it will impede his development in all life domains, as well as interfere with personal relationships and other therapeutic interventions.

Jared's defensiveness to touch was influencing his relationships with others, particularly me. In a 3/4 inch square patch of skin there are 9000 nerve endings and since I was the person who took care of his hygiene and grooming, touching his skin and hair, I was the enemy. And the less touch stimulation he got, the more defensive he became. It's a serious neural disorder — tactile defensiveness — and not to be taken lightly; even the mildest of cases should never go untreated. Studies have shown that when animals are not touched and handled during infancy, they fail to develop the ability to cope with stress and such an ability is critical to survival. Plus, the sense of touch is linked to the "emotional brain" — that limbic system again — and it's the emotional brain that is being wired during childhood and the place where we develop the feeling of empathy for others.

Every child is different in his or her degree of Sensory Defensiveness but for some children it can be eliminated, or at least decreased, quickly and efficiently by using an intensive approach and that by treating the touch system, something I had never done with Jared, the other sensory systems are influenced as well. So I immediately treated Jared's touch system with a very simple procedure which takes only 3 to 5 minutes from start to finish to do; any parent can do it unless physically handicapped. For seventy-two hours I treated his skin every two waking hours. By day three, his whining had suddenly ceased. I had become so accustomed to it, always hating it but ignoring it, that I didn't realize it still existed until it was gone. Finally, after five years it was gone. The love notes to me started coming in again, too.

His overall development, but particularly his emotional development, seemed to unfold then, slowly, but ever so naturally and with little input from me. Several people have commented on the level of his emotional maturity this year: relatives, teachers, the school administrator, even our neighbors. He no longer has to sit at the same spot at the table. "Remember when I had to sit at my own spot," he said one day while we were all around the table and me in his place, "that was because I thought if I didn't have my back to the wall the bad guys would get me." This summer when he cut his hand he did not cry, whine, or even yell. He simply looked at it and very calmly said, "Oh, I've cut my hand." Not that he doesn't have emotional responses at times to physical injury, if he didn't it would be cause for worry, but his responses are now more appropriate. He hasn't gone into his own little world in over a year and his fearfulness about "being alone" in a room by himself is gone as well. In fact, he has stayed home alone for up to three hours at a time on several occasions and he does fine, even at night.

This is when I realized the significance of the mind/body connection and its power to influence the perceptions of a child. Childhood is about first-time experiences and the forming of our perceptions; the perceptions that will then influence greatly how it is that we think and, consequently, behave as adults. Jared's mental health care demanded more than just the traditional psycho-therapy and I was awarded validation — my striving for his life skills acquisition and academic successes were, in fact, avenues in which to reach his psyche — the more organized he became in body, the more organized he became in mind.

The unfolding took time, though. For example, Jared fussed at first when he couldn't perform the movements of Taekwon-Do and cried over minor physical injuries, forcing me to question if the treatment had really decreased his touch defensiveness or if it was just my imagination. But I kept using the treatment. After the intensive treatment I used it three to four times a day just at key transition times for nearly a year: in the mornings, after school, before Taekwon-Do, and before bed. With exception to Joe, people thought I was crazy. In time we started noticing changes, big changes: more appropriate emotional responses to minor injuries, fewer behavior disruptions, less rigidity, and no yelling or angry outbursts when we touched his back accidentally with wet hands. In the past he refused to walk to the car in the rain without the hood to his coat up because the rain hurt his skin he said. He continued to complain that the rain hurt his skin even after the intensive treatment and he continued to be adamant about wearing his hood. Then one day, even though it was pouring down rain, he went out without his hood. Pretty soon he stopped fussing altogether and I had a different problem — he didn't care whether he had a coat on or not.

Jared's sensory integration problems were complex and they weren't treated in the correct order, either, evidently. Tactile defensiveness is only one manifestation of Sensory Defensiveness but it must be treated first and in conjunction with the Sensory Diet. Our keeping Jared moving and the climbing, the rough-housing, the swinging, the hiking, the jumping, and the bicycling, were all sensory diet type activities, I just didn't know it at the time; all I knew was that they seemed to help him (and his brother). In other words, the motor planning — the frame for Jared's house — seemed like a good place to start but the tactile defensiveness in combination with the overall Sensory Defensiveness was like the wiring and the plumbing; each should have been laid out and planned for accordingly before the frame went up and the work on the walls began.

The more I understood sensory processing and self regulation, the better I understood Jared. It had always been so much work for him to apply himself. And given that he was tired all the time not being able to sleep deeply at night, miserable in a body that hurt, craving sugar, and not able to "think straight," I suppose it was only natural that he would strike out and blame others for his problems; after all, his problems were invisible so somebody had to be at fault. He especially liked blaming me. I was putting demands on him, forcing him to use his brain and he didn't like that. I was too harsh with him also because approach is everything with a Sensory Defensive child. These problems in combination with the early neglect and trust issues, made him an extremely difficult child and very, very vulnerable.

In time his disposition began to change and his willingness to try new things expanded. When I first started treating his touch system he would make comments: "I feel so much calmer now Mom," he said one day. On another day it was, "I had more ideas at school today." Then one day, following the touch system treatment just before soccer practice, he said, "Now I can feel my toes kicking the soccer ball!" I realized then that he must not have been able to feel his feet and why it was that he liked the hiking boots so much — "They make my feet feel heavy," he had said. I didn't make the connection at the time, but the picture he drew of a person with only three lines for the body indicated he was not aware of or could not feel his own body parts; people who have had strokes will sometimes have this problem.

Eventually I could "see" the significance in using the Sensory Diet. Besides helping with the behavior disruptions, it helped to increase Jared's motivation. It also decreased significantly the verbal behavior disruptions in the mornings, making that time more bearable for me. Following a Taekwon-Do session he was more alert and interested in his studies or more willing to set the table, for example. Things kept getting easier and I stopped feeling so inadequate. After I treated his touch system he was better able to come up with his own ideas for the speeches for school. In time I came to think of sensation and the nervous system as the way in — the key to unlocking the spirit wherein lies the desire to learn and to love.

So I arranged for our daily living activities to take place around Sensory Diet type activities. For example, Jared's Sensory Diet required he have an hour of quiet time in his room directly after school and I came to plan for it accordingly. Jacob needed quiet time, too, and an hour of watching television became his favorite. We were finding balance and slowly but surely, the Sensory Diet became a way of life. When the boys fussed about having to go to Choir practice on Wednesday evenings, I took them out of it altogether; Jared couldn't keep up with the group and Jacob didn't need one more thing to do. It was wonderful not having to grab a fast food meal and rush to get to the practices. During the school year, when the boys are working so hard on academics, we stay home for the entire weekend at least twice a month — "home bodies" again. Those weekends consist of a lot of make-believe play, Lego constructing, and a very relaxed schedule — after the chores are done in the morning of course. The occupational therapists call this type of relaxed time "recovery time" and they know what they are talking about — without it the boys are fussy, cranky, and irritable. I, too, like it because now I don't have to feel guilty about not keeping the boys structured up constantly — maintaining the Sensory Diet and sameness in environments and routine provides just enough structure. Flexibility within that structure is important, also, which is not at all like I thought it had to be.

Finally, I had a framework within which to work. With the help of medication, purposeful activity and the Sensory Diet, I could face the future; I had a plan.

This last summer was the best ever for Jared in relation to making friends with his same age peers. He played and laughed and went to several slumber parties and birthday parties. Between he and his brother, they had friends over every day. When not at home they were running the neighborhood, riding bikes and playing. They are getting themselves to the Taekwon-Do studio, crossing busy streets, and going to the store on their own now. For the first time ever, they rode their bikes to the library, which is three miles from our house, all by themselves. Each took a dollar from his bank and Jacob put his watch on. They went to the library first, had pop at a corner store, and were home ten minutes early. I was incredibly proud of them and very pleased, it meant a new found freedom for me. It also meant hard work does pay off and that we are now more developmentally ready for the bigger mountains waiting to be climbed: shopping malls, movie theaters, peer pressure.

I'm not saying Jared doesn't have his social problems. He and his friends argue at times. He and his brother argue and fight. But it's normal for brothers to fight and for people to argue. I intervene very little these days — there were only two serious spats over the summer in which my assistance was required. It's typically kids Jared doesn't know very well and their parents whom we have problems with. Just last week a parent thought Jared was terribly "greedy" because he wouldn't let his kid have a turn on the computer. Jared takes care of himself first, unless in a giving mood, but he is not greedy-he takes only that which he needs. The problem is he has seldom experienced other children sharing their computer with him, so he thinks having an audience to watch him play is the way it's supposed to be. Sometimes he appears to be a show-off, declaring himself the one to be first with a given activity, which tends to annoy those who don't know him and how he operates. For example, he'll insist everyone stand around and watch him attempt to do flips on the trampoline. It never fails, in front of others he often has difficulty performing something new that he learned. So he'll keep insisting they give him the time he needs because he knows he can do it, but they get tired of waiting and the parents perceive him as "selfish" and "bossy."

Jared now knows his birthdate but he has no concept of time nor can he use a calendar. He is able to problem solve albeit in a limited way. If he wants to sit in a chair, for example, and there is something on it, he would find another chair rather than move the item. When faced with a problem solving difficulty in front of peers, he will act helpless or goofy; he's good at it, too. But people like him now, so he often receives help when it is obvious he is having a hard time. He can follow three steps to a command as long as it is a familiar task at hand. If it is something new, a three-step command will be overwhelming and he'll cry — it has to be delivered one step at a time. Placing his hands on the task and walking him through it using his senses is even better. He does not do well at all when pressured or stressed. He still doesn't play with anything the way it was meant to be played with but there are no broken and trashed out bits and pieces of things filling his pockets anymore. He cannot spell the word would. He cannot handle money. He can earn it and he can count it, but unless he puts it in his bank and leaves it there, he'll lose it. He won't know where or how he lost it either. The school continues to work with him on his money management skills and time concepts, but it's a slow process.

However, he has surpassed the predicted outcome of a fourth grade reading level, and now reads at an eighth grade level. The house doesn't have to be quiet anymore when he reads, he can read silently or out loud no matter what is going on around him. He reads for entertainment on a regular basis. Academically he is on equal footing with his peers and there are no more angry or emotional outbursts at school. On good days he writes beautifully, though slowly, but he can't spell very well. He is able to plan ahead somewhat and he is more inclined to use both hands when he works. These are all good signs of the brain functioning more as a whole. Not that there aren't restrictions. For example, when he is looking for something he won't always look to his left. People who have had strokes tend to do this, it's called "left-sided neglect." And until just this fall, he wouldn't answer the phone even if it was Joe or I calling. We had to tell him when we left the house to pick up the phone when we called. Everything has to be stated for him in very concrete terms. For example, I can't say "you're late for soccer practice, so hurry." I have to say "run across the field as fast as you can because you're late for soccer practice." The use of concrete terms and telling him how things should be rather than what is wrong are helpful techniques for effective communication.

Only once in the last two years have we found something he tied up. It was his pocket knife tied to a door stopper with rubber bands. I know it probably seems odd that I would even let him own a pocket knife but he is not a violent child and he uses it safely. Now, his make-believe play is violent in nature, the themes being acquisition of power and preparations for battle, and the sticks in the yard are actually pretend weapons, but that's what the men and the boys seem to like — they have since the beginning of time — so I don't fight it anymore. The main thing is that he can distinguish fantasy from reality now.

Until this school year, Jared's grooming and hygiene habits were sporadic. He would need constant reminders to put on clean clothes, take a shower, and brush his teeth. He took little interest in looking nice for school or outings. Now, with exception to the weekends when we are hanging around the house, he takes a great deal of pride in his hair and attire. To brush his teeth and wash his face, he has to use a mirror. I had heard that using mirrors is effective for children who learn differently. So one day I stood him in front of one and had him brush his teeth. He cried and yelled at me, saying I was hurting him and that looking in the mirror didn't help. But interestingly enough, two days later a small mirror miraculously appeared and was placed strategically at the bathroom sink. That was nearly two years ago and he has been using it every since. His teeth are still slightly yellow, though, which I have learned is primarily due to the fact that he has a thin layer of enamel. The fact that he didn't brush them well, only added to this problem. We are using an electric tooth brush now but he still needs that mirror.

There are things Jared cannot do yet but with the basics under his belt, he now has a solid foundation in which to continue to build new skills. He can make his bed, keep up his room within reason, empty the dishwasher, load the dishwasher, set the table, sort laundry, put his clothes away, clean the bathroom thoroughly, and make french toast although he'll say he can't. I write him a list when he has more than one chore at a time to do and it helps a lot. Some days the jobs get done really well. Other days he has to go back as many as three times to get it right. Sometimes I have to threaten to withhold his allowance but it's the only thing I have to threaten to withhold.

Jared has more on days that off days, now. And he finally got his own dog which he takes good care of. He and Joe wanted to train the dog so they checked out books from the library. *Good Dog, Bad Dog* and *Animal Happiness* were the books Jared chose. Like any child, he needs reminders to feed the dog but he walks him and he takes him out in the middle of the night when needed all by himself.

I know now why Jared was always getting bit by furry critters. He couldn't move his hands fast enough and he had a vision problem. Not the kind that requires glasses but a learning related vision problem in his brain. His eyes didn't work together as a team and his visual form perception was impaired — he couldn't translate object size, shape, texture, location, distance and solidarity into understood pictures and words. The year he was ten, we took him for vision therapy for nine months. Our pediatrician says she heard vision therapy doesn't work, but Joe and I saw subtle changes as a result of it. Jared stopped thinking cars were closer than they really were, he could distinguish one form from another, and he showed less frustration when playing Nintendo.

Not that he plays a lot of Nintendo because he doesn't. Nintendo and computer games are used in moderation at our house. Television is nearly nonexistent, except in the summer time. These activities are too sedentary for both Jacob and Jared. They get crabby if they sit around too much and then they will resist every little task; even something as simple as getting up to let the dog out. Plus, it's hard to pull them away from the television and the electronic games if they have been involved for hours without a lot of fussing on their parts and patience on mine. They are familiar with computer technology (Jacob is quite comfortable with it) and that's good enough for now. Childhood is about first experiences, the forming of perceptions, learning, problem solving, wiring of the brain for competency and Jacob and Jared need this time to learn how to do their own thinking.

Jared is still little and scrawny, having worn the same coat for four years. Now he is beginning to fill out. His muscle mass is heavier and that soft mushy feel to his muscles is gone. The primary physical problems are that of low stamina for physical labor and weak hands which means the tree farm business is not going to work for him. Lately I have been thinking along the lines of photography or some kind of graphics as his visual spatial orientation to things presents itself in unique form. There is time to prepare, that wall in his brain has been torn down "one brick at a time" and Joe and I are still chipping away. We'll never give-up and we'll never stop hoping for him either.

Six months ago Jared showed signs of hormonal changes. Since then, every other month or so, a cluster of dark hair appears above the top lip and then disappears a couple of days later. Jacob started early too. We are lucky; our pediatrician took it upon herself to explain to the boys the body changes that accompany adolescence so now they know a little about what to expect. Such changes are tricky though, because when the hormones change, the behaviors also change.

Jacob is moody, now, going into adolescence. Sometimes he laments "Nobody understands me." Fortunately, academics are still a favorite. He moved on this fall from Jared's school and now attends a more mainstream private school. He gets A's and B+'s but he has to work very hard for every one of them. The language arts skills as well as the memory techniques and organizational tools he obtained at the other school are helping him significantly to hold his own. The transition was stressful, he had to "rush just to keep up," but once he oriented to the environment and learned the lay of the land, he settled right in. Because he is so conscientious, he was spending three hours on homework every night, working during recess and lunch time, and not making friends. So Joe and I spoke with his teacher and requested less homework — expressing our desire for Jacob to have balance between work, play, academics, and art — and she was comfortable with that.

Joe and I have to help Jacob with his homework. Mostly it is just a matter of getting him started with the first sentence, first paragraph, or first math problem. Once started, he does fairly well. Even though he hates math story problems, his problem solving skills are quite good now. His primary problem is that of coping with stress. When stressed he will have problems stopping and bringing a task to completion. "He's obsessive-compulsive" some people continue to say. But he's not really, he's intense, and he learns differently. He will pour himself into a given project and mind every little detail until he feels it is just right. Einstein and Thomas Edison were like that — they learned differently, too. I used to think Jacob's explosive type behavior (he has never raged since *holding time*) was purely anger based but now I know it is also a reaction to being stressed and overwhelmed. It is as if he hits a wall in his brain and then he can't take on one more thing, one more challenge, one more demand. There are no more explosions at our house, however, because the Sensory Diet helped with that problem: weight lifting and bicycling on a daily basis.

Jacob and his brother are made neurologically different. "We're S.I. Kids," they like to say. Jacob likes it now. He says it is what makes him "unique." He is unique, too. The artistic, talented, and gifted type: sensitive, creative, spontaneous, temperamental, emotional, and very bright. He will have choices in life and he will go to college. I think he would make an excellent specialist. Music or writing will likely be his avenues for creative expression. With equal skill in both hands and perfect pitch, his piano playing is beautiful. The lessons are being given by an instructor who is calm, accepting, and non-judgmental. This fall he started cello lessons. Within three months he was transposing from piano to cello which is evidently difficult to do and uncommon for a boy his age. The day the music teacher said — "Do you realize your son has talent?" — was the day I realized our lives have definitely changed. Last year he was the Patrol Leader for his Scout Troup. Every year he has been one of the best players on his soccer team. For two years in a row he has played goalie. He is a pretty good horseman and he has a blue belt in Taekwon-Do. And guess who makes the scrambled eggs at our house?

Determined, caring, kind, committed, helpful, hard working, curious, creative, artistic and sensitive — these characteristics are what Jacob is made up of. He's a 'real boy' now — brave and unselfish — but not always truthful. I guess it was because I spent so many years controlling every cookie and every snack he ate — all in the name of "behavior modification" — that he became sneaky. It took him a while to "unlearn" that behavior once I started stocking the cupboards with nutritious snacks and then relinquished the control to him.

I am not afraid of it "all coming back at me in adolescence" anymore. Joe and I intend to keep the boys as close to us as we possibly can during those turbulent years. Like always, we will have to be involved, stand watch, protect, head off trouble, and say "NO," all those self-sacrificing duties that come with responsible parenting. I am preparing myself mentally of course, the adolescent years are typically hard on anybody, but whatever is in store I know we'll get through because of the depth of our relationships. Jacob and Jared both know they are loved and that their parents are on their side. We are a close knit group; bonded.

I never thought I would bond with Jared and maybe it's not a bond at all, just acceptance. But the respect is there — on both sides — and it feels good. The paranoia and accusations of deceit have dissipated; my suggestions are taken seriously; my intentions perceived as supportive; we now have a relationship. The day I realized our individual personalities and temperaments clashed was the day I realized we are "normal," whatever that is. I still get blamed when things go wrong — after all I'm the one who pushes him and he has to be pushed. If I push him too hard, though, demanding too much too fast, especially if his nervous system isn't ready, it backfires. And then I get *the words*. Last week it was — "My problem is you!" — and I was asking myself why the heck I bother with the kid. Joe says he has integrity — he says what he means and he means what he says — which is why I bother with him. He needs me, too: "I'm sure glad the adults are in charge, Mom." He is also determined, strong, understanding, forgiving, non-violent, sensitive, sentimental, and intelligent — he sees the big picture. I am grateful these wonderful qualities weren't spoiled.

I could have taken Jared to a psychiatrist for medications for the fears and anxieties. I know several children who take multiple doses of medications — up to five and six different kinds — something for anxiety, something for fear, something for depression, something for sleep, something to be still, something for the rages. And even though the medications have never been tested specifically for children, I know a four-year-old who receives Prozac, Dexedrine, and Melatonin — all in one day — and yet the behavior disruptions continue to wreck havoc on his young life.

I wish my children didn't have to take Dexedrine but at least we haven't had to increase the dosages — Jacob takes 10 mg. daily and Jared, 25. They can't concentrate in school without it. This last summer they didn't take it at all for the first time in years and they were a lot happier, enthusiastic toward life, and more social. I used the Sensory Diet to keep their nervous systems in that just right state and it worked beautifully — there was no impulsivity on Jared's part. They came when called to do their chores, focused on the tasks, and required no redirection from me. However, I let them sleep until 10:00, I let them work at their own pace, I put no other demands on them except for the chores — there was no artwork, piano practicing, reading, or new learning — and we stayed around the house a lot. Jared was very happy and pleasant company; he and I had no conflicts. It was a summer of fun-filled play and no stress. When I saw how happy they were without the pressures of life constantly pushing and pulling at them to keep up, perform, and compete, I wanted to give them summer vacation forever.

But life isn't a summer vacation and had I been working full time outside of the home and leaving the house at 8:00 in the morning, it would have been a very different situation entirely. I would have had to enroll them in numerous camps because if left to their own doing, Jared would have slept until noon and then laid on the couch and watched television all day while Jacob would have played computer games and not bothered to eat, open the drapes, or feed the dogs, and then to get him away from them when I came home would be a major ordeal. They would have wanted dinner at 10:00 at night and argued to stay up until 2:00 in the morning, too.

Ideally, Jacob and Jared would do much better if school started at 11:00 in the morning, if they could work at their own pace, and if they could do their homework at midnight; or better yet not have homework. But the schools aren't going to rearrange their timeframes to suit my children's needs, and we don't live in an ideal world. The world we live in today is moving fast, and picking up speed all the time.

I have to parent Jacob and Jared differently than I had wanted to. They would love it if I let them do whatever they wanted. Who wouldn't? But I can't do that. My long-term goals are still the same: capable children who can be self sustaining someday. Had Jacob and Jared been making the connections, grasping cause and effect, and orienting to environments and what goes on around them, I might have been able to relax. But they weren't. They needed intervention, help and guidance to learn, and now continuous years of practice using what they have learned as well as more opportunity to keep learning. I have to push — gently and supportively — but push nevertheless; everybody needs a little stress. It doesn't always feel right — it's a fine line between being a tough-love parent and a supportive ally — and it's work.

Now a friend of mine keeps saying "It all starts at home," Donna. It actually starts in utero, something I learned the hard way, I try to tell him, but he doesn't get it. "There are no family values anymore," he says.

On school days, and I'm pushing away, I buckle under the pressure of it all and yell sometimes. It's not the boys. It's the situation and I make sure they know that. Even still I feel like a terrible mom when I yell. But the boys are so sweet and forgiving; they're special that way. And according to them I'm "an excellent mom" because I keep them "going." Jared has often expressed his gratitude for all I have done for him. "You got me where I am, Mom," he says.

It wasn't just me, some of it was in spite of me. Jared would not be where he is had it not been for Jacob, Joe, "Mr. Rogers," Mrs. Pettit, the adoption subsidy, the soccer coaches, the Taekwon-Do instructors, and the teachers and the administrator at his special school. Love was a start, but without education, medication, behavior modification, holding time, play therapy, psycho-therapy, sensory integration, the sensory diet, the structure, our back yard, the play room, vision therapy, the Family Support program, the Partners Project, the special school, reframing, tolerance, acceptance, determination, hugs, kisses, apologies, ear plugs, and my Creator, I would not have made it.

I don't think Jared would have done as well had he been an only child either — he needed someone to model after. I didn't know it at the time, but the competition helped too. My keeping things fair helped to promote his well being until he and I had a relationship going, I think, but now he is "coming into his own" and I am letting nature take it's course — siblings are always competing. Most importantly, however, was the bond between he and his brother. It was stronger than all of the best of intentions combined and keeping them together was perhaps my smartest move.

People often ask me what I would do differently if I could do it all over again. That's a hard question and I don't know that I could have done anything differently given that I didn't have all the pieces. Not knowing about Sensory Defensiveness and how it is that the nervous system can impact behavior, left me at an incredible disadvantage. I would like to think I would have responded differently to Jared's fears and anxieties had I known about the tactile piece. I would have provided more sympathy for the tears; babied the "owies" like his brother did; wrapped the cuts and applied some deep pressure perhaps. I could have brushed his hair with tenderness. I might have prevented him scratching his back with the carpeting had I treated his touch system. By preventing the behavior disruptions, he might have been able to stay in the various early childhood development activities that he needed so much. I would not have worried about him staying in dark corners and I certainly would not have used aversion therapy. I don't think I would have had to work so hard because the Sensory Diet maintains keeping it simple. I would have had more faith in Jacob's character had I known what was really going on for him. It's hard to say — a lot of things might have been different — had I known about Sensory Defensiveness from the beginning.

But then again, even if I had had all the pieces, I still might not have done things differently. I didn't want something to be "wrong" with my children that love couldn't fix. I didn't want to think we couldn't get away from the past or that I didn't have all the answers, either. Jacob and Jared came with their already well established little personalities, and I didn't get to play a part in that. I didn't want to be a therapist; I wanted to be a mom and I was going to do it all just right. I didn't want my children to suffer under the burden of inequity. If you really love somebody, you want nothing but the best for him or her. Grief takes its own toll and requires its own time — it was a slow process for me.

I think a better question might be: What did I learn? I learned that raising a child is a very serious endeavor, the commitment lifelong, and the challenges never ending. I learned that children are not little adults and that shame is far more damaging to them than spankings. I learned that it's hard to know what a child really needs and somebody else will always think they know better. I learned to trust what my eyes tell me. I learned that motherhood is the most honorable position I will ever hold and yet I'm still trying to figure out how to do it. I learned that hard work on the frontend does pay off and that people can succeed if given the proper tools. When my dad died, I learned that if I am not functioning well, my children won't function well either. I learned that saying "I'm sorry" can mean a lot to a child and that forgiveness is a powerful tonic for the soul. I learned how to accept help and the value of teamwork. I learned about setting priorities — a well manicured yard isn't as important as spending time with a child. I learned that teaching a child to do the right thing is to be a part of something which is good and decent and honest.

When Jared said one day that the thing he remembers most about his "younger days" is when I played with him, while Jacob remembers holding time, I gave myself a pat on the back. I might have done a lot of things wrong but I did some things right, too.

There is one thing I do know for certain, however, and that is that I would do it all again for Jacob and Jared. Love gave me hope but they gave me something to believe in.

Love we are given, strength we lend.
Bring peace on earth to all good men.
author unknown

♡ X X X O O O ♡

Dear Mom ♡

I Love you with

all My Hart ♡

You mean a Lot

♡ to Me ♡

♡ You gide Me ♡

throo hard times ♡

when you're by my side

I don't tel carle X X X O O O

Jared

Dear Mis.
you are so patient
with me. I look forward
to writing class You
are special to me

Jared

Dear Mis.
you are so patient
with me. I look forward
to math. You are special
to me.

from Jared

HANK THE LORD WITH ALL YOUR HEART.

Dear Mom,

This year has been an interesting one so far. I have been doing pretty good, on my classes, and have gotten good grades. I have learned many new things at   H.K.   . It has been rough, though, and by the end of each day I am glad that I can go home. In this school, you have to rush around just to keep up. This part has been very hard for me. Some of my goals are: To be more open with people, to have better time management, and to learn to cope with the high speed of life. I think that this school will help me to know what life is really like. I know now that all those years at   M.C.   really helped me. I thank you for making sacrifices so I could come here. I am sure that   H.K.   will give me the skills that I need for life.

Your son,

Jacob

Jacob (left) and Jared, 1997.

Afterword

I am one of the bureaucrats in Donna's story, specifically, the administrator of the Partners Project which served primarily Jacob during a portion of the time covered in this story. I came to know and respect Donna in her role as a parent and as a Partners Project Parent Advisory Committee member. I thought I knew her story until I read it. There is so much I never knew. I am sobered and humbled by her story and the courage she and her boys and her husband showed on each page.

Donna continues to be a teacher through this story. As one who helps to plan and implement services across publicly funded agencies like mental health, child welfare, education, and juvenile justice, I realize there is so much to be learned from the story of Donna and her family's passage through our "systems." Donna has helped those of us in public service by writing her story and sharing it with us. Every teacher and social worker, therapist, psychiatrist, and case manager, should read this story as a part of their preparatory education program. If connection is a key to healing for the family, it is surely for the service providers as well. How we create this amidst our need for professional distance is the next struggle for us professionals.

Just as research into brain chemistry and neurologically based disorders is informing us about the reasons for some of the behaviors families cope with and how to treat them successfully, so is research investigating how to build a system of care around vulnerable families that helps rather than hinders. Donna's story shows us all that we professionals must work faster and better to have a positive impact and to avoid being part of the problem for families with children who are challenged.

The rules and regulations under which publicly funded agencies operate often create more stumbling blocks for families like Donna's and for those who try to serve them. The key in the next generation of programs targeted to meet the needs of children with emotional and behavioral challenges and their families is the creation of a service plan developed from the family's strengths which is built on the needs of the child and family, not the governmental regulations or agency traditions. Then a system which ensures that these plans are implemented with quality and timeliness needs to be developed to ensure that the innovations in service delivery are supported by organizations built on the same values and principles. Public agencies have more latitude than they are often willing to exert and there are many communities across the country who are creating a new and better image of the public service employee as a partner in the resurrection of healthy communities. The Robert Wood Johnson Foundation, the Federal Center for Mental Health Services, and the Casey Family Programs, are but a few of the many agencies and organizations funding such efforts in collaboration with local communities, counties or states.

Across the country communities are redefining the metaphor of help, basing it on a true partnership of publicly funded agencies with families served, recreating community on partnership instead of patronization. We providers of services need to demand that the funding of services be more flexible so we can end our turf battles and the practice of carving out family members who can receive services from those who can not, as happened to Donna's family. It is in this way that we are able to provide a truly seamless system of care for children and families and help to replace despair with a sense of hopefulness and possibility. Public and private initiatives across the country are working to reweave the social fabric around the strengths and needs of vulnerable families. It is stories like Donna's which carry the light into current practice and show us a way out of a tradition of learned helplessness into a more productive partnership with families and communities based on mutual respect.

What we are also learning is that the stigma of the child's emotional and / or behavioral challenges insolate the family and that our most lasting intervention is in providing opportunities for families to connect with one another, to break the stigma and isolation. We have also learned that the voice of the customer family, the people we serve, needs to inform us at every level in the organization, not just the service planning and delivery. We needed Donna's voice when we designed the Partners Project (it would have saved us so much time) and at the evaluation level as well as the governance or administrative levels. If everyone who worked to process a piece of paper that got a service to this family (or stopped one) had read this and known "the rest of the story," I hope we would have done a better job. Stories like Donna's bring hope to families and service providers alike and encourage our partnership so that more families experience the kind of triumph that Donna and her family experienced.

Elleen Deck
National Resource Network for Child & Family Mental Health Services, Washington Business Group on Health

Acknowledgements

Many people helped me with this book, either directly or indirectly. With appreciation I thank:

Tela Skinner for wanting a human interest story; Laurie King for sharing her knowledge; Molly McEwen for calling attention to the details; Sherry Knight for her intelligent feedback; Elizabeth Feddersen for her clarity and support; Susan Roth for keeping the faith; Bernadette Ericksen for teaching me the value of having fun; Rene Denfeld for being generous with her time, attention, and encouragement; Debbie Stockdale for teaching me that what I think somebody needs and what they really need might be two different things; Susan Suter for looking for the strength in families; Pam Zemke for being real; Donna Cutts for wanting to do it right this time; Mr. Miller for his attention to the human spirit; Brent Matthews for looking for the light in all of us and for speaking out for what is right; Mrs. Pettit for being who she is — with her all things were possible — may every child meet a Mrs. Pettit at least once in his or her life; Kathleen Krushas for her expertise and human caring; and Elleen Deck for her commitment to working for the good of humanity and for the integrity with which she serves.

With deep respect I thank Connie Schregardus — a real angel here on earth — for her continued inspiration.

Jared 1997

This book would have never been completed had it not been for my dear friend Anne Bowlden. Anne believed in the book from the very beginning. Always affirming its value and my observations when I needed it most; she stayed with me the entire way. She read each draft, analyzed, and made insightful suggestions. She never tired of listening. She kept me going.

A special thank-you to Joe, my husband, teacher, and friend, for his unfailing commitment and unshakeable convictions.

Finally, and with my head bowed in admiration, I thank "Jacob" and "Jared" for their willingness to share their story in the hopes that it might help others, and for giving me the gifts of grace and humility with which to continue to learn.

ORDER FORM

For additional copies of this book:

Fax an order to (503) 289-5201

Mail an order to:
LookAgain Publishing
P.O. Box 17332
Portland, OR 97217-0332

Name:

Address:

City: State: Zip:

Daytime Telephone (   )

Cost of book: $14.95

Shipping: $4 for the first book and $2 of each additional book.

Payment: __Check __Visa __Discover

Card Number:

Name on card:

Exp. Date: (month)/   (year)

Signature: